JUST THINKIN'

By

Hal Shearon McBride, Jr.

Cover Photos:
Front cover photo from the left: Pauline Martin Ross, Annice Martin Reynolds, "The Smith Boy", Ann Armstrong Farmer, Billie Martin McBride

Back cover photo from the left: James Lane McBride and Hal Shearon McBride, Jr. during World War II (1944)

JUST THINKIN'
An Inaugural Collection of Columns 2013 to 2017

You are bound to get ideas when you go thinkin' about stuff. - John Steinbeck

By
Hal Shearon McBride, Jr.

Published by Virtualbookworm Publishing

ISBN 978-1-949756-18-0 (softcover)
ISBN 978-1-949756-17-3 (ebooks)
LIBRARY OF CONGRESS CONTROL NUMBER
ON FILE WITH PUBLISHER
Copyright 2018 by Hal S. McBride, Jr.

McBride, Hal (1937 -)
Just Thinkin': An Inaugural Collection of Columns
1.   Hal McBride; 2. Billie McBride; 3. Stigler News Sentinel; 4. Stigler,
Oklahoma; 5. Sallisaw, Oklahoma; 6. Baseball; 7. Small town life; 8.
Christmas; 9. Thanksgiving; 10. Memorial Day; 11. Heroes; 12. Vian,
Oklahoma; 13. Television; 14. Weather; 15. Social Issues; 16.
Seasons; 17 American History; 18. Founding Fathers; 19. Education;
20. Family; 21. Rural viewpoint; 22. Politics

OTHER BOOKS BY THE AUTHOR

To Bear Witness: A Memoir (2009)
Who Be Dragons (2010)
Billie and the Boys: A Memoir (2011)
Gatewood: Tales from the Life and Times
of Charles B. Gatewood (2015)

DEDICATED TO
Mike and Cheryl
My invaluable, personal "uber" service.

Table of Contents

Government, Politics and Technology

SEQUESTERED TRYING TO UNDERSTAND SEQUESTRATION

March 1, 2013

Afflicted by both disorder and cure, between coughing, congestion and medication, a substantial thickening of my thinkin' has occurred. I am mostly confined to my comfortable chair. I have been sequestered.

So here it sat, trying to absorb the collective wisdom of the Senate testimony of Federal Reserve Chairman Ben Bernanke followed by a pleasant viewing to those two post lunch pundits, Hoda and Kathie Lee, with my wife. There is all this talk about sequestration.

Feeling I am sequestered, I thought I knew the meaning of the word.

I checked my old but dependable Merriam-Webster Dictionary. As I thought, it meant to seclude, to segregate, to impound or to isolate. You can sequester a jury. You can impound a car. With others keeping their safe distance, you may isolate a germ-infested man to his chair.

None of those seemed to fit the heated exchanges of dialogue I was hearing. So I checked Dictionary.com. I found a noun alternative that stated, "A general cut in government spending." Aha!

Being full of cough syrup and curiosity, I wondered about the origin of this noun. Where did it come from? My research suggested an origin in our Congress, in a bill titled the Budget Control Act of 2011. So it seems this problematic sequestration came into existence because our Congress actually passed a bill.

A long time ago, Will Rogers cautioned us about the dangers of allowing Congress to actually pass laws. But I thought he was joking.

It seems that this sequestration, this general cut in government spending, will put a lot of people out of work while cutting the pay of way to many others. I've have tried to pay attention, but I just can't hear where these pay cuts are going to bother that top 5% very much.

Now, the Good Lord undoubtedly knows, our federal government spends a tad too much money and often not very wisely. But it seems such a general spending cut could be a lot more general. It kept sounding like we should be reassured that the cuts would be somewhat gradual, but it kept sounding like a nurse saying it will be fine because she is going to pull the bandage off very slowly.

I am certain that the "drop dead" date will have come and gone by the time anyone reads these thoughts. We'll be scratching our heads and wondering that just happened.

A minute ago, I just got cold can of Coke Classic and poured it over several ice cubes. Don't you just love the way it fizzes when the cold coke hits the ice? I'll tell you I liked my Coke. It left a pleasant taste in my mouth. I can't say the same for this sequestration thing.

The significant problems that we face cannot be solved by the same level of thinking that created them. – Albert Einstein

ACTION, REACTION OR INACTION
September 12, 2013

I cannot recall listening to an advisory speech from a President of the United States of America, then sitting back in my chair and thinking now what was that all about. Was President Obama trying to convince me a significant number of innocent Syrian citizens were murdered with a poison gas? Well, I did already get that. I'm just not certain what the President was trying to say, maybe "Let's wait and see and then we'll react." Okay, I'm not for hasty premature actions.

Then, throw in seeking the approval of a Congress that hasn't agreed on anything in a number of years. Well, good luck with that. I didn't hear "If Congress says no, I'll do something anyway."

Does anyone else have this feeling that Vladimir Putin took an off-handed remark by Secretary John Kerry and efficiently turned it into a brush to paint our President into a corner, stalling any potential United States response?

As I think about it, maybe I just wanted him to be more direct, like say President Nixon when he said, "I am not a crook!" Course it turns out he was but at least I understood what he was saying when he was saying it.

Were we supposed to believe the threats of our Commander in Chief subdued a man who has been compared with the most brutal dictators in the history of mankind to meekly surrender his stockpile of weaponized poison gas? As I think about it, I feel as President Reagan said, "Trust, but verify."

President Obama said we were "war weary". I believe we are. How does weariness impact our moral responsibility? Do we have a moral responsibility? Maybe moral responsibility is more fluid than I thought. There was no moral outrage to respond in 1988 Saddam Hussein when used poison gas to murder more than three thousand

Kurds and injure about ten thousand more in northern Iraq. We all know how that ultimately worked out for us.

Or is it just all politics? All my life I've heard "All politics are local." Are problems also really local?

Our local newscasters in their nightly reports tell us of violent deaths in our own Oklahoma communities just because it is guns or knives; gangs or drugs, not governments. I am weary of hearing about "drug deals gone bad" as if there was are "drug deals gone good". We hear of children leaving school on Friday with a sack of nutritious food so they will have something to eat over the weekend.

Do you think maybe solutions like politics might just be all local too? Now I'm on the back porch sharing sips of an ice-cold Coca-Cola with my four year old Great-Grandson. Yes, he loves the fizz it makes when you pour it over ice too.

My youngest son, his grandfather, always gives him a word of the day. Most often it is the same word. We talk and I ask about the word. He answers, "Kind."

We share another sip of my Coke. In his huge smile and his bright eyes, I see hope.

Just thinkin' -- Does the best moral education take place on back porches? – I can't do much about Syria but I can see a kid in eastern Oklahoma gets a weekend sack.

Kindness is the language which the deaf can hear and the blind can see.
– Mark Twain

5

A BARRAGE OF BEFUDDLEMENTS

May 16, 2013 (printed September 27, 2013)

It is rare that confusing disclosures come at a rate that exceeds my capacity to absorb the befuddling events. I am certain that the truths are contained somewhere in the spinning selective presentations. I just can't find it yet. And there are so many of them.

The IRS was delaying applications for tax exempt status if the organization contains the words "Tea Party" or other such groups for the past 18 months. President Obama is said to be outraged by such improper targeting of the organizations. Now that suggests there can be a proper targeting of such groups. That really does confuse me.

Well, in response President Obama forced the resignation of Acting IRS Commissioner Steve Miller who was already schedule to resign in June. But he is going to remain on the job for a couple of weeks. That will teach'em!!!

Can you believe that a government agency has subpoenaed telephone messages of reporters of the Associated Press? I haven't figured out exactly why yet. I didn't see the Associated Press as a seditious or subversive organization. I suppose investigative reporting can be viewed in many different fashions depending upon the eye (and the political bent) of the beholder.

Now, add Benghazi. I struggle with the vigorous "political finger pointing" following an incident that cost fine men their lives. Obviously, something wasn't managed correctly. It is just not right.

Finally, there is our familiar friend, gasoline prices. After beginning with a gradual incline from $3.16 a gallon two weeks ago, the price per gallon for regular gasoline cut with ethanol increased by 33 cent a gallon in two days. I awoke this morning to find the price had reached $3.83 a gallon overnight. I knew I should have filled up yesterday.

Now Mike Thornbrough, the spokesman for QT, was quoted in the Tulsa World as stating, "We've got record low inventories coupled with planned refinery shutdowns and unplanned shutdowns." Now that is a real "head scratcher". He described it as a regional event.

I paid almost $4 a gallon for "real gas" this morning. The effected region was my billfold.

I think I will go to the back porch and see if an ice-cold reliably caffeine laced Coca-Cola can clear my mind. I have the feeling I'm going to enjoy my coke; looking at the flowers and listening to birds might help a tad. Just maybe the increased gas prices have reduced the traffic noise to the point the birds will sound more distinct.

Lord that is a long reach for a silver lining to this mess. But I was just thinkin'.

I'm not confused. I am just well-mixed. — Robert Frost

GAINING SUCCESS THROUGH THE FAILURE OF OTHERS

December 2, 2013

Is it just me or does President Obama have a sizable group of people cheering for each difficulty "Obama Care" encounters? I certainly acknowledge that the Affordable Care Act does not resemble the "universal" health care law I would have preferred. But it is what we got.

Is it better than what we had? Nobody knows, but there is no shortage of opinions.

Universal social welfare programs have historically been controversial and filled with conflicts. It is possible Social Security exists only because of the Great Depression. Was it President Lyndon Johnson's Great Society that gave us Medicare in 1965? Does Medicare work? It depends on who you ask. I sure like mine right now. My Physician, maybe not so much.

Virtually every President since Theodore Roosevelt has expressed the desire for a national health care system of some type. A newly elected President Bill Clinton valued it so greatly that shortly after his election that he placed his wife in charge of the effort to get Congress to pass such a plan. Drowning in a swamp of critics, ineptitude and lobbies, the noble effort was a spectacular failure.

Well, now we have "national health care" and no one seems happy about it. It is similar to the "Three Bears" model. There is too much or there is too little. The only thing anyone can agree on is that nobody got it just right.

How many people are there without access to affordable health care, but who are ready and able to pay a reasonable premium for health insurance? The number of people that went to www.healthcare.gov suggested a large number. So many we quickly discovered the site was ill-designed. While frustrating and disappointing, the website's failure provided considerable material for the late-night talk show hosts. Now, I am always in favor of a good laugh.

I do find it troubling that many people seem to believe that they only success comes with the failure of "Obama Care". But I have also heard grumblings about feeding children breakfast at school. I felt we all should know hungry children isn't acceptable in our country, just because it exists doesn't make it acceptable.

Can I only succeed if others fail? Is my solution the only acceptable solution? "I'm right, you're wrong!" To the extent you can trust political polls, everyone seems to have lost. I just refuse to accept the idea that my success lies in your failure. Just thinkin'.

I was sitting and sipping a Coke just thinkin'. It struck me, suppose the only way Pepsi could succeed was for Coca-Cola to fail. Now that is just illogical. It seems to me that we came out of the "Cola Wars" with two strong companies that employ a whole lot of folks. Thank God I don't have to destroy Pepsi before I can enjoy the fizz and flavor of my Coke.

Wouldn't it be wonderful if everyone in our country had the health care they needed? As my Grandmother Lane often said, "Seems the Christian thing to me".

WHAT'S IT GOT TO DO WITH THE PRICE OF MILK?

December 9, 2013

Have you ever noticed that some time we let our mind trap us into varying and seemingly unrelated concerns? Now and again, I suffer from the affliction. Since my gender doesn't multitask well, I seem to leave as I arrived, lots of questions and few answers.

I was listening to NPR and a question expressed the concern about the price of milk doubling about the first of the year, moving from $3.50 to $7.00 a gallon. My first thought was I like milk, but dang that seems like a lot. Then, this expert began an explanation. I thought now I'll get it.

She said the price of milk was tied to a subsidy contained in "the Farm Bill". Now, that sounded simple enough to me. Who is against farmers? As if she heard my question, she said the Farm Bill also contained the "food stamp entitlement" and that there was considerable opposition to this program. How about that?

I am certain that there is abuse of this "food stamp entitlement" program. It seems to me a small group of folks will always find a way to abuse a large government sponsored program. I know who pays for government programs. That would be us. But there are folks who need a little help. I especially like the school meals program. I strongly support the programs that send weekend food home with our school children.

Are those under the "Farm Bill" too? I don't know. I do know I can't stand the thought of a kid going hungry.

Another thing, did you see there was an objection raised to the Ten Commandments Monument on the grounds of the State Capitol. Who could have ever seen that one coming?

As I heard it, a Satanic group objected to the promotion of Christianity on public property. So, they want Capitol land to erect a monument promoting Satanism.

Just thinkin'. It seems to me Moses brought the Commandments down from the mountain. Now my Jewish friends assure me they have been blamed for quite enough over the centuries, so they'd just as soon be left out of this one.

See ladies, a man can think of more than one thing at the same time. Even though the end result is that I just confused myself.

A bone to the dog is not charity. Charity is a bone shared with the dog when you are just as hungry. – Jack London

FAIRIES, ELVES AND THE NSA

December 22, 2013

It is the customary season to expend considerable energy thinking about elves. Having a small child nearby seems to stimulate such magical thinking. Consistent with American legend and lore, the Christmas season is filled with images of bright stars in cold winter night skies, of angels and mangers scenes and visions of so many past Christmases. Christmas music ignites Christmas memories. The years seem to peel away and 40 years ago seems as yesterday.

Most of us are reminded of the spiritual depth of the Christmas season. It is faith and family, friends and food.

Then, there is that jolly old elf, Santa Claus. He is smoking a pipe and appears to be in need of cholesterol check. Beards do seem to be coming back into style. Shall we credit Saint Nick? Why not? If you have a 4-year-old running in and out, admiring Christmas trees and ogling the gifts wrapped and placed under the tree. He finds only harmony between the secular and spiritual components of our family Christmas celebration. With his grandparents, he will be a happy, jolly greeter at the early Christmas Eve service.

Fairies, my wife suggest that the "ice fairy" focused on our neighborhood and deposited more than our share of ice on our sagging and broken trees. For sure the ice found us. But the "power fairy" left our Christmas lights glowing. The lights from the Christmas tree look like a work of art when viewed from the street through ice covered shrubs and bushes. Like Santa, the Ice Fairy can do good work. That is if you don't find the cracking sound of branches too distracting.

Now, President Obama held his "paint the year bright and I'm off to Hawaii" press conference. It broke my chain of thought. Of course, some say I'm easily distracted. I contend I just think about a lot of things.

There were a number of questions about the National Security Agency and the Edward Snowden leaks. The NSA's phone data gathering program was at the core of these questions. Does it violate our Fourth Amendment rights? A Federal Court just said, "Yes". The Federal Government filed an objection. Should the government or a private company be allowed to stockpile our personal information? The recent Target incident suggests safety might be a myth. Huh, how about that?

I have a seasonal suggestion. It seems to me that Santa already has a comprehensive list of who has been naughty and who has been nice. If the NSA subpoenas the "Santa Claus Diaries", I hope they wait until after Christmas Day.

Merry Christmas and Happy New Year!
The McBride Family

THINKIN' ON TRAIN WRECKS

January 14, 2014

I think something about train wrecks fascinates us. Not necessarily those wrecks that occur on rails, but those seemingly self-inflicted ones that occur in people's lives. We are especially attracted if it involves people whose choices and ambitions have led them to dwell in the public eye.

I recently wrote some short thoughts suggesting there might be those among us rooting for the failure of President Obama's health care act. It was with the passage of time and continuing to think about it that I realized the President shouldn't take it personally. There are some of us who just enjoy watching "train wrecks".

Not all "train wrecks" are political. I understand that collisions, explosions and violence sell theatre tickets and video games and get viewers to press the buttons on their television remotes at a phenomenal rate. These permeate our entertainment culture.

Many of our entertainers seem to believe they are entitled to engage in poor conduct. Charley Sheen was trucking along playing himself in television's top-rated comedy until he found himself in a "train wreck" of substances, contract disputes and goddesses. Lindsay chose to "borrow something" from a jewelry store, a young celebrity relieved himself in a kitchen mop bucket, and then, very fitting for these thoughts, there is the girl who recently rode a wrecking ball somewhere or the other.

Most recently and still unfolding, is New Jersey's "Bridgegate" fiasco. A rising GOP star, the likable Chris Christie finds himself ensnared between what he knew, what he didn't know and what people believe he should have known. Now that seems a triangular trap harder to escape from than a sophisticated corn maze.

However, we can't forget there are those of us who just enjoy a scandal. Just thinkin' about it, but it seems most are quite forgiving if the peccadillo involves an inappropriate intimate relationship. We only have to think back to President Clinton or President Kennedy to see our willingness to forgive and forget such dalliances. Of course, Wilbur Mills of Arkansas set the bar pretty high. In a 1970's brouhaha, Mills and his mistress, Argentinean stripper Fanne Fox, had a car crash. A scuffle with the DC police followed. Ms. Foxe jumped into the tidal basin in an effort to leave the scene. This all concluded with Mr. Mills' re-election in which he received 60% of the vote.

Will Governor Christie survive this "train wreck"? Is this as bad as having your photo taken with President Obama after Hurricane Sandy? I do know it will continue to be fine fodder for the late-night talk show hosts.

Watching my Coke fizz and just thinkin', I might feel differently if I had been stuck on the George Washington Bridge. George Washington, I wonder if he really did chop down that Cherry tree?

No matter, it seems many of us just adore a scoundrel.

Unlike some politicians, I can admit to a mistake. --- Nelson Mandela

TO SPELL OR NOT TO SPELL.
March 9, 2014

Theodore Roosevelt, in one of my favorite quotations, points out the pleasure many people obtain from seeing the strong man fail. In the same passage, he makes it clear that he believes success is not possible without risk and failure.

It seems the letter E is especially troublesome for politicians. Vice President and Presidential hopeful Dan Quayle once added an E to the spelling of potato and President Obama omitted one E spelling respect as rspect. Now political cartoonists and late--night talk show hosts have again been delivered a bountiful harvest from comedic heaven. Politics – Saint George of Washington must be the Patron Saint of the humorist.

Do you worry just a bit about political pundits and satirist who behave as if an error in the spelling of single word in a casual environment merits the same scrutiny as decisions on the Ukraine or the Affordable Health Care Act or the not so simple balancing of a Federal Budget? How about the ability to remember who our friends really are?

Well, maybe is it just as T.R. stated, we just love pointing out were the "strong man has stumbled".

Maybe such stumbles just make us more secure about our own kerfuffles. Is kerfuffle spelled correctly? Is it even a real word? I hope so because I seem to make a lot of them.

Does anyone really believe that President Obama cannot spell the word respect correctly? I didn't think so. I want him to spell Medicare and Social Security. I want him to know his history as in "The Cold War" and the people behind the current events as in "Vladimir Putin".

Sometimes I get this uncomfortable feeling that while we are picking at each other over political trivia, there are movements, countries and individuals who really don't have our best interest in mind. And they are progressively creeping up on us. Or maybe I'm just a touch paranoid. Or as one late night talk show host at times observes, "The world is starving and we are holding cupcake wars. Now that is why the rest of the world hates us."

Let me think. Could I have written this piece without spell check? Hmmm? The answer is "No". Then again, this isn't all about spelling.

I think I'm thinking myself into a corner. Or maybe it is a circle. Have you ever noticed how you begin by thinking about one thing and end up thinking about something else?

"You must obey the law always, not only when they grab you by your special place." – Vladimir Putin

ENHANCED INTEROGATION AND CHRISTMAS

December 11, 2014

I am accustomed to our Congress providing me with a source of amusement, even on occasion fine performances of the ridiculous. Now we elected these folks, but they seemed to have been mired in inaction over recent years. So the least they could do is provide us with a good belly laugh along. They want to be disagreeable about healthcare. Well, I still believe a good laugh keeps the Doctor away.

I turned on the nightly news and discovered CIA had released a report. A fella could easily get the idea that a politically proper position for torture must exist. Excuse me, Enhanced Interrogation Techniques. Help me. Is this a part of the Democratic or Republican platform? Now for sure, Nancy Pelosi was railing against the failure of the Enhanced Interrogation Techniques.

The more I listen and the more I think about it does appear the big compliant is not on the morality of torture but that the techniques didn't work. It does seem I've heard this "End justifies the means" logic before. It seems just a bit ago that it was a method of "Keeping American Safe".

It seems another of the complaints is about hiring some behavioral scientists to design the program. Some eighty-one million dollars-worth of design and now Congress and the CIA can't determine if this group was expert in Enhanced Interrogation Programs. Huh! I guess there are experts in Enhanced Interrogation. All I ever saw in graduate school was guys I thought took too much pleasure in shocking rats. I'll bet the robed men from the Spanish Inquisition would have worked cheaper if they were still around.

Wait. Let me rethink this. The CIA needs help with interrogation techniques. Huh! I would have deferred to the Central

Intelligence Agency on any and all forms of clandestine information gathering.

Should the CIA and the Congress have a relationship? Why do I have this feeling that the answer will be "yes and no"?

I know he has made some remarks but I'm waiting on John McCain to make some direct remarks on the matter. He is a POW who was tortured and confessed to some fabrications. Seems he will have first-hand insight the rest of us are gratefully lacking.

This has been great weather for a back porch and a sweater; coffee and contemplation; sipping coffee and just thinkin'. Seems there is some line between justified torture and unjustified torture. You talk about a troubling moral and ethical decision, this is a WOW!

All this in the Christmas Season, there just might be an answer or two here. I re-read a Christmas favorite, <u>A Christmas Memory</u> by Truman Capote. It is a simple tale of an eccentric aunt, a little boy and the preparation of a Christmas cake to be mailed to the President. If you need a gift for someone special purchase a copy and wrap it in the lovely paper it deserves. In its leaves you might find an answer to interrogation.

It might just answer the question of how a free and spiritual people came to be asking themselves about the righteousness of Enhanced Interrogation Techniques.

It is inexcusable for scientists to torture animals; Let them make their experiments on journalist and politicians. – Henrik Ibsen

19

NOVEMBER 2016 – REALLY!

January 12, 2015

I have often expressed my thoughts on beginning the retail promotion of the Christmas Season before Halloween has even past, an impulsive premature collision. There is another season that seems to be moving from premature to perpetual. Presidential elections appear to have moved from seasonal to everlasting.

Sunday morning, I got some added prospective on the definition of the word premature. The Sunday talk shows were filled with Presidential speculation and interruptions of who had hinted at what. They were clearly unrelated to the sermons on salvation and social justice I receive from my favorite pastor.

While there were earlier hints of this fast approaching season, I guess I just wasn't ready to pay attention. I had been to the barber shop recently and I didn't hear a sound mentioned about a pending Presidential campaign. A cynical insinuation that the results of the recent mid-term elections really wouldn't change anything in Eastern Oklahoma emerged but that was about it. Sports trumped politics. Had I waited until later in the week, there would have been a considerable "Freedom of Speech" opinions expressed? How could there not have been when political cartoonists are murdered in Paris for drawing their opinions?

I swear I believe the politically ambitious never stop running for President of the United States. They are perpetually thinking about it, planning it, talking about it, raising huge sums of money so they can "get the message out" and doing it. Yet, even the Iowa Caucuses are over a year away.

It does seem like we are moving toward an election cycle that runs from one election until the next. I believe other things are important to the maintenance of our society, our culture and our communities.

Now I am as interested in our presidential elections as the next person, maybe even more than most. Still I know in most ways who is elected to local offices; county commissioner, state representatives and senators, district judges and almost every other position in the courthouse more directly affect my life.

How about sharing a cup of coffee and talking about how those guys and gals are doing at the courthouse? What was in the News-Sentinel or the Tulsa World? Do I want to talk about basketball and football? Pitchers and catchers are due to spring training soon. Do I want to speculate if Phil and Tiger, if Rory and Ricky be at Augusta in April? Read a good book? Like a new television series?

The answer is "Yes, I do." Not all that is serious is news.

Maybe I just don't want to have to think about the President and the Congress too long before I vote. I have found a protracted election cycle to be just downright mind-numbing. I guess it is possible that filling voting booths with anesthetized minds is exactly what most national candidates want.

Me? I just want time for a few cokes, a little coffee and some good conversation to clear my mind, a brain flush so to speak. There are creative wonders in an unclouded mind that I want to enjoy. I like voting with a clear mind.

Man is by nature a political animal. – Aristotle

IT IS EASY TO BE A CRITIC
April 13, 2015

I don't know if it is just me, maybe it is. It certainly seems that it is very easy to be critical. It is often easier to be against something than for it.

The national newscasts have been filled with coverage of the Obama administration's efforts to resolve the long-standing nuclear disagree with Iran. I would have thought a functional agreement is in everyone's best interest. There seems to have been no lack of effort from our Secretary of State John Kerry. An outline agreement was reached.

The BBC almost immediately reported that there were discrepancies between the US version and the Iranian version of the agreement. I just don't find that shocking!

Leading Republicans stated that Iran's Supreme Leader's version was "somewhat more trustworthy" than Secretary of State Kerry's version. Now there is a puzzlement. But then, the Senate vowed to reject the outline agreement virtually before it was read. On the other side, I guess even if your title is Supreme Leader you do have a constituency to satisfy.

If I ever got a title with Supreme Leader in it, I'd like it mean a bit more. My wife assures me I am safe from ever being faced with such a dilemma.

I know I don't care for the idea of Iran having nuclear weapons. I'll bet Israel isn't keen on the idea either.

With that said, all agreements between Nations are based upon trust and a capacity to obtain verification. Now that sounds reasonable to me. The "Death to America" signs that provide the backdrop for much of the television coverage of the negotiations do not evoke trust. Now I don't believe that any of those people holding the signs remember us as the nation that supported and sustained the regime of The Shah of Iran. I wonder who chooses the backdrops. How many "Death to America" signs can people just be carrying around the streets of Trahan? Huh?

Anyway, the Monarchy of the Shah was overthrown and replaced by the Theocracy that exists today. We stood down.

Despite a recent movie, I don't know how many of our fellow citizens remember that 52 members of U.S. Embassy staff in Tehran taken hostage, despite their pleas for assistance as the crisis evolved, and were held for 444 days. President Carter called our people "victims of terrorism and anarchy". The hostages were finally released minutes after President Reagan was sworn into office.

The Iranian high school textbooks have a chapter on this titled, "Conquest of the American Spy Den". Seemed odd, then I remembered that 60 years ago my high school United States History text had a large chapter on "The War for Southern Independence".

Again, maybe it is just me, but this is starting to sound a lot like the Arab Spring and our Consulate in Benghazi.

I've had plenty of time and no shortage of Coca-Cola and beautiful back porch weather for thinkin', it does seem that criticism comes easily to the critic. I think some folks just enjoy being contrarians. If the stance is "I'm right and your wrong" before the problem is even fully defined, well, nobody wins and everybody loses and nothing gets accomplished. But again, maybe it just me.

It is not the critic who counts, not the man who points out how the strong man stumbled or where the doer of deeds could have done better.

– *Theodore Roosevelt*

SEARCHING FOR UNDERSTANDING

April 29, 2016

Do you listen to the news about events in the Middle East because you possess great knowledge of the region? Me neither. I listen closely because I want to understand. To understand, I must learn. This is a region and a religion that holds long term influence on well-being of our nation.

Yes, it is about the oil. It is about the fervent desire of religious Jihadists to kill us. It is complicated.

When the media refers to a significant terrorist Jihadists group as ISIS, Islamic State of Iraq and Syria, while our State Department and our President refer to it as ISIL, Islamic State of Iraq and the Levant, it doesn't provide even a tiny bit of clarity. I've read several explanations of potential differences but ultimately it appears there is not a difference. They are a Sunni Islamic terrorist group. The United Nations and Amnesty International hold them responsible for war crimes and ethnic cleansing on a historic scale. Posting the execution of hostages for interviewing viewing must fit in that category.

It does seem to me that Sunni Muslims and Shiite Muslims have been killing each other for time immemorial. Actually, the Sunni-Shiite division began shortly after the Prophet Muhammad's death in 632 AD. The conflict arose over who would succeed the Prophet. The Sunni majority prevailed. The Shiite minority lost. The disagreement remains unresolved.

Now both have terrorist arms, there is the Shiite funded Hezbollah and to me al-Qaeda militants and ISIS are well funded Sunnis. They do share common enemies, the fundamentally Christian United States of America and the Jewish State of Israel. I don't know why we have any interest in the region beyond oil and a variety of self-protective motives. The Israelis want a homeland. They have craved it out and they intend to keep it.

24

Best I can see, many Muslims want to inflict all possible harm on Israel and upon us. I see American born and reared Muslims trying to go abroad to volunteer to fight with ISIS. It seems to me that I still missing something. For sure I don't understand suicide bombers, regardless of what might be promised in Paradise.

These are people who diverted jet airliners into the twin towers and the Pentagon. Courageous passengers sidetracked a third aircraft into a field in Shanksville, Pennsylvania. We have had the underwear bomber and a shoe bomber. Last week a planned attack on the Vatican was thwarted. And hostages – terrorist cruelty at the most personal and inhumane level, so may God's mercy watch over them.

I have thought long and hard about this. I have viewed it from as many angles as my understanding will allow. I know we are not without fault.

Nonetheless, I still just don't understand. In that sense, I have failed for the time being. But that is not an excuse to stop searching.

I certainly hope our State Department and our President aren't waiting on me.

HOW THE WORM BECAME A DIPLOMAT
March 10, 2013

"It is ridiculous," was NBA Commissioner David Stern's response when he was asked about the ex-parte pseudo-ambassadorial venture of Dennis Rodman into North Korea. Now, given his position, I would consider the Commissioner an authority on the ridiculous.

He is quite familiar with "The Worm", a rather peculiar nickname Rodman acquired during his college days at Southeastern State in Durant.

All the national media coverage of Rodman's international endeavors got me thinking. Exactly what positive outcomes might we expect from meetings between Rodman, the "Madonna trained king of piercings and self-promotion", and that the seemingly post-pubescent dictator of North Korea, Kim Jung Un? Let me think some more. Nope, I still can't come up with anything.

What position in our society does the young Un believe Rodman possesses? He seems to think Rodman has the number of the President of the United States blackberry on speed dial. On NBC's Today Show, Rodman stated that Kim Jung Un had asked him to "tell President Obama to call him". Really!

Un is young. Sometimes developing brains do confuse celebrity and self-promotion with intelligence and wisdom.

Let's see. In the time frame of Ambassador Dennis' visit, Un has spoken of launching nuclear missiles at the United States, declaring the cease fire that brought a halt to the Korean Conflict null and void, along with other unfriendly gestures.

This diplomacy and saber-rattling appear to have left North Korea's most important ally, China, scratching their heads. I can just see the leadership in Beijing saying, "Who?"

Yes, I do understand that Rodman was traveling with the kings of basketball comedy, The Harlem Globetrotters. I just don't think this trip will experience the level of success that "Ping-Pong Diplomacy" with China achieved.

The title of this piece suggests a children's tale. How does a worm become a diplomat? Self-proclamation! And make the proclamation in place an eccentric happens to be running the establishment.

I guess it would be unethical to tell the "early bird" where he lives. Can you put a worm in "time out"?

The cool thing about being famous is traveling. I have always wanted to travel across seas, like to Canada and stuff.
— Britney Spears

THERE'S TRAVEL AND THEN THERE'S TRAVEL

March 26, 2013

My wife and I were enjoying the last of our morning coffee and conversation. Then, on which ever morning television program had been providing the background noise for our oatmeal, a newscaster caught my attention. I thought I heard that our President was preparing to take a trip somewhere or another to promote some agenda or another. After a bit, they all begin to sound very much alike, but it got me to thinking.

I recently read about the President's armored Cadillac limousine, Limo One, breaking down in Israel. It stayed with me because a newscaster spoke of how fortunate we were that another suitable vehicle was readily available. I really started to think about how a Cadillac limousine makes its way to Israel. (what sea is parted)

I knew we bailed out GM. I am not convinced GM is so grateful they made an unlimited number of these reinforced Cadillac limos, a car in every port so to speak. Logic suggested that Air Force One does not have a tow bar or trailer hitch.

I poked around a bit. I found that Limo One is flown from location to location on a United States Air Force C-17 Globemaster.

At some point I begin thinking about the cost of Presidential travel. Let's just concede that it is a whole bunch. There must be a difference in essential and non-essential travel, between travels during prosperous times and – well, less prosperous times.

Each spring groups of high school and middle school students' travel to Washington, D.C., most come in yellow buses. Parents have likely sacrificed for their son or daughter to make this trip. They converge on our Capital and most take away a new appreciation of their country. This is all part of something called education. We hope these students will ultimately comprise an active, informed electorate.

President Clinton continues to point to a meeting President Kennedy while on a Boy's Nation tour as a pivotal moment in his formation.

This spring students are being told visits to the White House are not possible. They are told we just can't afford to take them on such a tour. It is called the People's House. It is like our kids can't tour our house. Peculiar concept!

Maybe rather than rolling out Air Force One and traveling some place to "sell a political agenda", he might just go visit with the people who have come to visit the White House. President Truman is said to have poured a glass of fine bourbon and stepped outside to visit those standing in line, people waiting for a White House visit. It is said he actually thanked people for coming to visit. And that man faced a few tough decisions during his Presidency.

Oh, well. Talk about a lousy job, how would you like to be assigned to inform groups of students they cannot visit the White House. I'm sure this will soon pass and barely be remembered. But it will be long remembered by some bitterly disappointed students.

I think I'm starting to over-think this now. I'm going to see if there is any coffee left in the pot.

Travel, in the younger sort, is part of education; in the elder, a part of experience.

– Sir Francis Bacon

THOUGHTS THAT GO BUMP IN THE NIGHT

November 2, 2013

Not that I believe you could have possibly missed it last Thursday was Halloween. In contemporary American, it is supposed to be the scariest of evenings. In my neighborhood, the sidewalks pulsated with small groups of zombies and monsters, with princesses and superheroes. Flash lights were like fireflies announcing their route.

They arrived at a door, passing ghosts and skeletons dangling from trees, skirting around large blow-ups of black cats or such, following pathways of lighted jack-o-lanterns. These denizens of the dark are easily bought off with candy. They smile and laugh far too much to pull off scary.

Technically it is All Hallows Eve. In ancient Christianity, it was a night devoted to the poor souls who were believed to be temporarily liberated from Purgatory and were free to revisit their homes for a night. Now if you really believed that it could make for quite a "fright night".

There are things that I find quite disquieting and they last longer than a single night. Had a "trick or treat'er" had come to my door in an Edward Snowden mask I'd have been concerned. He is supposed to be in Russia. Personally, I hope Moscow has the coldest winter on record.

It is concerning that this guy ever got employed by an NSA contractor. Now that is a scary thought!

But think about it, we are eves-dropping on our friends and allies. President Obama says he didn't know. Think about it, the President didn't know and a contract employee in Hawaii did.

How about that Affordable Care Act web page? More quality work from a federal contractor on a legislative showpiece, if that doesn't frighten you, it does me. Wouldn't you like to meet the wizard whose solution was to take the photo of the attractive lady off the web page? Well, maybe not.

Six citizens are signed up on the first day. By weeks end, millions are being notified that their existing insurance plans will no longer be offered. Those plans that President Obama assured us would not be touched. I'm glad I've got Medicare. I think. Could Washington mess with that? Now there is a thought that scares me!

You look to the horizon and like phantoms in the mist hangs visions of sequestration, budget balancing and debt default, their ominous return looming.

I just realized what a lengthy list I could make. That is scary.

I did enjoy Halloween. Our Congress is scary, the decisiveness of our Administration floats like a ghost in a fog.

Does it seem to you that we get the tricks and they get the treats? Just thinkin'.

The best minds are not in government. If any were, business would steal them away. — Ronald Reagan

AGING, AILMENTS AND POLITICIANS
8-15-2015

Let's talk. Nothing can get a guy to thinkin' like a political debate, a seventeen-candidate political debate. Even the NCAA couldn't set up a bracket like this one. I don't think. Well, maybe.

This one did seem to have something of "If ya raise da cash, you're in!" Hum, profits are possibly involved. Maybe Fox News did consult with the NCAA Basketball Selection Committee just a little bit. The candidate with potentially the most available cash did get to stand in the middle of the prime-time debate. It did seem that he got an awfully lot of television face time. Then again – maybe that is just me.

Did you notice the commentators kept talking about who was winning? I looked closely and I never did spot a scoreboard. Subjective scoring? From watching Olympic Ice Skating and Gymnastics to Boxing, I know how reliable and unbiased that can be.

The fair question is, "Why did I watch it?" The best answer is, "Curiosity". Would I have watched it if "The Trumpster" hadn't been involved? Likely not. I just suspected he'd find some creative fashion to confuse me as to what the hcck he meant.

Well, ultimately there will come a Tuesday in November of 2016 and we will get vote. There will be a winner. Wait – has anyone purchased Florida voting machines that don't produce "hanging chads"? Just askin'.

I have always preferred local politicians to national politicians. You know these folks; some of us see them at the grocery store and in church on Sunday. They do have to deal with local gossip but so does everyone in the county. It is rather recreational, "Tell me the dirt". There is local accountability.

Anyway, I looked at all those folks and the stage and tried to guess their age. If anything, I am becoming an authority on it is aging. The more I age the more ailments I discover have been lurking, hidden in my bones and joints and other provinces of my body. I'd like to blame all these ailments on national politicians but I just can't come up with enough rationalizations.

I gauged a number of the folks in the United States Senate or with presidential ambitions not to be many years younger than I am. Now the hair dye and make-up make cuts off a few years in appearance but the bones, joints and organs are not fooled. I know I'm tired of hearing my physician say, "You're in wonderful health. (Dramatic pause) For a man your age".

Logic leads me to conclude that physical challenges come to face each of us as we age. We attempt to mute their effects with a measured, directed activity or by medications. A good dose of psychological "flight and denial" might work a while. Politicians cannot have received some magical exemption.

Ever wonder about the medication regiment of the men and women on that stage? I know it is not something I speculated about at a younger age. Now having reached a certain age, it is hard not to speculate about such things. Plus, like watching these early debates does resemble a pre-season NFL game, it is just entertaining. Just think on it.

Thomas Jefferson once said, "We should never judge a President by his age, only by his works." And ever since he told me that, I stopped worrying.
– Ronald Reagan

ON CALLING THE CLOSE ONES
September 16, 2015

I didn't believe that the ladies and gentlemen's early campaigning for the office of President of the United States would hold my attention as it has. My history on such campaigning would suggest the contrary. Heck, I still haven't figured out the Iowa Caucus system. It seems that voters gather at their precinct, try to persuade each other through oratory, and then count heads. I guess it works for the people of Iowa.

Certainly, President Obama changed the course of history with his success in Iowa. After Iowa he was no longer "who?" and Senator Clinton had a fight on her hands.

I listen to the debates, read the newspapers and the more solid magazines. I am attentive to the Sunday morning talk shows. I was cynical about candidates rowing up to appear on the late-night talk shows. Vice-President Joe Biden's recent appearance on Steven Colbert has made me re-think this just a bit. For the most part, Colbert asked the right questions and stayed out of the way. The result was considerable insight into the "potential candidate".

Iowa's months in the sun completed, full focus moves on to New Hampshire and South Carolina. Now these primaries require an actual vote. I have always considered voting a good thing. The primary in New Hampshire seems civil but South Carolina is more often a no-holds-barred brawl. After these three primaries and even before Super Tuesday, the national media seems ready to proclaim the "Presumptive Candidates" for each party. I believe they might use some of those statistics I was thinkin' about last week.

I would like to believe that my vote in our Oklahoma Super Tuesday primary mattered.

I took a late morning break on our porch and poured a cold Coke over ice. I thought that what I had just written had a negative tint to it and that was not my intent.

I hate to even hint of complaining as we watch the other transfers of power around the world. I feel they voted and then descended into chaos. They take to the streets and hassle with each other. Violence begets violence.

Historians agree that we are indebted to the conduct of our first three Presidents, George Washington, John Adams and Thomas Jefferson, for sowing the seeds of a peaceful, orderly transfer of power. Washington stepped away from the Presidency after two terms because he believed that was enough for any man. John Adams succeeded him but lost to Thomas Jefferson after one term in the bitterly contentious election of 1800. Although their friendship at this time was quite strained and Adams was bitter about the campaign, there was an insistence upon a civil exchange of power.

Thank you, Mr. Washington, Mr. Adams and Mr. Jefferson. Personal differences were set aside and you provided the example of how civil men could act in the best interest of our Republic. We have trouble knowing when to start campaigning for an election. Thanks to such examples we do know when an election is over.

I'm glad I took a Coke break.

Our Constitution was made only for a moral and religious people. It is wholly inadequate to the government of any other. – John Adams (in an October 11, 1798 letter to his wife, Abigail)

The Constitution only gives people the right to pursue happiness. They have to catch it themselves. – Benjamin Franklin

THE GOOD, THE BAD AND THE INDIFFERENT

January 16, 2016

Did you watch and listen to President Obama's final State of the Union Address to Congress? I am always optimistic that I will hear or see something new, something that might make an actual difference in the "State of our Union". I suppose the optimism arises from my persistent belief that our system works.

I'm convinced that I would never continually watch a television program that I found below par. Yet, I watch this address. I would really like for it live up to its promise. I don't know for sure but I suspect many of you watch with the same expectation.

This year I found the speech to possess more of the hopeful confidence which enthralled many voters during his 2008 presidential campaign. I heard him say what was accomplished during his terms in office. I wish I could recognize these achievements in my daily life.

Oh well, the language of politics most often eludes me. What is the state of our Union? We are a government "of the people, by the people and for the people". We need to insist that our government meet more of our needs as a nation.

The day after the State of the Union address, I heard some friends talking about what I thought was the address. I found they were only discussing their hopes for a new television program titled Shades of Blue. Huh! Maybe I'm taking this "State of the Union" thing too seriously.

I did a little research and discovered the instruction in our Constitution, Article II, Section 3. The directive was not as clear as I had hoped. It said "He (the President) shall from time to time give Congress information of the State of the Union and recommend to

36

their consideration such measures as he shall judge necessary and expedient".

Do you see lots of room for interpretation there? I did. I found that historically others have viewed it that way too. George Washington and John Adams delivered speeches to joint sessions of Congress. In 1801, Thomas Jefferson felt the speech was monarchical. A letter was written and delivered to Congress, there to be read by a clerk.

The written word continued until Woodrow Wilson in 1913 decided to return to delivering a speech to a joint session. With few exceptions (President Carter in 1981) it has remained this way. A speech to the joint session is now our expectation although rarely has meaningful policy arisen from these words to Congress.

Are there merits of a return to the written form? I thought about it – and all the mail I get concerning Medicare, Social Security and such. Let's keep talking.

Forgive my cynical attitude but it seems most often centered on pointing out the differences between our political parties and blaming the other party for our problems. Politicians seem to be determined to make sense from nonsense. They fail but like me in my optimism, they keep trying.

The fizz of my cold coke striking my face I remembered Einstein's definition of insanity. "Insanity: doing the same thing over and over and expecting different results." Well, the old boy got me, at least me watching the State of the Union. Maybe he saw me talking back to the TV screen.

Two things are infinite. The universe and human stupidity; and I'm not sure about the universe. – Albert Einstein.

AN UNEXPECTED GIFT TO COMEDIANS AND COMMENTATORS

January 20, 2016

I enjoy observing unique politicians. I had decided I just wouldn't write about the presidential campaign of Donald J. Trump. It just provides too great a variety of temptations

I understand that for late night television, from talk shows to Saturday Night Live, any presidential season provides a wealth of enjoyable and humorous material. Trump's candidacy in particular has provided a treasure trove of material. The name recognition that his flamboyant celebrity provided has led comedians and commentators to refer to him as the gift that keeps on giving.

Interestingly his much younger wife has seemingly been off limits, at least up till now. This deference reminds me of the fashion in which presidential children are treated. I consider this an unusual level of discretion for the modern comic.

I have recently been reading some Will Rogers. He once said, "Everything is changing. People are taking their comedians seriously and their politicians as a joke".

Without doubt, Trump's repetitive themes such as "Make America Great Again" have had an unexpected and immense appeal to many people. Its consistent basic theme coupled with a constant evolution has given the candidacy a life of its own.

Without a doubt much of late-night television humor is dependent upon the news of the day for its comedic substance. Trump makes news, daily fodder to oil the wheels of the news/comedy machine. His actions are more fun than congressional inaction. Only the grim news from the Middle East breaks cycle. I think it is as Will Rogers noted, "Chaotic action is preferable to organized inaction". Our government has given us repeated examples of organized inaction, constant enough we are excited about any sign of productive activity.

Nonetheless, I was holding my ground of inaction, then ----
Well, Sarah Palin endorsed Trump. At this point I changed my
mind about writing about Mr. Trump. The man truly is a gift that
keeps on giving! I am certain Saturday Night Live has Tina Fey
handy for such opportunities. At least 7000 people piled into the
Mabee Center in Tulsa to hear Trump and Palin two days later. No
doubt the man is popular. He says the things many folks want to
hear.

There is also no question that political humorists of all veins
have received an unexpected wealth of material. Mr. Trump is a
proven celebrity and entertainer. Mrs. Palin seems always passionate
and funny, pressing her personal viewpoint.

Much of the humor of late-night television is dependent upon
the news of the day. Will Rogers understood this concept 75 years
ago. He said, "I don't make jokes. I just watch government and
report the facts".

I noticed a variable I hadn't anticipated. I know I should have,
I just hadn't. There was virtually independent commentary on Mrs.
Palin's wardrobe. Frankly no one had paid much attention to
Trump's ties. My wife confirms I should have expected a woman's
fashion sense to come under scrutiny. Now I do.
I should have paid more attention to Will Rogers advice, "Always
drink upstream from the herd". Think I'll just have another cup of
coffee and try to forget the whole thing.

If stupidity got us into this mess, then why can't it get us out?
– Will Rogers

SOLD OUT RALLIES AND INFINITE DEBATES
2016

The lines in Tulsa for a presidential candidate were very long. 8500 people ultimately got inside. After a one-hour speech inside this politician went outside and spoke to those who had been unable to gain admission, yet waited. Are politicians now the rock stars of a new age? I don't know but I'm sure thinking about it.

Another candidate advertises the quality of his education and his memory. Now I'm not going to make such proclamations but I just don't recall politicians drawing such large crowds. What I do recall is State Senators campaigning from the back of a flatbed truck in the middle of a field, using rigged speakers and passing out barbeque after the speeches and the music. I also remember the pie suppers.

Former Governor and soon to be United States Senator, Robert S. Kerr, walked the streets of Stigler going from business to business accompanied by a local handler who fed him the name of each businessman and woman. "Mr. Mac, I hear you are the only true Democrat in Haskell County." Change the name and add a slap on the back and you have the conversation conducted in each store in Stigler. That does seem like a fairly simple method of running a campaign.

I was asked what I thought about going to one of these huge rallies for Presidential hopeful. After thinkin' just a bit, I said "If I go see an event with a crowd of 8500, somebody is going to be dribbling a ball".

And how many Presidential debates can we have? I don't know but I think we passed too many a while back. Debates have been with us for a long time. The Lincoln-Douglas debates are the first debates of note I recall reading about. But that was a race for the United States Senate seat from Illinois.

And no, I wasn't seated in the front row.

I do recall watching the 1960 Kennedy-Nixon debate on a small black and white television set. The Cold War and Cuba were central topics. The Soviet launch of Sputnik in 1957 put the space race into play. Seeking the Presidency was changing.

I suspect the change was more gradual than I recall. Presidential candidates were once modest and reserved. They waited to be selected by the delegates, appearing as the party savior. They wanted to appear respectful and respectable.

Then, Harry Truman took a train ride. He actively and assertively pursued the Presidency from the back of a train. Dwight Eisenhower brought back the status quo. But John Kennedy went on television and it was never the same again.

Using the power of emerging technology, candidates enthusiastically sought the power of the White House. Television debates and huge rallies became the "king-makers". These things along with Iowa and New Hampshire and South Carolina.

I confess to thinkin' about this some. Worse I find many of the debate interactions amusing. Scary but entertaining. Just thinkin' and drinkin' a coke. Super Tuesday has passed. Want to have a pie supper and talk about it?

Elections have consequences. – Scott Walker

Don't buy a single vote more than necessary. I'll be damned if I'm going to pay for a landslide. – Joseph P. Kennedy

THE SEASON OF ANGST

March 27, 2017

Seasons come and seasons go. I heard that somewhere and I like it. Recently I've been focused on the personal pleasure this time of year seems to bring. I think spring and its whole sense of renewal just appeals to me.

Still I aware no term of time is perfect. Each season does offer the possibility of change, allowing us to experience something a tad different. This week I got reminded of another seasonal variation that is as regular as any solstice or equinox. Over the years this season has made me feel belabored, dependent and anxious. I don't find any of those emotions appealing but I am aware they are self-inflicted.

Okay, I'm talking about Tax Season. I don't believe that is a technically correct name but I sure know what it means. The boundaries of Tax Season are not governed by the laws of nature but by the laws of man. Just the fact that is imposed upon us by other men rather than by nature makes it feel arbitrary. It feels that way because it is. Those of us who are old enough remember when the date moved from March 15 to April 15.

Just thinkin'. Boundaries established by man are perceived as more arbitrary that those imposed by nature. Nature's physical laws seem logical and somewhat equally applied to all. It was arbitrary taxes and tariffs, perceived as unfairly levied, that led the American colonies to feel oppressed and unappreciated.

I will admit I discover complaining about taxes to therapeutic. The truth is I don't mind paying my fair share of the tax load. I have always enjoyed Oliver Wendell Holmes quote, "I like to pay taxes. With them I buy civilization.". As I look around our country today, I am unsure how civilization I am buying. Maybe it is just me but life doesn't seem to be all that civil anymore.

Where do I expect my taxes to go? I know public safety and national security must be secured. It would be naïve to believe we do not live in a dangerous world. Is it more dangerous than 1776 or 1861 or 1930 or 1941? Lincoln saw us a being constantly challenged to discover "if a nation so conceived and so dedicated can long endure." Perhaps we will forever be in the process of attempting to answer the astute question Lincoln posed at Gettysburg.

To me, it is naïve to believe that such a nation can be sustained without high quality public education. An educated, accurately informed electorate is vital. Can a viable democracy or a practical republic be sustained without it? Yes, I know how many of our federal officials are progenies of "Ivy League Universities". Now I do want our public servants to be the "brightest and the best". I also want public educational institutions to be adequately funded that every bright child can ultimately compete with those privileged few.

We do pay taxes for a reason. Are we getting what we pay for? I do believe that for what we are paying most of our public servants we are getting far better than we're paying for. Where is the rest of going? There has to be a rest of it.

I've got to think on this a bit longer. Gazing at the world through the fizz of my ice-cold Coke has only given me questions. I believe I have more to say about this. Can thinkin' too much give you a headache?

Death, taxes and childbirth! There is never any convenient time for any of them. – Margaret Mitchell, Gone with the Wind

Be thankful we are not getting all the government we are paying for.
– Will Rogers

UPON YIEDLING TO TEMPTATION
2016

I had promised that I would resist the temptation to write about national political gatherings. I told myself that it would be akin to shooting ducks relaxed and floating on a farm pond. I agreed with myself that these conventions were designed for the entertainment and consumption of the party faithful.

I didn't anticipate such temptations as an attempt to over-throw the presumptive nominee by applying a creative approach to the rules right out of the Republican gate. Oh, who can't write about a lady, a chant leader, in a lime green baseball cap? Then there was the guy who each evening appeared as Abraham Lincoln from beard to stovepipe hat. The Texas delegation wearing shirts appearing to made of the Texas State Flag. They rise and cheer in unison. It seemed a little – well, a lot too organized. They reminded me of something. Oh, I got it. What was the name that highly structured fraternity in "Animal House"?

Just when I didn't think it could get any better, it did. The presumptive nominee's wife spoke. It all seemed consistent with all the other "wives' speeches" I had heard over the years. Then, I found out why. Mrs. Obama had recited the exact lines in her convention speech in 2008. Now you talk about fodder for the late-night talk show host, this was beyond their wildest dreams. Just play segments of the two speeches simultaneously and you have a comedy segment in itself.

Plagiarizing a speech might be new for a prospective First Lady, but it certainly isn't for a politician. Again, the political prognosticators launched their searches of past "political plagiarizers". They were abundant. I was good until somebody pointed out that Johnny Cash had lifted much of <u>Folsom Prison</u> from an earlier song, <u>Crescent City Blues</u>. Johnny Cash settled the matter for $65,000. I don't like it much when politicians start to tarnish the name of a favored country/folk singer.

If you recall, Vice President Joe Biden withdrew from the 1988 Presidential race over allegations of plagiarizing from RFK, JFK and HHH. I always thought it spoke well of Joe in that he went after the really classy stuff. And no, I don't mean to suggest in any fashion that Michele Obama isn't one well-educated and classy lady. I know she is both.

All this stuff isn't new. It is said Thomas Jefferson borrowed direct quotes from Thomas Paine and John Locke in writing the _Declaration of Independence_. However, the _Declaration of Independence_ doesn't say "By Thomas Jefferson".

Vladimir Putin borrowed many phases found in his theses from two University of Pittsburg professors. I would say politicians are politicians except I like politicians.

Well, this has been too much fun and silliness. I'll have to go to the porch, have a Coke and slap the back of my own hand. It was like shooting ducks on a pond.

Art is either plagiarism or revolution. – Paul Gauguin
Genius borrows nobly. – Ralph Waldo Emerson

AND THIS TOO SHALL PASS

November 2016

It doesn't seem to matter much who you strike up a conversation with it quickly turns to the outcome of the Presidential election. Frankly, I have just about been talked out on this topic. But I have discovered what seems to me to be a rather odd phenomenon. The harder I try to avoid the topic the more it gets thrust to the forefront of a conversation.

Every time I've tried to write this column, I found myself looking at the word election on my computer screen. That is just not normal. Is it?

Ever ask yourself how do I walk away without appearing rude? I really don't wish to be rude but I don't want to talk about anymore. Still here I am writing about it.

So, what do I want to talk about? How about the Dallas Cowboys? This election will not affect the NFL. Are you certain? There was that locker room talk? Oh, come on, who do the Cowboys play this week? What do you mean you don't know?

Forget the NFL. I know the Panthers and the Lions picked up big playoff wins Friday night. Maybe the weekend talk will move to playing the Purple Pirates at Panther Field. Let us hope.

I'd like to think that come Sunday I will stand on the steps of the church and no one will mention the "top of the ticket".

There are certainly "down ballot", local elections – Sheriff, County Commissioners and State Questions – that will affect our daily lives in a more meaningful fashion. I know I researched and gave considerable thought to these people and our State Questions before casting my ballot.

It is in our best interest and the best interest of our friends and foes that each person we voted into office will succeed. If our office holders succeed, we thrive as a city, a county, a state and a nation. I will always contend that the center of meaningful government is at the intersection of "Main and Broadway".

Oh, did I mention that I voted? I preserved my right to complain. I think I'll go to the back porch, pour a Coca-Cola over some ice and see if I can divine the future through the fizz of my Coke.

Popularity should be no scale for the election of politicians. If it would depend on popularity, Donald Duck and the Muppets would take seats in the Senate. – Orson Welles.

WHERE DO WE GO NOW?

January 2017

How long can a guy keep his head stuck in the sand and act as if he doesn't know what is going on in the world? Here is a suggestion. Until your wife comes in says, "You should see all the women marching in the streets in Washington". This means your wife has seen something on the television that you need to know and understand. To secure best results, go watch.

Just in case you missed it let me tell you there were a lot of women and not just in D.C. It seemed there were marches all over the United States, women out in the streets holding up homemade signs protesting whatever was on their mind. I thought these homemade signs were much more effective than those mass-produced jobs you see people waving at other marches and rallies. The concerns of the marchers did seem diverse. While I have no proper data to support my hypothesis, I believe the perception that our newly inaugurated President Donald Trump does not have a suitable understanding of women's issues is a vital element. I am convinced the marcher's feel misunderstood, unheard and unappreciated.

If I had to categorize their concerns, I would lean toward issues that could and would be impacted by the appointment of Supreme Court Justices. It is certain our current President will make at least one such appointment. It is likely he will make more. The appointment of two Supreme Court Justices is a lot. Three is enormous. Now just sip a cold drink and think about that for a bit. I am.

I understand almost everything a President can do requires some sort of Congressional approval. In their wisdom, the Founding Fathers created a government based upon a system of "Checks and Balances". What can a President really do? You know during his first week in office President B.H. Obama signed an executive order requiring that Guantanamo Bay be closed. Guess what, 8 years later, it is still open. Did you hear President Trump wants to move our Embassy in Israel from Tel Aviv to Jerusalem? Congress authorized this move in 1995. Now, Presidents W.J. Clinton, G.W. Bush, and B.H. Obama refused to act upon this directive because they each considered it to be an infringement upon the power of the executive branch. Our President can nominate Justices, declare War, influence the Federal Reserve and guide Foreign Policy. But those all require Congressional approval and/or oversight. Guess nobody really likes being told what to do. Congress doesn't like the President telling them and the President doesn't appreciate Congress leaning on him. People are just funny that way.

I printed a copy of this and took it out to the back porch to proof read it. Can you believe a 70-degree day in January? I was just thinkin' and I realized that I have started to get more my news from Seth, and Stephen and SNL. It sounds just like a lot of people who once listened to Will Rogers on the radio. Remember Will said, "I don't make jokes. I just watch government and report the facts." Laughing is healthy.

It is a good thing we don't get all the government we pay for. − Will Rogers

Even though you're on the right track you'll get run over if you just sit there. − Will Rogers

WHO IS YOUR ENEMY?

2017

I was recently asked, "Where did the quote Enemy of the People come from?" While it was familiar, I couldn't place it with a quotation. The more I thought about it I realized I didn't recall it being a quote but rather the title of 1882 Henrik Ibsen play. A play titled An Enemy of the People.

I first became aware of Ibsen's play when the American playwright, Arthur Miller, adapted it for the Broadway stage in the early 1950's. I always considered the play to be a blend of dark comedy and classic drama. The tale is set in a town whose major source of revenue is dependent upon tourists coming to bathe in the town's "healing warm water baths". The baths have been rumored to be contaminated. The central character, a Doctor, test the waters and determines the baths are polluted. He is celebrated by those who had contended such difficulties existed. As Doctor prepares to release his findings, he is confronted by the town leadership stating that he will be responsible for the demise and collapse of the town's economy.

The people who get ill are not citizens of the community but rather are outsiders. Sacrifice a few outsiders for the benefit of the town. After all, not too many die, most just get ill.

When the Doctor insist on publishing his findings, the town leadership declares him an "Enemy of the People". The truth is denied, then a barrage of falsehoods damage the man's reputation beyond repair. The "healing" baths continue to operate.

I am often reminded of the town councilman in Jaws when, fearing the tourist would stay away, he demanded that the beaches stay open. Suppose the shark had just swum away to open water, that a "bigger boat" was never needed but the town's tourist industry was permanently damaged. Would the police chief become the villain of the piece?

Ah, the relative nature of the truth. Can the truth be based upon a fluid set of information? Do facts change? At what point does your friend become your enemy? What is an enemy? Webster's says it is a person who is actively opposed or hostile to someone or something.

I enjoy pointing out that at one time in their life Thomas Jefferson and John Adams were intense competitors, political enemies. Both were right, both were wrong and both grew from their experiences. By the end, they had become close friends. I submit that neither were ever "enemies of the people".

Of course, we could consider President Nixon's feeling about Woodward and Bernstein. This just gets confusing. I think I'll go to the porch and drink a Coca-Cola.

Hum, I'm pretty sure Nixon viewed the Washington Post as his enemy.

I am in revolt against the age-old lie that the majority is always right
— Henrik Ibsen
You should never wear your best trousers when you go out to fight for truth and freedom. — Henrik Ibsen

WHAT DO YOU THINK?
July 21, 2017

It is difficult these days not to think about how downright ugly national politics is. I feel we awaken to it and we go to sleep with it. Now, I'll confess I prefer the humor I go to sleep with to the unbelievable stuff I wake up to. And Lordy, the national news before dinner can give you indigestion.

A member of my family asked me a logical question. "If you find the behavior of our current crop of politicians, from Congress to the Executive, to be so inexplicable and incoherent that it aggravates you to your core, then why not stop reading the newspapers and listening to the news?"

My answer? I told them I felt I had a moral and ethical obligation to be informed if I intended to vote. And believe me I intend to vote! I have no idea how I will vote in any future election but I know why I will vote. I have a responsibility as a citizen to cast an informed ballot. But dang, right now the truth seems to be meandering along more erratically than the Arkansas River as it leaves the Rocky Mountains and heads for Lake Keystone. I have never seen so many "alternative truths".

I believe I have an obligation to be actively attentive and intellectually engaged. I know the truth is here somewhere. I just must work harder to find it.

The truth. Why am I hearing more of the ghosts of Presidents past saying, "I am not a crook!" "I did not have sex with that woman."?

You know Presidents really do have to be thick-skinned. SNL, Letterman and Leno had great fun at the expense of George W. Bush and Bill Clinton. When Letterman referred to "Bubba" everyone knew who he was talking about. SNL's skits hinted that "W" was intellectually inept.

You know if I can I'm going write about our founders. A peek at the Presidential election of 1800 between Thomas Jefferson and John Adams seems to fit here. This duel might be the father of all campaign nastiness. Jefferson hired one James Callendar. Devoid of morals, Callendar with a cadre of his cohorts spread blatant lies about Adams throughout the taverns. Jefferson won the election, Callendar went to jail for slandering Adams, Adams went home to Massachusetts.

In 1802, the vengeful Callendar was released from jail and published the story that President Jefferson was having an ongoing affair with a slave, Sally Hemmings. The story dogged Jefferson and his legacy until DNA testing in 1998 proved it to be true. So, not all "lies" are lies.

You would think it would be hard to lie about people but it isn't.

I submit that the taverns of 1800 have morphed into the social media of 2017. What do you think about this hypothesis? Seriously, what do you think?

As evil a man as ever drew a breath wrote in his guidebook to securing power, "Make the lie big, make it simple, keep saying it and eventually they will believe it".

Maybe we could agree to follow the Ninth Commandment, "Thou shalt not bear false witness against thy neighbor". It seems to me that should cover all kinds of lying. What do you think?

History repeats itself and that is one of the things that is wrong with history. – Clarence Darrow

EVERY BULLY IS A BULLY
August 17, 2017

Have you been keeping up with this North Korea thing? I find I have been thinking more about "school yard bullies". I am coming to realize that many bullies are long past school age. But a bully is a bully is a bully. In the logic of a bully, there is one correct opinion and it is their opinion.

There is a certain "been there and done this" feeling to it all this. I don't know exactly why but this week has felt unrestrained.

Even in October of 1960, when Khrushchev was banging his shoe on the desk at the United Nations, I felt there was measured restraint on our part. Many said Khrushchev had chosen his time well. Our President, Dwight Eisenhower, was in the final months of his Presidency. John Kennedy, the Junior Senator from Massachusetts and Vice President Richard Nixon were locked in a highly contested battle for the Presidency. It was an election in which each party had a foundation for great optimism.

The election was incredibly close. Kennedy received 303 Electoral Votes and won the popular vote by the slimmest of margins, barely 100,000 votes. The Republicans, perhaps with some merit, felt the election had been "stolen" from them by the "big city political bosses", especially in Chicago by Mayor Richard Daly.

Despite banging his shoe and being something of a bully, Khrushchev was a measured man. Buoyed by the United States failure at the "Bay of Pigs", he waited until October of 1962 to test the young American President, before bringing the world to the brink of nuclear war over the placement of missiles in Cuba. The resulting 13-day stalemate is well documented.

If you recall or may have read, during "back door diplomacy", President Kennedy received 2 letters from Khrushchev, the second letter seeming to retract favorable elements of the first letter. The second was more the letter of a bully, a shoe banger. On the advice of his brother, Robert, President Kennedy chose to ignore a "second Khrushchev letter" and respond only to the first. Most historians agree that this restraint was the critical difference.

I'm wondering how much restraint does a bully possess?

Well, anyway, today seems reminiscent of this yesterday. Every nation and every culture have it bullies. So here we are. Guam is much further away than Cuba but it is us.

I don't think we are back to telling our children to get under their desk and to not look toward the flash. About 25 years ago an author, Robert Fulghum, wrote <u>All That I Need to Know I Learned in Kindergarten.</u> Play fair, clean up your mess, don't hit people and so on. Every kid knows who the bullies are.

About this school yard wisdom, we advise our children to ignore the bully. Don't give them credibility. That still seems good advice. Well, that and take a nap every afternoon.

Back to that school desk thing, it is a good thing kids are kids. They know how to sit on the back steps and drink Coca-Cola and giggle at the ridiculous. I hope I never forget how to laugh at the absurd.

The truth is that all men having power ought to be mistrusted. — James Madison

If tyranny and oppression come to this land, it will be in the guise of fighting a foreign enemy. — James Madison

VOYAGES TO NEW WORLDS
2016

Have you ever wondered how on earth the sailors with Christopher Columbus viewed their trip? I don't think the far side of the world held much gold and glory for these guys. Perhaps they were just sailors. We know a great deal more about the men who followed Lewis and Clark up the Missouri River, across the mountains and came out on the Columbia. It was a new world except to the native Americans for whom it was just home.

Think about this. The world of modern medicine has made many of us adventurers. While commonplace to the physicians who "live" there, it is a whole new world for the rest of us.

On my most recent journey into the mysterious land of medical miracles, I again wondered about Columbus and the boys. Just as they had sailed other seas, I had experienced somewhat similar medical adventures. Of course, now a colonoscopy is akin to sailing a rowboat across Lake John Wells not taking to the high seas. There was a day watching the monitor was an exciting new view of an old world.

Now the preparation is still no walk in the park but it is no longer misery. Do you think any of Columbus' guys were first timers, hanging over a bucket throwing up? I'm told it was likely.

I believe strongly in regular physical examinations once you pass a certain age. Every half a decade a complete examination is prudent. As some of you might have seen from an advisement my eldest granddaughter recently purchased in the Stigler News Sentinel, I have just had one of those "zero" birthdays.

Beyond the internal adventures that one comes to expect, I discovered new lands. I swallowed a capsule. I swear I opened the box and there it was for all the world looking like a space probe headed to photograph Mars. On one end was an eerie blinking blue light sending out a beam of piercing light.

Swallowing equated to blast off. It is a large capsule but manageable for most. The thought that this capsule was making its way from one end the digestive track to the other, taking photos like a Martian tourist and transmitting them back to earth as it traveled along its prescribed pathway. It felt like an adventure. There is great anticipation waiting to receive the photos. Like Columbus' crew, I got to go along for the voyage.

As with most trips, the preparation still leaves something to be desired.

From a personal health standpoint, I recommend such a regular routine physical examination to each of us. Oh, I know many of us have to make the magical inquiry before undertaking such a quest. "Will Medicare pay for that?"

In wisdom gathered over time I have found that every experience is a form of exploration. – Ansel Adams

I never thought I'd miss the quiet dignity of Anthony Weiner. – Stephen Colbert

BEFORE.COM
2017

Over recent months I have been asked what apparently is an increasingly common question. "What was life like before the internet?"

I suspect that the color of my hair and along with other miscellaneous physical features makes me appear as though I might have the answer to the question. I can't say that their logic is flawed.

"Internet" suggests speed, the rapid generation and transmission of Information and written communication. Our obsession with speed seems to multiple disproportionally. Remember when "dial up" was considered state of the art for connecting to the internet?

Alexander Graham Bell had already given us real time auditory communication between established points. However, recently fewer than 50% of the American households had an actual land line. What a marriage the internet and the cell phone have formed! A farmer in his field inside his tractor can check the stock market and issue a buy/sell order and never miss a furrow.

Speed. Studies suggest that hurried responses open the door for emotions to come into play. Emotions can push aside reasoned logic. I believe if we reply to a communication within mere minutes our thought processes are more vulnerable to the frailties introduced by impulsivity.

Let me think. Life before the internet. Written communication was slower. Life somehow seemed more permanent. Words like solid, durable, stable, predictable and honest jump to mind. You talked to people face to face, eyeball to eyeball.

Your wait for a response was days or even weeks, not minutes. Gratification was delayed, not instant. Patience and anticipation were nurtured by the very nature of life. We expected things to take time. Yes, when we could afford it, we could make a long-distance call. But even that wasn't as satisfying as a letter. You can remember a telephone call but you cannot re-read it until the paper is worn at the corners. A text message certainly does not get the job done.

Letters were written with considerable thought. There was no spell check or synonym finder, you were on your own. A letter was somehow permanent once you signed your name to it. You mailed it and you were committed.

It was slow but thoughtful. Thoughtfulness breeds effectiveness and accountability.

Information was saved on paper, it existed. It was tangible. It was in books and journals.

Let me think. This whole idea of life before the internet is going to take more words than this one writing. I wonder if each technological advance prepares us for the next. I've got a Coke and I'm headed to the back porch to think about this a bit. I'm leaving my iPhone in the house.

The problem with quotes on the internet is that it is hard to verify their authenticity. – Abraham Lincoln.

TELEVISION

LIVING IN THE AGE OF MEDICATION COMMERICIALS

October 7, 2013

Ever think about how much television commercials for a medication might cost us per pill?

I suspected no-where near the cost of the research and development. Then, I found that many medications were the result of slight change in chemical formulation as a patent prepared to expire and generics become available. Virtually same drug, with the same degree of effectiveness, but now marketed with a different name. How about that?

I have noticed an increasing number of television commercials are for "age related diseases". I suppose as we live longer, we noticed more aches or pains. A friend suggested that his were from boredom and thought a pill being hyped on television might help. A physician in the group made a diagnosis, rather than a medication he should consider "getting a life". After some thought, he gathered his wife and went to the bright lights of the desert for a few days. He left with visions of winning, fine dining and romantic evenings. He returned with considerably less money and colitis, his aches and pains had grown worse. I thought it would be rude to ask how that romance thing worked out for him.

Still I find cures for a number of diseases advertised that I didn't know existed until a drug company found a cure for it. Restless Leg Syndrome can be a superior rationalization when your wife accuses you of "hogging the covers".

There was a time medicine was only to cure disease or mute pain. Now many medicines seemed to promise to allow us to avoid the routine discomforts of life. Having carefully examined several wooded wheeled, iron rimmed wagons in which our ancestors came west, I am convinced if it hadn't been for the patent medicines that were a blend of 70% opium and alcohol, we would have never breached the Mississippi River.

Now that I consider it, having at least my share of the "aches and pains of age", you might be able to sell me a bottle or two of patent medicine.

I suspect there is some crude correlation between the number of commercials and the demand for product. The heated advertising challenge between the "blue pills" and the "twin bathtubs" suggest these companies have tapped into a high demand arena. There seems to be no shortage of commercials for diabetes, anxiety and depression. Of course, there is educational value, otherwise how would we know about SSRI's (Selective Serotonin Reuptake Inhibitors).

Then, they always suggest we discuss it with our physician. I once went in and ask my Physician about some newly hyped cure. Knowing me well, he used a single word to refer to me as a male mule. Nonetheless I'd enjoy hearing Dr. Thomas' view on this advice.

Weather's cooled but an afternoon Coke is still very good when I'm just thinkin'.
Want to come out ahead on this deal? Buy stock in a drug company. If they are advertising it like crazy, we have got to be buying it.
Always laugh when you can, its cheap medicine —Lord Byron

PURCHASE IT, PURCHASE IT NOT
2016

In a recent writing, I acknowledged a lengthy love-hate relationship with television commercials. In doing so I realized there might be a very thin line between over thinkin' a matter and being obsessed with it. Some obsessions are clinically diagnosable. Others just irritate those around you.

As I thought on it a bit more, I realized I'd reached a time in life that my joints were like a Rice Krispies commercial, when I move, they go "Snap, Crackle and Pop". I also believe it is an age that it is okay to write about an obsession or two without it bothering me a lot. So, I will!

The AFLAC duck has to be enjoyed. But it is the black gentlemen with his completely befuddled expression whose closing cameos add the exact spice that make these tasty pieces memorable.

Then, there is the budding Gordon Gecko, that stock market addicted baby with all his technology, who I feel at any second will announce "For the lack of a better word, greed is good". But the greedy little devil is cute.

Some advertising genius detected our enjoyment of the plight of "bad boys". Perhaps he simply watched Charlie Sheen's repetitive rendition of himself in Two and a Half Men. Before Charlie personally wrecked his train!

In applying his skills, he put Alex Baldwin and Charles Barkley together. Some casting just seems to fit together properly. Do you suppose Sir Charles really has a hot dog warmer or mustard bottle under his suit coat? Even when you know the lines by heart, there is a chuckle. I'm sure many of you know but I can't tell you the product they are hawking. But by not letting the product get in the way, they have become belly laugh funny.

Coach Knight and Coach Phelps appear to be making an appeal to our desire for civility. Alas, civility is only skin deep, ultimately requiring Coach Knight to calmly instruct his cohort, "That's not how to throw a chair".

Car commercials are a television staple. I find cars that intrigue me, I am unwillingly to buy. The cars can I easily afford don't intrigue me. My wife says it is guy thing. I'm good with that.

Ah, television commercials that influence a purchasing decision. Maybe.

A passion about something strips our sophistication. I love the whole idea of bacon frying in a skillet. While it smells so much better in Billie's kitchen, I find visions of bacon in a television commercial agreeable. It is so agreeable that I almost fell for the Bacon-Flavored Scope commercial on April Fool's Day.

I still find this topic to be "quite a mouthful" but commercials reach out and involve me. Now that concept requires a lot more thinkin' on my part. Thinkin' can get confusing, like trying to understand why a certain cure requires an ending in two separate bath tubs. Separate you say. Just thinkin'!

Tell me and I forget. Teach me and I remember. Involve me and I learn.

IN THE FLICKERING LIGHT OF LATE NIGHT
March 20, 2015

Well, in not many nights David Letterman will be leaving us. How many years has he been with us now? I know that it is not too early to thank Letterman for the Late Show. He was a skilled interviewer and fine comic. That seems the ideal blend for a talk show host. I am anxious to see what Stephen Colbert brings to Late Show desk.

Jimmy Fallon, the current Tonight Show host with a Saturday Night Live pedigree, is bringing a different flavor to his show. I like "Thank you notes", but I guess I'm just slow to warm up to "Jimmy's celebrity beer pong" and other such celebrity games. His interviews seem more about entertainment than information, and that isn't an inherently bad thing. It is just different.

In thinkin' while writing this piece I realized a truth. We are still "Carson" people. The more I wrote, the more I thought of Johnny Carson. Remember Johnny Carson? For generations he was the Tonight Show, he was late night television. How many viewers remember him now?

Ed McMahon introduced him each weeknight, extending the first word, and saying "Here's Johnny!"

Carson was the consummate host and interviewer. The guest was treated like a guest.

Remember the great cast of Johnny's characters and skits? There was "Floyd R. Turbo" with his red plaid hat and his ultra-conservative positions. There was the mustached pitchman "Art Fern" and his busty co-host who introduced America to the "Slauson Cutoff" and "when you come to the fork in the road, take it." Aunt Blabby and the Mighty Carson Art Players appeared regularly. There was Carnac the Magnificent, a psychic who divined the question when provided the answer that had been "sealed in mayonnaise jar on Funk and Wagnall's front porch since noon today".

Johnny took time off but he never left us with re-runs. He left us with guest hosts like Bob Newhart, Joan Rivers, Jerry Lewis, McLean Stevenson and of course, Jay Leno and David Letterman. It provided his fans with a new show each night and invaluable opportunity for his fellow comedians.

Just thinkin' on it, I suspect I've painted Johnny with the satisfying tints and hues that time provides. Billie and I agree that we laughed away many late nights with Johnny, then David. I'm glad we did. I'm thinkin' a lot of folks did.

I want to thank David Letterman for his contributions to our quality of life. Alright! Alright! I still miss Carson. But that does not mean I can't miss Letterman too.

I wish Stephen Colbert great success in replacing him. I like late night talk shows. I miss David Letterman and he isn't quite gone yet. I hope he stays well and enjoys his years with his son, Harry and his wife, Regina. I have rarely seen a child so change a man. I am optimistic about Stephen.

I suspect David Letterman will find retirement difficult. In fact, "I wouldn't give his troubles to a monkey on a rock".

Who can follow Carson? Well, believe me, somebody can — and will. — Johnny Carson.

ALRIGHT, ENOUGH ALREADY!

February 12, 2015

Now I know I have considered my "love-hate relationship" with television commercials before. However, when a six old boy becomes your frequent viewing companion – well, you just have to think about it again. Perhaps it is just me but the new breed of television commercials seems to increasingly involve physical relationships or aggression.

I am not talking about Scooby Doo or Ninja Turtles. I am thinking about sporting events of all varieties and much regular programming between 7PM and 9PM. Six-year-old ask questions.

The "What is ED question?" was manageable. Manageable until this lady in the blue silk showed up, crawling and expressing what she had rather be doing. I didn't know if a six-year old notices such things. But they do. Input from classmates make things more awkward, saying that it is make-believe like Scooby-Doo isn't working as well for me.

My wife told me that sending him to ask her was not an acceptable option. I said "I understand."

The Super Bowl commercial in which the "blue pill" rolls out the bedroom window, over the roof top and ends up in the gas tank of a small car has helped. The car grew bulging muscles. I liked that one; it provided support for my "Scooby Doo" hypothesis. Even a six-year old knows cars don't grow muscles.

Just when I thought I was good to go, here comes an advertisement for a cream that will help attractive ladies with an activity that becomes painful with age. Enter – inter – something or the other.

I think I'll save the ads for "aggressive video games" for another time. I need to get my Sports Illustrated out of the mail box and put away. It is the swimsuit issue. Buddy and I won't be "reading" stories and looking at photos from this issue.

Obviously, I need to think about this a lot more. It is confusing.

P.S. on gasoline: A few weeks ago I had some thoughts on the price of gasoline. I said I was going to keep my tank topped off. I tried but the gas went back up faster than I was driving it out. Oh well, I hope you fared better.

All television is educational television. The question is: What is it teaching? – Nicholas Johnson

CAN A JIMMY EVER BE A JOHNNY?

February 10, 2014

I suppose you heard that Jay Leno, apparently with considerable reluctance, is leaving the Tonight Show. He is giving way to a younger man with a Saturday Night Live pedigree, Jimmy Fallon. I must say that in recent years we have been a "Letterman Household". If The Late Show was in reruns, then we would watch "Leno".

As I thought about it a bit I realized that is only partially true. We are still "Carson" people.

As NBC's changes at the Tonight Show materialized, the more I thought of Johnny Carson. Remember Johnny Carson? For generations he was the Tonight Show. At its onset, it was a one hour and forty-five-minute show in markets with fifteen-minute nightly news cast. It was an hour and a half in other markets.

Ed McMahon introduced him each weeknight, expanding the first word, and saying "Here's Johnny!"

In our home we rarely were awake at end of the program, but always listened to the monologue. The monologues were not as cynical and sarcastic as we hear today.

Remember the great cast of Johnny's characters and skits? There was "Floyd R. Turbo" with his red plaid hat and his ultra-conservative positions. There was the mustached pitchman "Art Fern" and his busty co-host who introduced America to the "Slauson Cutoff" and "when you come to the fork in the road, take it." Aunt Blabby and the Mighty Carson Art Players appeared regularly. Perhaps the most memorable was Carnac the Magnificent, a psychic who divined the question when provided the answer that "sealed in mayonnaise jar on Funk and Wagnall's front porch since noon today". The audience enthusiastically participated in "Stump the Band".

Johnny took time off but he never left us with re-runs. He left us with guest hosts like Bob Newhart, Joan Rivers, Jerry Lewis, McLean Stevenson and of course, Jay Leno and David Letterman. It provided his fans with a new show each night and invaluable opportunity for his fellow comedians.

Do you remember the night George Gobel followed Bob Hope and Dean Martin, he sat on the couch between them and ask, "Did you ever feel like the world was a tuxedo and you were a pair of brown shoes?" Or perhaps the Ed Ames Tomahawk Toss?

Remember Bette Midler's rendition of "One More for My Baby and One More for the Road" on his final show?

Just thinkin' on it. In this erratic weather the steam off an extra cup of coffee has replaced my Coca-Cola. I suspect I've painted Johnny with the satisfying tints and hues that time provides, but Billie and I agree that we laughed away many late evenings with Johnny. I'm glad we did. I'm thinkin' a lot of folks did.

I hope

Who can follow Carson? Well, believe me, somebody can — and will.
— Johnny Carson.

TO BUY OR NOT TO BUY
2015

Every think much about the commercials you see on your television screen? I am convinced that I have love-hate relationship with them. There are those where I find the sales pitch quite palatable, others not so much. Some are funny, some are silly, and some insult the intellect of a four-year-old. Other commercials hawk products that I don't presently wish to explain to the four-year-old that frequents our home. Hopefully not belaboring the point, television commercials seem a quite diverse lot.

Logic dictates television advertising must be effective. Corporate America would never spend such great sums of money without the reasonable expectation of a profit. The creators of advertising are unquestionably skilled at their craft.

Illusions have always been sold. In the beginning, cigarettes were sold with images of social sophistication and good health. Beer is now sold as cure for all our social insecurities. Some poor dog named "We-go" was recently dragged into the beer arena.

Drug companies want us to believe our life will be better because we purchased their pills. We consider their pills despite the long list of side effects provided us in monotone voice while visions of the surf and beach continue to flood the screen. I wonder if we knew about "restless leg syndrome" before a drug company discovered a cure for it.

I know I am no longer in the target audience of most ads, the eighteen to forty-five-yea- old crowd with their exuberant willingness to part with disposable income. I am in the target group of some, those commercials often end with "- and we will bill Medicare." Or maybe address some element of bowel function.

I confess the ad where the lady stands before the city council and inquiries about their colon health does amuse me. Has this been on the agenda of the Stigler City Council? If not, should it be? Just askin'.

Now I got to thinking, what advertising influences my shopping? I can't recall buying something because I saw it on television. I do carefully look through several inserts in the Sunday Tulsa World. Mother and Dad always waited for Shelton's ad in the News-Sentinel.

This is about the point I realized I had really "bitten off more than I could chew". I still want to consider local furniture merchants and automobile dealers whose commercials tend to wear me out. Especially those who I obviously have mislead into believing I wanted to see regular doses of their children.

Believe I'll go get a coke, sit down and watch the Cardinals for a while. Then, maybe I can think about this a little more.

The difference between almost the right word and the right word is the difference between the lightning bug and lightning. — Mark Twain

THE EVOLUTION OF LATE-NIGHT TELEVISION

August 20, 2015

If you have watched any CBS television programming over the past few weeks, you know that Stephen Colbert will soon begin his tenure at the helm of the Late Show. The quality and format of this show has yet to be disclosed. The good news and the bad news is that will likely be different than David Letterman.

How will he complete for ratings against NBC's Tonight Show with Jimmy Fallon or even compare with Seth Meyers in NBC's later time slot? They are part of a multitude of comedic graduates of NBC's Saturday Night Live. Colbert will come from the newer school of late-night programming championed by Jon Stewart.

Fallon has broken with the format of Leno and Letterman. Both Leno and Letterman were students of the "King of Late Night", Johnny Carson. Carson believed the keys were razor sharp and flexible interview skills coupled with a format of well written and well executed skits. His fans came to feel they knew the characters in his skits personally.

Thinkin' on that, I realize it is possible that I am setting myself up for the doom of disappointment. I want the impossible. I want Johnny Carson back.

His monologues could cut like a straight razor yet not be cynical or sarcastic.

Remember Johnny's skits? First was "Floyd R. Turbo" with his red plaid hat and his ultra-conservative positions. There was the mustached pitchman "Art Fern" and his busty co-host who introduced America to the "Slauson Cutoff" and "when you come to a fork in the road, take it". Remember Aunt Blabby? However most memorable was Carnac the Magnificent, a psychic who divined the question when provided the answer, information that had been "sealed in mayonnaise jar on Funk and Wagnall's front porch since noon today".

Letterman retired and left us with a summer of crime drama re-runs. This decision compelled many of us to a summer of watching The Tonight Show with Jimmy Fallon. Being vacation season, Fallon and Meyers were often also re-runs but my wife and I had the opportunity to preview Fallon's version of The Tonight Show. We just haven't warmed up to the silly games he plays with the star guest. But as I recall it took us a bit to embrace throwing melons, cans of paint, buckets of super balls, etc. off the roof of the Ed Sullivan Theatre. By the end, we considered it something of a modern art form.

Late night television has significance in our home. Johnny Carson took over as host of the Tonight Show in 1962. Our children are young and it was before the days that 9,000 networks were available through cable or satellites. This was intimate, private entertainment time; time a young couple could smile and relax together. So, the quality of late-night shows is important in our home.

We hold out hopes for Stephen Colbert. We might grow to like Jimmy Fallon's silly games. Seth Meyers has great promise. Yes, we know there are 9,000 other channels but we like the traditional late-night show.

I like to smile as I doze, then snore.

We'll adjust.

Who can follow Carson? Well, believe me, somebody can — and will.
— Johnny Carson

DO TELEVISIONS COMMERCIALS EVER FADE TO BLACK?

Oct. 2, 2015

At the closing of a television program, I frequently notice the screen fades to black. This signifies a clear conclusion to the program. Now the commercials we see during the intervening time show no such courtesy, they simply run one on top of the other. In a past column I had written about a generic and somewhat indiscriminate dislike of certain television commercials. There are television advertisements for given products or market segments I find bland or distasteful. Furniture ads often head my list of the consistently bland. However, recently one furniture pitchman showed up in a bowling shirt. I chose to take it as an obvious nod to television's most immoral reprobate, the Charley Harper character on <u>Two and a Half Men</u>. I thought that was subtle and creative and maybe purely accidental.

Having previously expressed my negative feelings about medication advertising campaigns, especially those directed at biological dysfunctions that appear as the human body ages and that would better addressed at a later time in the evening. Anyway, I wanted to express my admiration for some commercials I enjoyed a whole lot more. Advertisements that brought smiles, that made my wife and me feel better just because we watched them.

We are completely taken with the small white dog with the green cast on its right rear leg. As other dogs joyfully sprint by the dog and his owner, a sad expression crosses his face. The owner takes out his smart phone and places an order. To the lyrics of "I was born under a wanderin' star" from the classic western musical <u>Paint Your Wagon,</u> dog and owner reappear with the dog in a front baby carrier, man and dog all smiles.

And I suspect thinkin' about old Lee Marvin singing that song in the movie version of the play has to bring a smile. Stimulating fun memories is a fine thing.

The best thing is that you have to look very close to know this an ad for Amazon.

On a more serious note, the pharmacy commercial for "get a shot-give a shot" promotion is cute and kind. The children are troopers. The red adhesive bandage with the big white W is gently applied. You are helping your child and another less fortunate child. All good stuff.

Then there is the thirtyish dancing couple. After a "feeling it" beginning, she hurls herself through the air with the belief he will gracefully catch her as she sails toward him. A landing more awkward than elegant brings a crash and fall into the table and then to the floor in grand slapstick humor. In the concluding consultation with their United Health Care online physician she explains, "I came in too hot". The perfect description.

I confess. I enjoy television commercials even those I find annoying. I like kids and dogs and adults who don't take themselves too seriously.

The temperature on the back porch is ideal for a coke and a snooze. Fade to black.

I must say television is very educational. Every time someone turns it on, I go to the library and read a good book. – Groucho Marx

OH PLEASE, NOT AGAIN
2015

I don't believe it is a revelation that I find both enjoyment and annoyance in television advertisements. I am adequately obsessed with them that I would collect them if I had a way. Unable to accumulate them as one would collect coins, I write about them. If you write about a topic, people will ask you about the topic. I have come to enjoy such communications.

If a couple of folks inquire about a topic, a reader who has made it to this point knows they are going hear a little more about television commercials. It is a bit like asking about someone's grandchildren. In the flash of an eye you can see everyone reaching in their pocket and retrieving their phone. It always strikes me as "a gunfight in an old western movie." Now, make no mistake, I've developed a competitive quick-draw.

I have written and discussed enough about television commercials that I have had to consider how I became so intrigued with them. I was almost in my teenage years when television first entered my parent's house. The television set created static on my FM radio so it rather aggravated me. Given my age, I now suspect that my parents found me equally irritating.

Anyway, I know Ford Motor Company always presented their product with a lovely young lady draped across the hood of a vehicle. Teenage boys notice such things. I'm sure I was disillusioned to find such a young woman was not standard equipment on any of the Fords at Doyle Sewell's dealership. Anyhow, seeds of expectant disappointment or deception were sown or something akin that.

Moving on, I found that I really enjoyed some advertisements despite this predisposition. Anticipate anything with kids and dogs to receive a positive 5-star review. I really like kids and dogs. I am convinced that it is impossible to see considerable humor in the commercial with AFLAC duck working out in a cross-training gym, especially when he pops from the stack of tires or startles the man while dosing in a stack of towels.

Have you seen the newest Dick's Sporting Goods ad? It is a very well-crafted commercial that celebrates all the positive aspects of participation in athletics by all genders and all ages. Almost as an aside at its conclusion, it is mentioned that Dick's has all the necessary equipment you could ever need.

It is a rainy day. I can sit on the front porch partially obscured by our thriving Japanese Maple tree, lovely as rain collects and then falls from the leaves. I always think about what I have written. I thought about television advertising television. Huh? A new trend I think but HBO to Showtime to Netflix is also advertising on network television. And movies. I finished my tea and returned to the keyboard.

It seems that there is now a steady trend toward television networks advertising their own programming. While these are equally creative, how many times can you watch a "nude" woman covered with tattoos come from a zipped bag in the middle of a street? It is all about the numbers of viewers. I pay for HBO and so forth, network programming is still supported by advertising. So, it is about the numbers. I'm sure many a television executive is thanking the good Lord for the arrival of "election season" with its bounty of advertising dollars. A buck is a buck.

Advertising is the art of convincing people to spend money they don't have for things they don't need. – Will Rogers

THE NEW TELEVISION SEASON
2016

Do you recall when the beginning of a new television season was highly anticipated? There was adequate cooperation between the 3 major networks and each had a week to present their new lineup. There were only 3 networks plus PBS. It was all over the air and the air was free. Of course, in Stigler we needed a substantial antenna to pick up an adequate signal. I believe early on these extendable metal poles with linear bars at the top, stabilized by guide wires attached to each corner of a house, were something of a status symbol.

My dad had returned from World War II with substantial knowledge of the workings of radar so he understood the technology behind television. Dad and Paul James of Oklahoma Tire and Supply pioneered the sales and installation of early Haskell County television.

While I still preferred radio, there was a magic to television. I can't tell you how many people knocked on our front door and ask to see "the television". The picture was snowy but you were able see the people. It seemed miraculous and mysterious; mystifying yet gratifying.

I have heard recently of a number of households returning to an aerial in their attic. Dang, television is still free if you only need about ten channels rather than "ten hundred".

Okay, back to the new season of programming. Over the years I have gotten considerable pleasure pointing out how easily television heroes accomplished their task. Physician friends have often been an easy target after watching *Marcus Welby, M.D.* to *Code Black*, from *M.A.S.H* to *St. Elsewhere*. I confess *Nurse Jackie* provided a different prospective. Attorney programs were even better from *Perry Mason* to *Ally McBeal,* from *Boston Legal* to *The Good Wife*, the humorous comparisons to the day to day life of an actual attorney was fertile ground. I believe there will always be law enforcement programming from *Dragnet* to *Law and Order* to *CSI* to *Hawaii 5-0* a couple of times. I have known a lot of physicians and attorneys, fewer in law enforcement but enough to provide me with good times.

Now I assume you've heard those sayings about "pay back". Well, it true. Now if I was teaching and I only had to deal with *Welcome Back Kotter*.

In the mid 1970's, immediately after I completed my Ph.D., I started practicing with a psychiatrist in Tulsa. Her practice was focused on forensic matters. I actively assisted her in the emerging science of jury selection. I only did it for a short time before beginning to focus on another arena of forensic practice.

Well, this fall a television program titled *Bull*, allegedly based on Dr. Phil's early career, appeared on the schedule. Gosh, some people I've enjoyed heckling over the years have awfully long memories. That I initially think *Bull* is bull makes no difference. I know some folks are going think vengeance is sweet. Maybe the program won't last.

I think I'll go to the back porch, sip a Coca-Cola and enjoy this fall day. Maybe I'll think of some solid retorts just in case.

Well, I'm not sure what pop psychology is but I don't like it.
– Phil McGraw

THE JFK CENTER HONORS
2017

Over recent weeks I have heard considerable discussion about Presidential legacies. I believe a legacy is a plausible perception of who we were and what we valued during a particular time in our life.

Now I understand that much of this discussion is fueled by pundits obsessed with the drawing an audience to their own essays or television programming. Authentic historians enter the discussion more carefully.

Oh, I have no doubt that Presidential legacies exist. Some are created by a careful manipulation of facts yielding a positive or negative perception of events. Legacies do not require consensus. Who and what was FDR? This is a question that remains the focus passionate historical debate. What about Thomas Jefferson and his ownership of slaves? Thinking on it I have concluded that for each man legacies (plural) exist rather than a legacy (singular). Further, none of these men, these high achievers, were without flaw but neither were they without passion.

It seems to me that the more lasting of these legacies occurs through an uncomplicated acknowledgment of a Presidential passion. The 35th President of the United States, John Fitzgerald Kennedy, was passionate in his love and admiration of the performing arts. Each year since 1978, the Kennedy Center Honors have been awarded to performing artists for their contribution to the American Culture.

What better legacy can a person have than to be remembered for their passionate admiration of the achievement of others?

These Honors involve a weekend long ceremony that includes a State Department Dinner, a White House Reception and the Gala Performances at the Kennedy Center for the Performing Arts. Since its inception, each President of the United States and the First

Lady have taken an active role in the honoring these individuals who have made such enormous contributions to our culture. Certainly, our last 3 Presidents seemed to have cherished their role in these presentation ceremonies.

Maybe any really lasting legacy just occurs, it is not actively sought. A Kennedy Center Honor is considered the most cherished award a performing artist can receive. I think President Kennedy would have quite pleased to have his name attached to such a prestigious honor.

That our country and our culture so values the performing arts and artists that we so honor them in such a fashion speaks volumes about us as a people.

Such a legacy cannot be synthetically created by the man. That they are a reflection of his deeds, his personal values, perhaps so. In honoring them we honor ourselves and our culture, our way of life.

In the relativity of time, Henry David Thoreau, fishing on Walden Pond, would approve. Had it been around I think Thoreau would have enjoyed viewing life through the fizz of a Coca-Cola. Just thinkin'.

I think this is the most extraordinary collection of talent, of human knowledge, that has ever been gathered here at the White House, with the possible exception of when Thomas Jefferson dined alone. – John Fitzgerald Kennedy (White House Dinner honoring Nobel Prize Winners, April 29, 1962)

I look forward to an America that will reward achievement in the arts as we reward achievement in business and statecraft. – John Fitzgerald Kennedy

The Fall Commercials Season

October 24, 2017

Once upon a time the television season began in the fall and concluded in the spring. New television programing came as winter increasingly confined people to their homes, more of a captive audience. Summer was for being outdoors. On occasion, we would watch reruns. The programing seasons were crisp.

Remember when <u>Dallas</u> had left you in suspense as to "Who shot JR"? That fall I was hanging over the fence at a football game when the PA announced who had shot JR. I was not a follower of the program and for all the world it sounded to me like "The Christians shot JR". I found that confusing. My wife placed me on the right path before I said something embarrassing.

Well, I hope you get the idea that we really did wait for a new season.

As I recall, the new commercials also came in the fall. It was long before the Super Bowl Grand Prix of Commercials commenced. I was enthralled by commercials and how they are selling us what. I still am.

Like the times, commercials were once simple. A new car commercial with an attractive young woman draped on the hood was a straight-forward sell. Every 16-year-old boy with a new driver's license in his pocket was a prime target. Subliminally convinced if you buy the car, you get the girl, he couldn't wait to afford such a vehicle.

It seems as if I have always been a fan of television commercials, some I like and others I don't like so much. I understand that like those old automobile commercials, we are being sold a fantasy.

Nonetheless, I enjoy creating a list of my favorites and my least favorites.

My cotemporary favorite begins with two cars, same brand, park beside each other on a bluff overlooking the surf. A grandfather and grandson emerge from the cars. After shaking out his wetsuit, the old man is standing beside his grandson at water's edge.

The young man asks, "Tell Grandma you were going fishing again?"

The old man, face deeply lined and heavily tanned, replies, "Maybe."

In the closing frame the pair are paddling out toward the surf.

I find the series of Extra gum commercials in which emotion is conveyed through a young man's simple drawings on the inside of gum wrappers. The subtle joy on the young woman's face when she discovers the drawings that have been left for her is a treat. Makes a guy wish he could draw!

Then, there is the man driving in heavy traffic belting out his rendition of "Sweet Caroline". The early reviews are critical. Then, he stops beside a lady and a brief duet ensues. The light changes and they move on.

On the low end of the spectrum, I rank the self-gifting smart phone ad for a mysterious "34-day anniversary" near the bottom. I place it just above the football official in the restaurant. You know these are just my opinions.

I am just passing over medications this time. This year I started looking up the average price of the drugs in the better commercials. I understand why they can afford such expensively crafted advertisements. Even a perfect fall day on my back porch with a cold coke can't make me feel right about the price of some of these medicines.

Finally, have you seen the new beverage commercial that involves the phrase "Dilly, dilly!" It is either sheer genius or incredible stupidity. I just can't decide. Just sayin'.

The greatest deception men suffer is from their own opinions.
– Leonardo da Vinci

On Sports

BULLIES, CONCUSSIONS AND FAN AMENSIA
November 8, 2012

Doesn't matter if you listen to Brian Williams or Scott Pelley, to CNN or ESPN, the seemingly poor behavior of a Miami Dolphins player has reignited a heated discussion of the culture of NFL football. Inevitably the dialogue made its way into NCAA athletics. Locally, like a waterfall, talk of the recent Sports Illustrated article on Oklahoma State football experienced a rebirth. Dez Bryant and Justin Blackmon's current difficulties didn't help.

As with every effective organization, leadership starts at the top. I propose that the play of the New England Patriots reflects a consistency of ownership and coaching. Being prepared to dodge the boots that might be hurled my direction, I hypothesis the same is true of the Dallas Cowboys. And the Miami Dolphins.

Just thinkin', you notice how quickly the fans have forgotten and forgiven the New Orleans Saints for "bounty gate". Perhaps we do view these athletes as mere performers, entertainers. As a society we have been notoriously forgiving of "movie stars" multiple and repeated transgressions. Are they entitled to blanket immunity for poor conduct because God has blessed them with exceptional talents?

Physical aggression is encouraged and prized – and well paid. The Dolphins have shined a light on verbal aggression. You have to admit announcers enjoy saying and fans get a chuckle hearing "It's getting a little chippy on the field". Taunting brings a yellow flag.

Just a moment – I'm thinking about the difference between taunting and bullying.

NFL football, given the size and strength of the players, is a violent and collision- based game. Management of injuries is vital to a team's success.

Well, it is all part of the game. Right? It is the violent collision that excites us. "Did you see that hit? Dang, that was something! Just a minute they will replay it."

A man of letters recently suggested these people add color to our otherwise drab and colorless lives. I rejected the suggestion. There are more honors in a laborer's calloused hand or in the tired aching feet of a saleslady than in any touchdown pass ever thrown or caught.

Something about all this bugging me. Are there life lessons being learned by adults playing the game for money? I haven't found them yet.

What really troubles me? What do I resent?

I resent these greed driven elements of professional and collegiate football are a threat to an invaluable school boy sport. In the interest of full disclosure, I love high school and middle school team sports, especially football, basketball, softball and baseball. I'm warming up to soccer but haven't gotten there yet. Unlike golf and tennis, these are not lifetime activities, they are developmental activities available to us for a brief time of time.

But football, so many students can participate. There is ultimately a place for everyone who commits themselves to the game. Cooperative efforts are valued, we learn to appreciate the diversity of skills required. Offensive lineman, defensive lineman, skill players and those who really decide the outcome are in the trenches. Everyone contributes.

Just thinkin'. Bands are so similar. It takes tubas and trumpets, the woodwinds and the percussions to obtain a pleasing end product.

The more I think about this, the more certain I am that the answers are inside the gates of Panther Stadium. The games can teach life lessons to our children and bind us a community. It is everyone's team.

The NFL is simply a social anomaly. It is not where we learned to love our games. **Go claim your seat at Panther Stadium**! Enjoy an authentic football game, community, friends and yes, popcorn and Coca-Cola. Get there early enough and you'll see a guy about my age making his to the press box. Stop him, thank him and ask the "Voice of the Panthers" if you ever stop being a Panther.

I know the answer.

Never, never, never on cross-examination, ask a witness a question you don't know the answer to. – Harper Lee in To Kill a Mockingbird

BASEBALL AND ANOTHER CLASSICAL FALL
October 18, 2013

The baseball playoffs are upon us. Baseball is a game of skill punctuated by bursts of great athleticism. It is a game of stamina and persistence, those with long and hallowed careers were successful only 30% of the time. A team that wins 60% of its games will experience considerable success. It is a game of strategy, statistics, superstitions and traditions. Our family is filled with such opinions, rites, rituals and superstitions surrounding baseball.

Some people believe baseball is too slow, it is not. It is deliberate. Contrary to the clever series of ATT commercials that lead children to the conclusion that faster is better, there are times that slow is better. Don't nurture your children in a hurry. Fine wine and superior Scotch whisky is aged. I wonder if it is the same with the human brain. If I can remember I'll let you know.

Oh yes, back to baseball. What other game will entice a four-year old to sit in the lap of seventy-six-year old and listen to an explanation of the game. "A pitch or a throw?" "Hit is fair or foul?" "Run, batter, run…. Go sit down!" Leaping from my lap, he dashes across the room and slides under an ottoman. I signal him "Safe!" He leaps to his feet and shouts, "Go Birds!"

Baseball is an interactive experience.

You can discuss hair, hats and beards. The Red Sox have taken that beard thing really seriously…and superstitiously. It entertains me and makes the boy in my lap cackle as between pitches we try to decide what animal a player resembles.

Baseball contains a sociology education.

President Ford once said, "I spent hours watching baseball on the radio." Me, too. I sat with my Grandfather while he colored the word pictures being described by the St. Louis Cardinal announcers.

Traditions are treasured, not because we are told they are important, but because they are important. They make us feel a part of the game. Some traditions are newer than others. The fans sing "Sweet Caroline" at Fenway Park while Cubs fans serenade the ivy walls with "Take me out to the ball game".

Baseball is a multigenerational experience. It has no gender boundaries; just ask renowned American historian, Doris Kerns Goodwin.

Come spring, don't forget there is a very nice baseball facility west of Stigler High School in Rose Park. You don't have to travel far to get a Coke and sack of popcorn, lean back in the bleachers and enjoy baseball.

Meanwhile, it looks to me like the football Panthers are doing well.

"Every strike brings me closer to the next home run."
– Babe Ruth

AND SUPER MEANS?

February 3, 2013

For food consumption, a day second only to Thanksgiving, a day on which a nosebleed seat fetches $3400, a price far too rich for the blood of the loyal season ticket holder of either team, untold amounts of money will be wagered by days end, and a football event will occur in a venue far, far away. Who does actually fill the stadium? It beats me.

There has been much written about the impact of violence found in television programming, movies and video games. My wife certainly believes that after an evening of <u>Justified</u> or <u>Boardwalk Empire</u> there is adequate blood flowing from our television set. How should the NFL be considered? "Bountygate?" It is the violent collisions that make for animated Monday morning water cooler talk. What social values are we redeeming? Well, I don't know.

For contrast, let's go to a local high school football game. Buy a coke and a sack of popcorn, visit with some friends on your way in, find an available seat, settle back and enjoy the game. After all it is a game and such games were intended to be played by boys, to teach a fundamental relationship between effort and outcome. There is little more gratifying than to see a young man make a play after having failed on previous efforts. The greatest pride comes not from defeating an inferior opponent but to have won as a team against a more talented foe. We did not receive an equal measure of physical coordination at birth. But in some fashion, we each learn contribute. We can discover things in ourselves we did not know we possessed.

Despite the jokes, character is built on these playing fields. The rewards are intrinsic to playing the game.

Did I mention that it is most probable that none of the young men will play again after their final Friday night in red and white? Honor their efforts.

A grassy field with imperfect lighting but filled with eager young men willingly learning lessons that they will unsuspectingly apply to situations throughout their lives. The educational quality of such participation is boundless.

And don't forget the Coke and the popcorn.

In life, as in football, the principle is to hit the line hard.
— Theodore Roosevelt

THE SOONER SCHUFFLE
January 6, 2015

Discussions of religion and politics are often considered taboo topics when it comes to the public expression of thoughts. In discussions of national politics Social Security is often referred to as the "third rail", making an analogy to the lethally charged direct current carried by the third rail of rapid transit system.

On occasion, for the many fans of the University of Oklahoma football, the existence of a "fourth rail" can be observed. If you can believe what you read, the rail is don't disappoint us and don't embarrass us by getting soundly beaten at the hands of a defensive coordinator that two years ago the faithful were convinced had to forced out of the program. This seems a move that worked out far better for the Tigers than for us.

While aware some players failure to compete, of the impact of roster reducing injuries and that emotionally disturbing year ending bowl crushing defeat in some Florida bowl or another, Head Coach Bob Stoops has decided it was time to make a couple of changes to the staff. His first conclusion was "I'm not the problem, so I'm staying." In a meeting with the press, in a rare flare-up of cynicism he sniped, "When I was hired, I was told all you have to do is beat Texas. You see where that is."

Well, if you re-create the Dragon, then you have to feed the Dragon. For those of who can recall, even Coach Wilkinson and Coach Switzer out stayed their welcome. The noise was the same, "The game has passed them by." As I think on it maybe they were devoured by their own pet Dragons. Now the University places bronze images of them near stadium entrances. Perhaps history does provide prospective.

The temporary solution seems to be "Let's throw an assistant coach or two under the bus". A teammate and fellow defensive back at Iowa, Jay Norvell, and the juco transfer who quarterbacked

Oklahoma to its last National Championship and had rapidly risen to Co-Offensive Coordinator, Josh Heupel, were selected.

I have been looking at the coke tinted ice cubes in the bottom of my glass, somewhat similar to reading tea leaves, and thinkin' about what I have written. I noticed that like college athletes not all the ice cubes were equal. I thought I have to be on the practice field to really understand what an ice cube can really do. I watched the ice cubes roll around the bottom of my glass. I hope it all works out.

I hope Jay and Josh find their "Clemsons". I hope The University of Oklahoma wins a National Championship.

I promise to wonder about Oklahoma State in the future and believe me I have already spent a great amount of time scratching my head about The University of Tulsa. I just want to see Oklahoma teams win and Oklahoma kids play well.

Pressure is something you feel when you don't know what the hell you're doing. – Peyton Manning

Composed in memory of Jimmy Thomas, SHS Class of 1955

ON BEING A FAN
January 15, 2015

This is the season that makes you consider the definition of being a fan. I suspect we are all fans of some variety of another. Personally, I'm a fan of jelly beans and Brach's peppermints, of Coca Cola and hot coffee, and of teachers and decent books. I am a fan of high school athletics.

Technically the term fan is derived from the words fanatic or aficionado depending on which source you are a fan. A fan is marked by an excessive enthusiasm for a team, a person, a group or a product. Right now, it is sports fans I have in mind.

The college football season has concluded with a four-team playoff. The NFL is in drawing down. Conference play in college basketball is underway. The NBA is approaching the all-star break. Hope springs eternal in the hearts of da' Cub fans as pitchers and catchers report in few weeks. Professional sports seem to persistently overlap one another. I believe in part fueled by seemingly inexhaustible amounts of money available to be paid for television rights.

It seems we can make a competition from any related endeavor. We have fantasy football leagues and even Super Bowl advertisements have become a contest. Fantasy? Just thinking on it a bit, hadn't considered the possibility fan comes from fantasy. We assign a number of traits to our heroes that they do not possess. Some live quite vicariously through their teams. Why else would someone paint their body green and gold and top off their head with a hat that resembles a triangle of cheese and sit in a negative twenty-degree temperature? I considered fans to be those sat in marginal temperatures while struggling with TU through a 2 and 10 season. Did I almost break my arm patting my back? Well, I shouldn't because I had a great time. Football, family and popcorn.

OKC Thunder players are well paid to put on a show and they do. It appears you can't buy or steal a seat for a Thunder game while OU, OSU and TU seats go begging.

But let's get down what being a fan is really about. Have you been to a high school game recently? Make a football game this fall? Attended a basketball game yet? Of all the levels of sports you can follow, I'll tell you which players have the most appreciation of your attendance. And their parents and grandparents appreciate it. I don't make my way up bleachers easily anymore, but I can give the front row holy heck. I repeat I am a fan of high school athletics.

My family said if I was going to write about positives of being a high school athletic fan, I had to disclosure that I rated high school venues on the quality of their popcorn. I do. Buy a bag of popcorn, a Coca Cola; lean back and enjoy the purity of high school athletics.

I can accept failure. I cannot accept not trying. -- Michael Jordan.

CHANGING OF THE SEASONS

March 19, 2015

Mid-March brings us to a change of seasons. I'm not thinkin' weather.

Selection Sunday and the Conference Tournaments have been completed. A common and persistent question is being asked. "Have you filled out your brackets yet?" The NCAA basketball tournament has a considerable fan participation ingredient to it, "the office bracket". If one or two of your favorites made the field, there is an additional vitality as we attempt to determine the best manner for them to win and move on. College basketball's grand finale is up on us.

Then, on the same day, it is announced the best pitcher on your favorite American League baseball team is headed for "Tommy John" surgery and will not be available this season. It does feel like baseball season outside. It is warm with a cool nip riding on the southern breeze. Spring training games, hopes in every camp are on the rise. Every team is conjuring up a scenario under which they can win the pennant this season. This is the "next year" we have been waiting for since last fall.

Oh, did you hear the Tulsa Drillers are now the LA Dodgers Double A affiliate? That could be exciting. Minor league baseball is still an affordable family outing. You can go to a number of games each season. Can't make it up to Tulsa? Let me suggest Roye Park. Go see the Stigler Panthers play and I'm sure there will be summer leagues. The fresh cut grass smells the same. The popcorn and coke will taste great. You'll only miss the sound that wood makes when it solidly connects with the ball.

Baseball is baseball. How did someone in the mid-1800's lay out the ideal field for the "perfect game"?

But first, we have to conclude the NCAA basketball season. March Madness is here. Every fan, player and coach is optimistic.

The pessimist points out that every team is going finish their season with a loss except for one. Only one team can win the National Championship. Nets must be cut down and "We are the Champions" must be played.

"Tis the nature of Bracketology." Is Bracketology really a word?

I know there are some in Oklahoma who will contend that basketball and baseball are just there to keep our brains warm between football seasons.

I strongly disagree.

If the old ash tree at 605 NW A Street ever goes down, I'd like to get enough wood to have a bat milled. There could be nothing better for a dreamer's back porch than a Coca-Cola and ash baseball bat, a 34" Mantle model Louisville Slugger. Now that would have to improve the quality of the little bit of thinkin' that is takin' place.

"It ain't over till its over". – Yogi Berra

ONCE UPON AN AUGUST AFTERNOON
August 4, 2015

When I write columns like this, I always warn myself of the perils of writing a tale of "walking miles to school in the cold and wind, uphill both ways". It would be foolish not to acknowledge that such a risk does exist.

Let's save a discussion of the explosive expansion of curriculum for another time.

Then as now, the beginning of football practices heralded the pending arrival of the formal academic year. In 1951, enrolling freshman got their first introduction to organized football. There was no grade school or junior high football in Stigler.

Football coaches around eastern Oklahoma were an interesting lot. They might have played a little football here or there. However, their service in World War II or Korea dotted the interval between their playing days and their coaching time. Their conditioning philosophy was adapted from various World War II physical training programs. Many coaches proudly acknowledged their conditioning programs were adapted from a Marine boot camp training mentality.

Players were taught thirst was the demon that could mentally weaken you. During a hot, dry August practice you must overcome your desire for water. The practice field was on open land just to the east of the city cemetery. An oval shaped grassy boundary surrounded a large practice area. Years of Panther football teams had worn this grass-free zone into the shape of a shallow bowl. Several inches of dust had collected in the center of the basin, now after many years affectionately dubbed the "Dust Bowl". I don't know how the dust remained when each day so much of it was carried into the WPA gym bleachers that served as a dressing room.

Our equipment looked to be relics from the 1930's. The equipment that worked its way down to the freshman was all pre-

War. 1951 would be the last year the Panthers played in black leather helmets. Plastic shell helmets, Riddell Suspensions became available. Let me assure you there have been tremendous strides in concussion safety. It is unclear that having "your bell rung" and concussions are the same thing or even similar. For sure both left you unsteady, but any coach of the era would tell being a little dizzy might actually improve the quality of your play.

Freshman pads were often seemed to be a shell of hardened cardboard and lined with layers of felt. There was no fashion in football.

No one is more thrilled for school to begin than football players. Practices had to end in time for bus students to make their bus route.

One thing everyone who ever played football has in common is a distain for August practices. There are memories, stories and friends we will never forget.

Baseball players are smarter than football players. How often do you see a baseball team penalized for too many men on the field? – Jim Bouton

"SAY IT AIN'T SO, JOE."

June 25, 2015

My phone beeped and I read a most distressing sports news update. The St. Louis Cardinals were being investigated by the FBI for hacking into the computers of the Houston Astros. The Cardinals! If you grew up in Stigler, Oklahoma in the 1940's and 1950's you were likely a Cardinal fan. Maybe you even joined a group of males of all ages and sat on the curb outside Zenos Garland's domino parlor and listened to Cardinals game on a radio blaring out the windows.

You could go inside and reach into the icy water of the Royal Crown cooler and retrieve an ice-cold Coca-Cola. Zenos would tell you as you paid the nickel to remember to bring the bottle back.

As you reclaimed your seat, Harry Caray would describe a baseball stadium you only dreamed of ever seeing.

Not the Cardinals. Not baseball. This is kind of thing football teams do. Are the Cardinals the New England Patriots of baseball? No, the feds weren't inspecting the air pressure in footballs.

I feel akin to the small boy who asked "Shoeless Joe" Jackson of the Chicago White Sox as he left the Cook County Courthouse in 1919, "Say it ain't so, Joe."

I tried to rationalize that it is not the players but the "money ball" computer whizzes, the carpetbaggers who now infest the game's front office management. The players just comprise the team on the field. Of course, that is just my opinion. I want to believe that is the way of it. I think it is that way.

What should Major League Baseball do? Well, this seems to have been made a "Federal Case". The Cardinals are accused of hacking into the Astros' computers to obtain scouting data and such. The violations sound more like corporate America. I guess an uncomfortable truth is that baseball teams are corporations. Corporations that pay established players big bucks, unestablished players not so much. Maybe it is a federal case. But the players still play the games.

I do enjoy the Texas Rangers and the Kansas City Royals. It isn't their fault they aren't the Cardinals. Even as older men we cling to the teams of our boyhood. And to baseball, the game that lets us remain young forever. The perfect game.

I find pleasure watching young Oklahomans progress in and into the major leagues. How can you watch Dallas Keuchel pitch and not feel good?

I could never abandon the Cardinals, even if they were letting the air out of the balls. Oh wait, I'm confused. Anyway, can this be a federal case? By the FBI!

"Just say it ain't so, Joe."

I see great things in baseball. It's our game – the American game. – Walt Whitman

God knows I gave my best in baseball at all times and no man on earth can truthfully judge me otherwise. – Shoeless Joe Jackson

THE USGA'S FATHER'S DAY LESSON
June 2016

Those of you who may not be avid golf families are unaware of a Father's Day ritual that is almost like turkey on Thanksgiving. On Father's Day, pending the cooperation of the weather, the United States Golf Association (USGA) hosts the final round of the United States Open Golf Championship. It is a real big deal for a lot of us.

This Father's Day brought a perfect storm when the NBA basketball championship series went to a 7th and deciding game that evening. Although I'm not a big NBA fan, it just doesn't get any better than two major athletic championships on the same day, Father's Day.

Our Father's Day dinner found every member of our family in attendance. Two television sets coupled with creative dining arrangements provided all with a nice view of the activities.

Sunday afternoon I recalled golf's advent on the television screen. Television was black and white. Broadcasters kept you abreast of the leaders as you watched each twosome play the final 3 or 4 holes. I would intently watch the screen for the slightest suggestion that Arnold and his army were nearing visibility. To be sure this coverage consumed only about two hours, not today's all-day events. I waited for an update of a Palmer charge.

It was 1960 and the US Open was at Cherry Hills in Denver. The coverage had expanded and many of us expected the challenge to our populist hero, our shining, cigarette smoking, knight with the unorthodox swing, to come from Ben Hogan, the old warrior who lost his prime years to the military service and his body was reconstructed from a horrible car wreck. Hogan off his courageous return to golf did not win but he did not disappoint. Few expected the challenge to come from a chubby cheeked amateur from Ohio but Jack Nicklaus forced Palmer to bring his "A Game". Arnold did. He shot an exhilarating 30 on the front side and a steady one under par on the back on that final day to achieve a two stroke victory. His army roared. The "Golden Cub" progressed toward becoming the "Golden Bear". Ben Hogan, the old "Hawk", circled looking for just one crack in the crystal mountain sky. What a Championship!

I believe the courtship between television, money and golf began at Cherry Hills. Arnie pocketed $14,000 for his win at Cherry Hills. Dustin Johnson received $1.8 million for winning the US Open at Oakmont this past weekend. How about that?

It seems the relationship between golf and television has grown and grown. Grown until finally, in my opinion, the USGA made an effort to "shoot off the foot" of their game. Remember this is a gentleman's game, a game where players call the penalties on themselves.

This Sunday on the 5th green, as Dustin Johnson settled behind his putt the ball rotated parallel with the putter head about an eighth of an inch. Johnson summoned the official walking with him – yes, a USGA official with each player. The result was agreement that no action on Johnson's part had caused the ball to move. So, the ball was played from the spot it had come to rest. The option was to have returned the ball to its original place and a one stroke penalty would be assessed. That was not the ruling of the USGA Official on the spot, who could see the grass and feel the breeze or the player. Consistent with the popular term, it was "settled law".

However, at the 12th hole another USGA Official informed Johnson that after further review he might be assessed a one-stroke penalty. They'd let him know after the round. Now, that just might affect a guy's game plan as he clings to a lead in the US Open. And all the other competitors don't know right away that they may or may not be closer to the lead that they believe. Oops!!

Oh yes, the reviewers did not include the golfer nor the USGA Official who had been on the spot.

So what was "settled law" on the 5th wasn't on the 12th and ultimately Johnson was assessed a one stroke penalty. For golf's sake, I am glad Johnson won by 3 strokes.

Johnson said he didn't cause the ball to move. That should be enough. I hold that honor is important than instant replay.

The most important shot in golf is the next one. – Ben Hogan.

FRIDAY NIGHT LITE
2016

I really enjoyed watching the University of Tulsa and Southern Methodist University football game Friday night. There were multiple lead changes before TU finally won 43-40 in overtime. The game was exciting and lengthy. Wait a minute it is Friday night.

Should I be watching college football? Is that Coors Lite they are drinking? Let's just hold on a bit. It seems that Friday nights were or should be reserved for high school football. It seems almost as if there is a sacred trust being violated. Friday is for high school football, Saturday is for college football and Sunday is for the NFL. In my mind that is the natural order of football.

So, what happened? I guess the roots can be found in the early 1970's when ABC in an effort to secure a piece of the NFL pie launched Monday Night Football. It interfered with nothing and with NFL greats like Dandy Don and Frank Gifford, with the blustery Howard Cosell and gifted broadcaster Al Michaels a fan following was quickly established and this programming flourished. Sunday Night became "Football Night in America" and then Thursday Night football appeared on the NFL Network. The NFL is now a true "cash cow".

The lessons were not lost on the NCAA and the various football conferences. "Ya gotta have a tv contract". Friday night NCAA football was created to accommodate the cash needs of mid-size conference members.

But Friday night? On 5 Friday nights each year every small town in Oklahoma should be aglow with the lights of the high school football stadium. These events are a vital part of the every student's education. After hours of practice bands march and blare fight songs, cheerleaders and pep clubs make their presence felt, Homecomings are held and football teams compete on the largest stage most athletes will ever experience. Grade school students have accessible local heroes they can emulate come Monday recess.

Adults, many of whom played or cheered under these same lights, gather with a sense of community that it is difficult to achieve in other settings. You know you belong. As many of you know I have a great passion for the value of high school athletics and their role in educating our sons and daughters. Not all vital life lessons are academic.

I want to mention again, take your spouse and go to Panther field. Buy a large box of popcorn and a couple of cokes, get up in the stands beside a group of your friends and have a great time. Do you know how important every person in a crowd is to those kids performing? Stay in your seat and watch the band! All these students have worked hard to put on a fine show for you this Friday evening.

Finally, don't yield to the temptation to sit back in your lounger and watch two college teams you don't really care about. I have no excuse for this past Friday beyond TU athletics brings me considerable pleasure.

Also, at Panther Stadium or any other high school stadium do you don't have to dodge Lite beverages being sloshed around. I don't want to get too harsh here. The playoffs are coming and the weather will be bitter cold. On such nights a hint of brandy in the air when the cap is removed from a thermos can be forgiven.

When somebody says it is not about the money, it's about the money.
– H.L. Mencken

PLAYERS OR TEAMS IN THE BIG TIME
2016

I believe I am suffering from "World Series hangover". I can't get a formal diagnosis but some such thing afflicts me. I know that after 108 years the Cubs won the World Series. With the series over, it is time for the "hot stove league" to begin. At times I wonder if that league still exists.

In the 1950's most boys were avid fans of the St. Louis Cardinals. You followed teams rather players. You never thought about a player leaving the team, they were Cardinals. Their contracts said they were. Regardless all winter long around a hot stove the upcoming baseball season was discussed.

You could follow an American League team with out being considered a traitor to the Cardinals. I liked the New York Yankees. I suspect in part because they were winning but also because they owed some of their success to 2 Oklahomans, Allie Reynolds and Mickey Mantle.

The group that would gather outside Zenus Garland's domino hall during the summer months, sit on the curb, drink sodas and listen to the Cardinals game on the radio considered it privilege to play major league baseball. The players must have too. Most had off season jobs in the community. Even baseball players had to make a living.

Yogi Berra and Phil Rizzuto were at work on their off-season job a week after leading the New York Yankees to a fourth World Series Championship. They sold suits at the same men's clothing store in Newark, New Jersey. My boyhood heroes, Stan Musial, Red Schoendienst, Marty Marion and Terry Moore of the St. Louis Cardinals sold Christmas trees at the same St. Louis lot to supplement their income.

Just thinkin' about it, we were coming off the Great Depression and World War II with its severe rationing. Well it just seemed okay that people had to work a full year to make a living. So what if the owners were making a lot of money, they owned the business and it was their money at risk. Plenty of baseball teams went bankrupt.

In 1969 things changed. Curt Flood of my beloved Cardinals sued baseball and won. Free agency became the "law of the diamond". Player's salaries sprinted upward. In 1955 the typical player earned $5000 a year. Today the minimum for a major league player is $500,000 a year.

At the stadium everything from the price of tickets to the cost of a coke and a hot dog skyrocketed.

While there are still some restrictions, players now come and go from team to team. I find myself being as much a fan of individual players as of a "special baseball team", especially players with Oklahoma roots. Young pitchers like Archie Bradley (Broken Arrow) of the Diamondbacks, Dylan Bundy (Owasso) of the Orioles, Jon Grey (Shawnee) of the Rockies and 2015 Cy Young Award winner Dallas Keuchel (Bishop Kelley) of the Astros. When they are pitching, I'm interested in those teams.

Maybe I'm as capricious as the players. Clearly it is now about the money. I protest! I never turned down a change to play ball. If anybody suggests paying us to watch, let me know! Baseball is the perfect game.

"I'd walk through Hell in a gasoline suit to play baseball." – Pete Rose

IT'S A PITCHER'S YEAR
2016

I know some of you looked at the calendar, then stepped outside to confirm the arrival of springtime. A few of you knew it was just a matter of time until I'd feel compelled to write about baseball – again. I'd write about why baseball is perfect game. Well, you were right and here it is!

Baseball came back in a rush this year. Have you noticed how baseball can permeate our life at so many diverse levels? Baseball is a family thing. What else can involve the youngest of us with the oldest of us? I now find myself sitting on the first row of some wooden bleacher to watch my great-grandson play baseball. The first row because that is the only seating level I can "climb" to. It works fine until I try to get up. Oh well, each stage of life presents its own unique challenges.

After a season of watching first grade basketball, "machine pitch" baseball is remarkably organized. I think perhaps it is because baseball itself is organized, it has fixed positions. A boy plays first base while another boy plays shortstop and so on. Each boy is learning he has a responsibility to the success of the group. A layout with players in their proper spots lends to the illusion of competence and organization. The batter swings, a ball is hit or not and everyone knows what is expected. If you forget that the boy in centerfield is who is swinging his glove like he is swatting at flies or the third baseman making a small pile of dirt with his foot, it looks like baseball. Players are in their correct place. What can I say? It just looks right.

I glance at the scorebook to my left. It is covered with familiar scratches. Any game at any level is scored the same. A 6-3 groundout or K is always the same. Be it kids or be it men playing a kid's game for big bucks, baseball is baseball.

Talking about the dollar signs, are you following the major-league pitchers with Oklahoma roots? Regardless of any intense loyalty to a team, it is nice to see local or regional players do well. Dallas Keuchel (Tulsa Bishop Kelley), 2015 Cy Young Award Winner, is off to superb 3-0 start, with an era under 1.00, with Houston. For those of you who are interested in such crass things, this is Dallas' contract year and he is staring down the barrel of some really big bucks.

Dylan Bundy (Owasso) is in the Orioles starting rotation and just picked up a nice win, throwing 7 shutout innings, against the Red Sox. Archie Bradley (Broken Arrow) has recovered from getting hit in the face with a line drive and appears solid out of the pen for the Arizona Diamondbacks. Fun thing about following a reliever is you check each morning to see if he threw the night before. Also, Jon Grey, a Chandler native and former OU player, seems to now be settling in with Colorado Rockies.

I promised pitchers at the top and pitchers it is. Even if I did start with a pitching machine. And yes, Coca Cola, popcorn and baseball is a triumphant trio, I don't care what you hear about hot dogs and peanuts and crackerjacks.

When a pitcher is throwing a spitball, don't worry and don't complain, just hit the dry side like I do. — Stan Musial

Seasons and the Weather

AUTUMN COLORS

September 5, 2017

Each fall, in eastern Oklahoma, thoughts turn to the colorful beauty of leaves. On a good year we can expect bright reds, oranges and browns. There will be talk and planning around the family table of drives through Ozarks, the Ouachita's or maybe just a quick drive over the mountain to Red Oak or up around Lake Tenkiller. On the latter drive, if the leaves aren't just right there is always the rich reddish orange, the crusty brown and white of peach cobbler at the Dairy Princess.

If it is a true family outing be prepared to answer the age-old question arising from the younger set in the back seat, "Are we almost there?" Of course, if they aren't there, we would miss them. Remember the play, <u>On Golden Pond</u>? Ethel ask her daughter, Chelsea, "We knew that all these years all we needed to do to make Norman happy was rent a ten-year-old boy?" When those voices of complaint don't arise from the back seat, you will miss them.

The significant fall colors in Oklahoma are not limited to the colors of the foliage. Amidst green fields there appears Crimson and Cream, Orange and Black and Blue and Gold. For some, these colors reflect a preference requiring unyielding loyalty. These are the colors of the 3 Oklahoma schools playing NCAA Division I football, some of us have alma maters that require a commitment of primary loyalty. For many us, the colors represent our Oklahoma schools, to the football world all 3 reflect "Oklahoma". For me, unless OU or OSU are playing TU, I'm in their camp big time.

University football is of considerable importance here. With my SHS teammates I saw my first college football games. After the Poteau game in 1951, we left Stigler early the next morning. We traveled by "yellow hound" to Stillwater to watch Oklahoma A&M lose to Arkansas on a Pat Summerall field goal in the closing

113

seconds. Then we returned to Tulsa to watch the Golden Hurricane trounce Hawaii. I was impressed.

However, honestly, it was not as impressive as my first trip to Owen Field – yes, for those of us of a certain age it will always be Owen Field. There are few spectator experiences like an OU game.

With all that said, I'm convinced that it is high school football that really matters. An eastern Oklahoma fall, as sure as the leaves turn attractive colors, will include the sound of a band playing our National Anthem followed by a whistle and the thud of a football being kicked. A game begins teaching lessons with practical application though out life.

Let's not forget our current role is to be there. And don't forget to buy a coke and bag of popcorn on the way to your seat.

Sport is a preserver of health. – Hippocrates

If it is a cliché to say that athletics build character as well as muscle – then I subscribe to the cliché. – Gerald Ford.

COLD IS JUST COLD

September 13, 2017

Labor Day has come and gone. Unofficially it is the final day of the vacation season. I suppose it is not odd that the school year seems to dictate our vacation travel. Then again maybe we like to travel in the warmth of summer and it just so happens that school is also out.

Personally, I'm okay with that because I'm not a avid fan of winter travel. I don't care if you are going skiing, cold is cold. While I know it has its great admirers, you might say I never warmed up to winter camping. If I'm going to sit on a bluff and enjoy a vista, I want to feel the warm summer sun on my back. In the winter, I could sit wearing a great coat and wrapped in a blanket in front of a fire and it still wouldn't be enough to block the frigid air blowing down a mountain slope. Have you ever looked at a Coors commercial, one of those with a beautiful mountain stream slicing through snow, and thought "Boy would I like to go swimming"? Me either. But I do have the feeling that if that same stream was racing over boulders on a hot, lush July day I would digging for my swim trucks.

However, like most things in life, I believe choosing to be out in the cold has a clear degree of selectivity to it.

I can sit in my warm home, sinking deep into my comfortable chair and wonder how fans in Green Bay or Buffalo can sit all bundled up and enjoy a football game. For me, maybe I just need a "dog in the fight" to do that. I have sat at high school football games in the most miserable of weather you can imagine when I had grandson playing. How bad you ask?

Do you remember that nasty early December ice storm we had about 10 years ago? I sat out in a freezing fog in OKC at the State Championship game as that storm arrived. I had every electric gadget available in my socks while clutching a hot pack inside each glove. No Coke, just a thermos of brandy laced coffee.

Oh, I remember sweeping snow off the seats at Oklahoma State before the Championship game with Davis when Bobby Cariker was Superintendent of Schools at Davis. Davis won.

How did I get from holidays and summer vacations to football games? I don't know. Maybe I'm trying to say there are some things worth getting cold for. Naw -- If you haven't figured it out yet, I believe the only thing that should be ice cold is a Coca-Cola.

I'm glad football season is here. I'm happy my wife enjoys football. What do you think the chances are that it will remain warm through Thanksgiving?

Nothing burns like the cold. — George R.R. Martin

Christmas

HOW MANY SHOPPING DAYS LEFT?

November 18, 2013

The Christmas season is filled with rich and meaningful traditions focused upon the religious significance of the celebration. There are also many Christmas customs with a more secular focus. Not judging, just observing.

It seems I saw Christmas advertising before Halloween had been observed. The concentration on the commercial aspects of the Christmas season has steadily intensified as the days passed. This week I have read several commentaries on "big box stores" opening on Thanksgiving Day. I found that to be cause for indigestion.

I always considered Thanksgiving to be a special holiday. Thanksgiving seems an observance of faith, family, food, and friendship. The afternoon often filled with revolving game of touch football or driveway basketball, laughter and conversation.

Thanksgiving properly celebrated, the Christmas season would commence.

Do you remember when we found out the number of shopping days left till Christmas on the front page of the Stigler News Sentinel or the Tulsa Daily World? Sundays were not counted as shopping days.

I recently heard on public radio that online shopping was growing by leaps and bounds. Researchers provide some seemingly large projection as to the amount of shopping would be conducted on line. The suggestion that all of your Christmas shopping could be conducted on Amazon seemed virtually appalling.

Should purchasing a gift require more than clicking "Add to Basket"?

100 years ago, you could shop in a Sears and Roebuck catalog. The purchase would be delivered to your home. My Grandmother Lane, as I sure many did, referred to it as the "wish book". Sounds like Amazon without a website. Not the same but close.

As the son and grandson of merchants, I still make every effort to shop locally. Is Walmart more local that Sharps? I don't know. I can't walk in the store and visit with the owner or see them at church on Sunday or see them at a Friday night game. But they do have managers and many employees that are certainly local.

Believe me I know the world of retail has changed. But it is still the Christmas season that turns a retailer's ink black, local or chain. I need to think about this a bit more.

How about we get Thanksgiving properly celebrated. It is such a fine holiday. The quality of visiting might just be unsurpassed...... and at my house the food is grand.

I'm looking forward to Thanksgiving.

Then, I'll think on this some more.

Christmas is a season not only of rejoicing but of reflection. – Winston Churchill

A FAMILY CHRISTMAS

December 15, 2014

There is little better than children and Christmas. If you want to feel better about the world sit a five-year-old in your lap and read <u>The Night before Christmas.</u> The excited voice of the child saying, "Read it again!" for the fifth time is all the affirmation you will need to be assured your reading has been a triumph.

The fact that the story is read from the same book you read to you children, then your grandchildren and now your great-grandchildren suggest you anticipated success in the endeavor. Now a Nativity story must be adlibbed. Some children like bright stars and sounds of angels in the night skies, others like the donkeys and the mangers. One year I told it from the viewpoint of the donkey. When the time is right, I want to do that one again. Wise men bearing gifts are always enthralling. Kids like Christmas gifts. Regardless, if it is donkeys or angels, get a lot of emphasis on the baby Jesus. After all for us Christians this is an important religious holiday.

The younger adults, now parents and grandparents themselves, recall and recite their recollections of Christmases past. Tables are cleared and board games come out. The sounds of the games reach the level that a teenager lays down their tablet and comes over to check it out. Now there is a Christmas miracle for you.

Most families have their Christmas Eve and/or Christmas Day traditions. There are not correct ones, only those that fit our families. It is important that time we all settle in our beds feeling snug, safe and loved.

I opened a Coke and re-read what I had written. As I sipped on the Coke, I realized that in writing about a family Christmas, I had let an essential portion slip through my fingers. The trouble with thinking is that sometimes it makes us uncomfortable.

Now sitting with a five-year old does make you feel better about the world, but it is a temporary fix. Oh, you hope that five-year old will make the world a better place but like all else in life there are no guarantees. There are just hard questions to answer.

Have I done everything I can do to make another families' Christmas warm and safe?

Have I forgotten the men and women, feeling everything but safe themselves, who are far from home in the hope that we might feel warm and safe?

We can do no less than include them in our Christmas prayers.

It would be okay to pray for a little Congressional wisdom too.

Merry Christmas!

Happy Christmas to all and to all a good night.
– Clement Clark Moore

NIGHT Before CHRISTMAS

HOLIDAYS: BEGINNINGS, ENDINGS AND FRESH STARTS

December 2015

The winter holiday season, Thanksgiving, Christmas and New Year's is officially underway. I'm sure a large percentage of the state would lobby for the inclusion of Bedlam Football. I'd consider it next year since the game will return to early December, not bumping into Thanksgiving as it does this year.

Thanksgiving has been a family favorite around our home. Thanksgiving is about family, friends, food and family. Yes, about 50% family seems right. You can visit with family without the excessive inclusion of gifts or alcohol. Talking over a table of food surrounded by family, that is good stuff... and good stuffing.

I don't want to downplay the value of visitation on "Friday Pizza night" or a Sunday dinner. But Thanksgiving, when family members with a knack in the kitchen labored intensely and with such pride have set a magnificent table, is about the enjoyment and acknowledgement of each others efforts. It is about appreciating and acknowledging the efforts and the individuality of our family members. Talk a little, listen a lot and be very grateful for the uniqueness of each member of our family. I promise that next year I'll be even better at that.

I do not consider "Black Friday" to be a holiday. First and foremost, it is a difficult activity to participate with young children in your life. If a child spends on rainy night camped on the concrete in front of big box store, I do not believe a family tradition will be formed.

I'd more be in favor of "Small Business Saturday" being anointed a holiday. It is just more to my intellectual liking. Yes, I recognize that what I'm really saying is that I still object to the commercialization of Christmas. Yes, I know that ship sailed long ago. Even when I suggest to our family that we draw names among the adults for Christmas they look at me like some of my cogs may have worn dull. Oh, well.

In writing this, I started to wonder if there is a clear end to Thanksgiving and a beginning of the Christmas Season. In Utica Square, the Christmas lights are turned on Thanksgiving evening. That is before we have even had a good dose of leftovers, so that doesn't seem right.

I have to write a column like this before the spirit of Christmas overtakes me. Before I become taken by the true meaning of Christmas, by the great optimism of the Christmas message has for us Christians. Because then I also fail in being cynical about the commercialization of the season.

Maybe the Spirit of Christmas shouldn't have a beginning or an ending. I couldn't think about that concept and not think of the great comedian from another era, Bob Hope. Try to remember where Bob Hope spent his Christmas Seasons. If you don't know, ask a veteran. Maybe it is just time to start thinking about helping someone who needs help.

My idea of Christmas, whether old fashioned or modern, is very simple: loving others. Come to think of it why do we have to wait to Christmas to do that?
— Bob Hope

EXCERT FROM A CHRISTMAS PAST

(And Billie and the Boys)
December 2015

While there might be some his equal, I don't believe anyone enjoyed Christmas mornings more than my father. He couldn't stay in bed much past five AM despite my mother's best efforts to control him. Christmas mornings found my father in his glory.

He would go to the kitchen. There he would put on the coffee and place some type of sweet rolls in the oven. If you ignored the aroma of Folgers coffee and the loud clanking of pots and pans arising in the kitchen, he would come to your bedroom.

He would whistle, creating an ear-splitting sound that had once been used to summon James and me home from blocks away. The sound virtually echoed through the house and the head.

Now convinced that he had some type of audience, he'd yell, "Santa's been here."

This was combination guaranteed to awaken any child. It extracted groans, along with substantial derogatory commentary form every other adult in the house except my mother.

The smell emanating from the two fresh perked pots of Folgers continued to creep through the hallway and met you as you emerged from the bedroom.

It seemed almost instantaneous, but my mother would have retrieved the orange juice pitcher from the refrigerator and begin stirring it. At Daddy's encouragement, she clanged the large spoon into the side of the pitcher, creating a bell effect. She would be setting out small glasses, several which had contained chipped beef in a previous life, by the pitcher. She would hand a glass of orange juice to each member of the family as they made their way into the kitchen. It was at such times I had no question as to how genuinely happy my mother was.

126

This morning, as on all Christmas mornings, I can remember at 607 NW "A" Street, Dad had closed the doors adjoining the kitchen and the living room. The kitchen was now abuzz with excited children while frazzled adults sipped on hot Folgers and hoped for the best.

The Christmas morning of 1958 was no exception. My father was thrilled to once again have child in the house.

From the bedroom window, I could see Mema Mac's bedroom light was already on next door. Daddy had called her. Her crippling arthritis now made the simplest of movements a struggle for her and would soon put her in braces. The doors to living room, to the Christmas tree, would not be opened until she was seated, her coffee and orange juice on a table by her side. While she would live to see three more Christmas Days, I believe she would have considered this to be her last.

Our first son, at 14 months old, had the concept that what was on the other side of those doors was exciting. He was right.

He got a red Radio Flyer wagon, a football, and a small train that traveled in circles. The gift that ultimately enthralled him was a yellow turtle whose green head bobbed in and out as it rolled across the floor. He pushed the turtle all over Mom and Dad's house. The turtle captivated him.

Mother prized the watercolor we had bartered to acquire from a Navajo artist. Billie and I were proud of the gift. Over the years it grew on Daddy. Still, in his mind, it never acquired the esthetic beauty of his two mounted bass.

The smells of sausage, bacon and ham frying would now overwhelm the remaining scent of perking coffee. Soon the breakfast table would be surrounded by clattering family. The meats along with eggs, waffles and sausage gravy would be devoured. The chatter of family talking all at the same time and over each other consumed the room.

Above all other family gatherings, my Daddy and Mother loved Christmas morning. They shared their excitement with us, an enduring Christmas gift to us all.

Merry Christmas from Hal, Billie and family!!!!!!!
Dedicated to the memory of my parents, Follie and Shearon McBride.

FAIRIES, ELVES AND THE NSA

December 22, 2013

It is the customary season to expend considerable energy thinking about elves. Having a small child nearby seems to stimulate such magical thinking. Consistent with American legend and lore, the Christmas season is filled with images of bright stars in cold winter night skies, of angels and mangers scenes and visions of so many past Christmases. Christmas music ignites Christmas memories. The years seem to peel away and 40 years ago seems as yesterday.

Most of us are reminded of the spiritual depth of the Christmas season. It is faith and family, friends and food.

Then, there is that jolly old elf, Santa Claus. He is smoking a pipe and appears to be in need of cholesterol check. Beards do seem to be coming back into style. Shall we credit Saint Nick? Why not? If you have a 4-year-old running in and out, admiring Christmas trees and ogling the gifts wrapped and placed under the tree. He finds only harmony between the secular and spiritual components of our family Christmas celebration. With his grandparents, he will be a happy, jolly greeter at the early Christmas Eve service.

Fairies, my wife suggest that the "ice fairy" focused on our neighborhood and deposited more than our share of ice on our sagging and broken trees. For sure the ice found us. But the "power fairy" left our Christmas lights glowing. The lights from the Christmas tree look like a work of art when viewed from the street through ice covered shrubs and bushes. Like Santa, the Ice Fairy can do good work. That is if you don't find the cracking sound of branches too distracting.

Now, President Obama held his "paint the year bright and I'm off to Hawaii" press conference. It broke my chain of thought. Of course, some say I'm easily distracted. I contend I just think about a lot of things.

There were a number of questions about the National Security Agency and the Edward Snowden leaks. The NSA's phone data gathering program was at the core of these questions. Does it violate our Fourth Amendment rights? A Federal Court just said, "Yes". The Federal Government filed an objection. Should the government or a private company be allowed to stockpile our personal information? The recent Target incident suggests safety might be a myth. Huh, how about that?

I have a seasonal suggestion. It seems to me that Santa already has a comprehensive list of who has been naughty and who has been nice. If the NSA subpoenas the "Santa Claus Diaries", I hope they wait until after Christmas Day.

Merry Christmas and Happy New Year!
– The McBride Family

MUST HAVE BEEN CHRISTMAS

December 2016

I put down the phone after reading <u>The Night Before Christmas</u> to my great-grandson and good buddy. I knew he enjoyed it but I also knew he wanted to know about "shutters and sashes", "sugarplums". What is this "down of a thistle" stuff? What is a "Courser"?

Now I read many short stories to him. I have to adjust a lot of the words. Over recent days I have been reading to him from Rick Bragg's book <u>My Southern Journey</u>, a collection of his columns from <u>Southern Living</u> magazine. Gerald Kirk's daughter, Lisa gave me my copy.

Anyway, I adjust the stories on the fly for 7-year-old ears. Most recently we read about 13 Crazy Cats and a coyote named Sylvester Highstockings. While what we read resembled Bragg's southern tale, it now made perfect sense to a first-grade intellect – and to that of an old guy enjoying the telling of a tale.

But to adjust any Christmas tale requires some courage. With hopes of avoiding plagiarism I started to give it thought for the next night's telling.

It was Christmas Eve. The lights of our Christmas tree greeted us as we came through the door, returning from an evening of Christmas Carols at our church. As coats were being hung in the closet with care, a child asked with concern, "There is no snow, so how can Santa drive his sleigh to Sallisaw tonight?"

Relying on what I had just heard in church, I replied, "It is a miracle."

Children often accept what we cannot understand. I'm glad.

The fireplace crackled. Its light made our children's stockings appear as large as their eyes on this night.

Cups of hot chocolate were joyously gulped as we chattered. The story of Mary and Joseph and baby Jesus was told as if it was all that mattered. The final sips passed our lips, followed by good night wishes.

"Merry Christmas, Merry Christmas, now it is off to bed you go."

We headed to bed with Silent Night echoing in our heads. I kissed "Mrs. Claus" good night and pulled the blankets up nice warm. I thought, "It really is a wonderful life".

The children were tossing and turning in their beds. Visions of peppermint canes, lovely dolls, balls of all shapes and remote-control toys careened through their heads; of the gifts each carefully wrapped and placed under the tree. Dare they dream of a bicycle?

Our eldest wondered if Santa had gotten his letter in time. Oh, if Santa ran short of a particular toy, well, Mrs. Claus always selected well in its place.

I had just settled into a sound sleep when from the street came a clattering and clanging, maybe a backfire or two. Now fully awake, I jumped from the bed and ran to the window.

I raised the blinds and what did I see? To my great surprise I saw Santa driving a pickup truck followed by a half dozen elves. With his window rolled down, Santa was barking directions and pointing to this house and then that. I tried to make out the markings on the side of his truck. For the life of me it looked as if Santa had borrowed a Western Auto pickup truck.

At Santa's direction, elves placed two bicycles, no assembly required, on our front porch, and then each tossed a handful of gravel upon the roof making a sound like reindeer hoofs.

They dashed up and down the street. I opened the door as they were almost out of sight. Santa stuck his head out the open window and I heard him shout, "On Ford, On Chevy, On Dodge and Jimmy."

I brought in the bicycles. I knew now there was a secret to Santa's prairie deliveries. I scratched the stubble on my face and thought about what I had witnessed. I now knew it was a miracle.

Well, this is the tale I chose to tell, more filled with truth than not. I cannot wait to tell it to a "smarter than average 7-year-old".

And I tip my hat to the Golden Days of Western Auto in Sallisaw, to Ray and Cherry Farmer, to Jay and Bobby Reynolds and the rest of us who on occasion got to make such midnight Christmas deliveries. They understood the meaning of a joyful Christmas.

At Christmas, all roads lead home. – Marjorie Holmes.

SEASONAL SHOPPING IN REVIEW

December 2016

It is about this time each year that I realize that I am not an imaginative shopper. Over the years I have learned I should be listening for subtle hints that might have been dropped over the course of the previous months. I have concluded female ears would have detected these understated suggestions as if they were played on a bass drum. Men don't do quite so well. I started to write that we don't listen as well but there just seemed to all sorts of downsides to such an observation. But from a personal level, it seems these discreet clues just miss my conscious awareness. In short, most often I just don't get it.

I do pretty well with books. I do pretty well with rituals. My family expects an <u>Arizona Hiways</u> calendar. The ladies truly enjoy Lee Williams annual cookbooks each of which Lee has always been kind enough to personalize. Rituals might not be creative but they are comfortable.

So, what does the inept shopper do at Christmas time? Well, you look at the Sunday newspaper ads more closely and listen to the television commercials more closely. I have yet to buy a chia pet but I never rule anything out.

Many of you know I have something of love-hate relationship with television commercials. I don't care much at all for jewelry commercials. Irrationally, they make me feel guilty because I can't afford the 6 carats diamond my wife obviously deserves. Why are there so many TV ads hyping Lexus and Mercedes? Would no one be interested in a Ford or Chevy for Christmas?

With all the uncomplimentary sniping going on today, it was nice to discover the Amazon commercial with the Priest and Imam. After an older Priest and Imam have spent an evening together eating good food, discussing their religious practices and the aches and pains of their advancing age, they part company. Independently thinking of the needs of the other, each man places an order with Amazon. The ad concludes showing that each has ordered knee pads for the other making prayer easier on their well-worn, maturing knees. Now that commercial pleases me.

Gosh, it is Christmas Eve and I've got to do something. I think I'll go over and check out Williams-Sonoma. Might not be the best place, my wife knows that inventory by heart. Chico's is right there. A jewelry store is close by.

Oh, Russell Stover's is right there. I wonder if they have any of those chocolate covered cherries my Grandmother Lane liked so much. Pure sugar and cherry syrup covered in chocolate but my Grandmother could eat a whole box.

Next year I have to start shopping earlier.

Maybe Christmas, the Grinch thought, doesn't come from a store. – Dr. *Seuss*

SANTA'S SHOPPING LOCALLY

December 9, 2017

Christmas is growing closer. More trees are appearing in the beds of pickup trucks and in car trunks; ready to be decorated in homes all over town. Boxes of lights and ornaments appear from storage. Thoughts of sugar plums and peppermint sticks; dreams of Christmas morning gifts fill the heads of the kids, so excited they can hardly remember their lines for the church Christmas program.

The media is filled with reports of Santa Claus sightings at Christmas parades. What a schedule that man keeps! If this magical elf is like most guys, well he'd never keep that timetable without Mrs. Claus waking him up, feeding him and getting him off to work on time. She knows that NORAD will be following him as he circles the globe on Christmas Eve night.

Perhaps a fantasy story but I'm sticking to it. Just thinkin' – I might have discovered "authentic fake news". I pray no child of any age reads this cynical disclosure.

All those gifts. How on earth does this delightful elf pull off that magical trick? Here is a thought I found in the fizz of my coke, this saintly elf is one smart guy. He contracts the acquisition and transport to local contractors. I want to emphasis the LOCAL.

It seems every small city and town operates some sort of campaign encouraging us to shop with local merchants. I think locally owned businesses (along with our schools) are the life-blood of every community. I have heard that these local businessmen and women represent considerable civic involvement. Their children attend our schools and they worship with us in our churches. They run for school board, for city or county offices. They vote.

It is these local elves who deliver Christmas gifts. They are an irreplaceable resource for those who are afflicted by a shopping disorder known as "Christmas Eve Panic". Being a notoriously late and lousy shopper, I know about such things.

I received Christmas bonus at the end of business on Christmas Eve. I shopped at "Head's Pharmacy". A carton of Camels for my dad, a box of Chocolate Covered Cherries for each of my grandmothers, a Whitman's Sampler for my mother. Gifts for my Granddad and my brother would already be under roof.

These small businesses employ people and are very reluctant to lay anyone off. It is tough to fire a friend. Heck, they usually try to give someone the chance to pick up a little extra Christmas cash.

I don't mean to ignore all those local businesses who sell services rather than merchandise. Now in my mind there was nothing like Christmas season at Hays & Buchanan or the Stigler 5 & Up. On the other hand, I don't remember any one buying gift certificates from McBride Radio and Television Repair.

Not all local businesses sell goods. Like my father, many provide essential services, from physicians to vets to attorneys to electricians to plumbers to police officers to – well, you get the idea.

There have been years I could have used a gift certificate to our veterinarian. My wife alleges our dog received better treatment than – ah, let's just forget this one.

Anyway, fill your cart at home as much as you can. I can't see online carts or clerks. I like visiting with the clerk who is checking out my cart.

Instead of cursing the darkness, light a candle. – Benjamin Franklin

A CHRISTMAS MORNING RECAPTURED

December 21, 2017

In many ways, Christmas as we think of it is constructed of our individual memories. Sustaining our family traditions as we move through life becomes increasingly vital. We do strive mightily to preserve our family rituals, many of which have been in our families for generations. As our roles change, from married to parents to grandparents to great-grandparents, our obligation remains unchanged. We feel compelled to sustain the traditional while embracing the new each generation introduces.

Change is hard when we feel preserving our family institutions and rituals are so important. Oh, there will be a generational evolution but we can save the core. Our senses are our allies in this effort. Unbox our family lights and decorations, the sights are pleasing. The smells of pine, sausage, bacon and coffee are the same. The sounds of children tearing paper doesn't change. Best of all – Laughter! There is people's laughter I miss yet I can still hear it.

Christmas is holy. It is fun. We pray and we laugh. Each year provides a mark on the Yule log of life.

As I thought about Christmas approaching, I reached back and thought of stories I'd already shared in a book called <u>Billie and the Boys.</u> I was surprised at the number of Christmas stories that it contained.

Anyway, here is one of those stories I'd like to share.

While there might be some his equal, I don't believe anyone enjoyed Christmas mornings more than my father. He couldn't stay in the bed much past 5 AM despite my mother's best efforts to control him. Christmas morning found my father in his glory.

Escaping the bedroom, he would go to the kitchen. There he would put on the coffee and place some type of sweet rolls in the oven. If you ignored the aroma of Folgers and the loud clanking of pots and pan in the kitchen, then he would make his way into the hallway.

Then, he would whistle, creating an ear-piercing sound that had once been used to summon James and me home from blocks away. The sound literally echoed through the house – and the head.

Now convinced he had some type of audience, he'd yell, "Santa's been here."

This was a combination guaranteed to awaken any child. It extracted groans, along with substantial derogatory commentary from every other adult in the house except my mother.

The smell emanating from the two fresh perked pots of Folgers continued to creep through the hallway and met you as you emerged from the bedroom.

It seemed almost instantaneous, but my mother would have retrieved the pitcher of once frozen orange juice from the refrigerator and began stirring it. At Daddy's encouragement, she clanged the large spoon into the side of the pitcher, creating a bell effect. She would set out a diverse array of small glasses, several of which had contained chipped beef in a previous life, by the side of a side of the pitcher. She would hand a glass of orange juice to each member of the family as they made their way into the kitchen. It was at such times I had no question as to home genuinely happy my mother was.

This morning, as on all Christmas mornings I can remember at 607 NW "A" Street, Dad had closed the doors adjoining the kitchen and the living room. The kitchen was abuzz with excited children while frazzled adults sipped on hot Folgers and hoped for the best.

The Christmas morning of 1958 was no exception. My father was thrilled to once again have a small child in his kitchen, racing from door to door hoping for just a peek.

From the bedroom window looing next door, I could see Mema Mac's bedroom light was already on. Daddy had called her. Her crippling arthritis now made the simplest of movements a struggle for her and would soon put her in braces. The doors to the living room, to the Christmas tree, would not be opened until she was seated, her coffee and orange juice on a table by her side. While she would live to see three more Christmas Days, I believe she would have considered this to be her last.

David, our 14-month-old son, had the concept of what was on the other side of those doors was exciting. He was right.

He got a red Radio Flyer wagon, a football and a small train that traveled in circles. The gift that ultimately enthralled him was a yellow turtle whose green head bobbed in and out as it was rolled across the floor. He pushed the turtle all over Mom and Dad's house. The turtle completely captivated him.

The smells of sausage, bacon and ham frying would now overwhelm the remaining scent of perking coffee. Soon, the breakfast table would be surrounded by clattering family. The meats along with eggs, waffles and sausage gravy would be devoured. The chatter of family talking all at the same time and over each other consumed the room. Laughter could consume the room.

Above all other family gatherings, my Daddy and Mother loved Christmas mornings. They shared their excitement with us all.

I hope you found some things in these paragraphs that you enjoyed, that triggered some pleasant memories from Christmas' past. Our Christmas have evolved from 1958 to 2017, roles have changed. Prayers and children and laughter has not. Can you smell the coffee and hear a child giggle with joy?

MERRY CHRISTMAS!!!!!

Christmas is a season not only of rejoicing but of reflection.
— Winston Churchill.
Christmas is the day that holds all time together. — Alexander Smith

Thanksgiving
New Year's
and Other Holidays

A SEASON OF CHARITY AND BLACKEYED PEAS

December 31, 2013

Christmas has passed; the Grinch has changed the center of his attention. It seems to me the Grinch is now focused on stealing unemployment. No, let me rephrase, unemployment is still with us, it is the payment of certain benefits Grinch wishes to stop. Maybe it isn't the Grinch but rather our Congress dressed as the Grinch. They do seem by nature to be an ill-tempered group who can agree upon little. That seems "Grinchy" enough for me.

I've never been unemployed but I find the thought of it unnerving. I'm told the unemployment benefits lengthened during more difficult times are designed to be temporary. Congress has decided that times are no longer as thorny, so it is time to cut off the extended benefits. Huh! These less thorny times "trickled down" to you yet?

At times I think can understand the obscure motives of our Congress and our Executive branch on such issues. Now the Republicans speak in terms that warn us against creating a society of "Dependents". I do believe most of us have become dependent upon eating and sleeping under some type of roof. Democrats are accused of desiring to secure a reliable bloc of voters who are dependent on government assistance.

All I can say for sure is that "I hope you weren't planning an unemployment check to help launch you into a happy new year". Because it appears that Congress got together and decided to allow elements of the unemployment act to expire during the holiday season. I'm sure I should feel encouraged that our Congress agreed on something, but I don't.

It seems the Christmas season filled with charity and "good will toward men" has passed. Nonetheless, it looks like we're headed into the New Year with those who are "down on their luck" still there. Except there will be less change in their pocket.

Over the holidays I met a friend for conversation and a Coca-Cola. In listening, I believe I found something. I know unemployment and underemployment are not the same. However, it seems unemployment and underemployment must feel a whole lot the same. I think we all need to think on that some. I know I do.

The New Year is here. I hope you didn't forget to eat blackeyed peas. Maybe that will fill our pockets with lucky pennies. If it happens, don't forget to share.

Cessation of employment is not accompanied by cessation of expenses.
— Cato

FINDING THE NEW IN NEW YEAR'S
January 2016

Do you ever think about why we celebrate the arrival of the New Year, especially on New Year's Eve? Yeah, me too. The view from one angle says we can put aside our mistakes from the previous year while resolving to do better in the coming year. Then I consider the likely result and think "Boy is that a bad case of self-delusion".

There is another school of thought that simply says, "We made another 365 days and are still here. Let's celebrate!" I suppose there is some merit to toasting our survival. We do always seem compelled to acknowledge for a final time those who did not make it to see the New Year. We toast those who did not live to tell more tales. A few moments for such remembrances will enhance the quality of our lives.

It seems rather like a Tontine where groups, veterans to clubs, purchased a bottle of very expensive booze for the last survivor to open and drink a shot in remembrance of each individual in the group. I do think we have an obligation to ensure that those we loved are not forgotten within our family circle. I want something more lasting than a ritual involving a shot of good whiskey. To resolve to record a collection family stories for our descendants' overflows with good intentions. Let's all do that.

Back to celebrating the New Year, there are those who commemorate the holiday by attending worship services at their church. There is no better place to seek forgiveness for the mistakes that dot our previous year and resolve to do better in the coming year. A younger demographic prefers large public gatherings such as Times Square in New York or assemblies such as found in Memphis, New Orleans or Key West.

I enjoy the idea of a mountain New Year where a large lighted pine cone is lowered for the top of a local hotel at 10PM (12 EST).

This allows warmly dressed children to take part in the festivities and be in bed at a reasonable hour. I like that, a family outing and still have the children all snug in their beds at a decent time. As I just said, I like that.

Now Billie and I have reached a place in life where we enjoy watching the Times Square Ball being lowered at midnight from the warmth and comfort of our bed. Although fighting off drowsiness, I did see the ball descend this year but I had to ask Billie if "Anderson and Kathy kissed". In good humor she suggested that if I wanted to know such things, I should consider staying awake.

I find that after Christmas I do reflect on the previous year. It seems to be more of a season that an event evolving around the final seconds of a year ticking away. Maybe it just takes me extra time to think anymore.

Many of us can now drink our Coca-Colas plain. We have little or no concern about the contents of some magic elixir that relieves a thumping, throbbing head; an aversion to bright light. We can just sit back and focus on upon the New Year's Day football games. A new-fangled New Year's ritual, bowl games, it seems harmless enough to me.

Be at war with your vices, at peace with your neighbors and let every New Year find you a better man. – Benjamin Franklin

HOW'S THAT RESOLUTION WORKING?

January 17, 2018

Ah, it was mid-January, the sparkle of the holidays had past, college football's National Championship had lost its luster out in sunny California, and 2018 was taking shape to be not unlike its predecessor. The night was bitter cold outside while my bed was toasty warm. I blessed the inventor of the television remote as I turned off our bedroom TV, remembering a time I would have had to dash across the cold floor to find the knob on the side of the set, only on rare occasion stumping my toe in the suddenly dark room.

As my Grandmother Lane would say, "That's a man who deserves an extra star in his crown."

Anyway, I was all snug and comfortable, just soundly dozed off for a night's sleep when from somewhere deep in my mind I heard crashing noise. Dreamlike but not gentle, the sound was reminiscent of the blending of a car crash and a vision breaking. Its theme music sounded like it had escaped from Stephen Stills asking, "Hey, what's that sound, everybody look what's going down".

Fully awake now, I tried to tune my ears and listen more carefully. In clearing my mind, I searched for possible matches of sounds and causes. Then, a flash of clarity it hit me. It was the sound I imagined a half-a-country would make as their New Year's Resolutions came tumbling down, mashing into bits as they collided with the unyielding floor of reality.

New Year's Resolutions. An odd piece of holiday hope and fine wishes. We do mean so well.

Did you make any New Year's Resolutions this year? It seems to me these promises made by us to us most often prove problematic. You know if you make them and publicly declare them, somebody will expect you to keep them.

Is that fair for someone to keep reminding you of your resolutions? Is it reasonable for them to keep saying, "Well, you made it not me?"

What did we expect when we committed ourselves to these glorious goals of self-improvement? I do believe the original intention was good. Ah, but once again we have set ourselves up for failure!

How can something that sounds so reasonable at the time become so problematic? We promise ourselves to eliminate behaviors that we truly don't like in ourselves and we are determined to get rid of those unappealing suckers. When we resolve to cease smoking, chewing or drinking we know it would make us healthier. Losing weight, working out at the gym – we know these activities would make us healthier, improve our appearance and strengthen "a general sense of well-being". We want to learn how to control our temper; just learn to be nicer to other people.

Me? I gave up making New Year's Resolutions many moons ago.

I'm happy I didn't resolve to give up Cokes or seeking wisdom in the cool fog of Coke fizz. And I didn't resolve to cease thinkin'.

In victory you deserve Champagne, in defeat you need it.
– Napoleon Bonaparte.

146

'TIS THANKS I'LL BE GIVING
November 2016

Well, Thanksgiving is here. I think I have bored you enough with my displeasure over our uniquely American and my favorite holiday being relegated to some hiccup between Halloween and Christmas. I know many of you are thinking "yes but you managed to slip it in again anyway". Mea Culpa.

Anyway, I'd rather talk about blessings.

Only half of the pilgrims and the Mayflower crew lived to see their first New England spring. Having survived a harsh winter, they had experienced successful hunting, fishing and growing seasons. The Plymouth Pilgrims had much for which to be thankful. In my mind that seems to be a good basis from which to express one's gratitude.

I am convinced there is no incorrect way to articulate sincere thanks.

The lore of a successful summer appears to be true. Squanto, an American Indian who had been an English slave, had "saved their bacon". It is well documented that he taught them how to cultivate corn, use maple sap and fish the rivers. He also taught them how to avoid poisonous plants native to the region.

So, in the autumn of 1621 records indicate that the Plymouth settlers and the Wampanoag Tribe held a three-day feast. I think there would have been merit to naming the feast after Squanto but certainly every Plymouth resident had reason to give thanks. Gosh, three days. I suppose some of us do get a long holiday. But if you're working retail – well, Black Friday is looming before you can finish warming your leftovers.

1863 in the midst of the Civil War President Abraham Lincoln declared Thanksgiving to be a National Holiday to be celebrated on the final Thursday of November. It stayed there until FDR tried to advance it to early November to stimulate depression era Christmas sales. How about that?

After strong objections, the holiday was only slightly moved, to the fourth Thursday in November.

Thanksgiving is American. Our Native American and European forefathers unintentionally got the whole thing started. We have preserved it, adjusted it and modified it over the centuries but we never lost the core. We should give thanks for the blessings we received over the previous year.

If you want a day to observe our ill-fortunate over the previous year, go find another day. Just because times have been tough don't act like your life was without blessings. Okay, maybe some years we do have to hunt harder than others but I still believe they are always there for the finding.

May I give another hint? Thanksgiving will always be special because on Wednesday, November 21, 1956, Billie Jean Martin of Sallisaw, Oklahoma married me. This is unquestionably the greatest single blessing of my life. That year the 21st was the Wednesday before Thanksgiving.

Guys, it makes remembering your anniversary really easy. That can be a blessing.

Family, faith, food, football and fun. Happy Thanksgiving!

We must find the time to stop and thank the people who make a difference in our life. – John Fitzgerald Kennedy

LAID UPON A SOLDIER'S STONE
May 2016

Write enough and there will be times you'll have to clarify yourself. In discussing Memorial Day, I closed a column with "Never forget your own but take the time to find a soldier's stone and leave a coin upon it". It seems while many are well aware of the tradition, others are not. To me, it is a custom worth knowing and retaining.

The practice of leaving coins upon the markers of fallen soldiers has been around since Roman times. It is does seem that the practice has evolved over time. This acknowledgement of fallen military never fell from favor; it experienced a significant revival during the Vietnam War. Historians credit the revival to the politically contentious nature of the Vietnam War.

The coins allow the family to know their loved one has been visited and honored. In National Cemeteries, the coins will ultimately be picked up and placed toward caring for the grounds or for assisting in the burial of an impoverished veteran.

There is meaning assigned to the denominations of the coins. A penny is left by a friend, even a visitor who did not know the soldier but paused to pay their respects. A nickel is left by a fellow soldier who went through boot camp or trained with the soldier. A dime is left by a person who served with the man or woman. A quarter is placed on the stone by a fellow soldier who was with the fallen fighter when they died.

Since the 1960's many vets view the coins as token of respect and a payment toward a drink or a game of cards when they meet at some future time. Some have now individualized their remembrance, leaving a half-dollar or a dollar coin one of our several efforts at creating a useful dollar coin.

Over recent years, availability making them more accessible, Challenge Coins have begun to appear on some graves. Originally the coins were given by commanders to soldiers as a special recognition. The coin could be used as identification and presented as documentation if "challenged". Now they can be purchased on the internet or in a variety of gift shops. Regardless of its origin, a Challenge Coin of the First Marine Division left upon a stone can be quite meaningful to a family.

Families may remove the coins they consider to have unique meaning; that is okay. However, there is a special place reserved in Hell for those who might steal the coins.

I find it impossible after writing these columns not to sit on my porch and contemplate the pain and loss a family must feel. The coins only represent a small acknowledgement of our appreciation. I believe it is a tradition worth keeping and nourishing.

It is foolish and wrong to mourn the men who died. Rather we should thank God that such men lived. – George S. Patton

THE TRICKS OF OCTOBER'S FINAL NIGHT

October 2016

Just in case you aren't aware, it is almost Halloween. This year seems different. Oh, it is not that the ghost and goblins appear to be in any short supply. I have seen parents bringing home <u>Frosted</u> wigs and ballerina dresses, anything <u>Star Wars</u> already seems in short supply. I've been told I'd only have to go walk the isles at Walmart or Target to get a preview of what is going to appear at my front door this year.

Billie and I are going to have to make a Sam's Club run to secure an adequate candy supply. Now adequate here means each child can have several candy bars. I enjoy being generous with the candy. The smile on a child's face when you stay "take a couple more" is worth any price.

I just don't know why my family accuses me of stashing a few Snickers and Butterfingers for myself. So, what if I do have a six weeks supply of my favorites left. I didn't want to run short.

The few of you who know me from back in the day just noted my taste in candy bars has not changed a lick over the years.

Another thing, have you noticed how many adults are now dressing up in costume to celebrate Halloween. I don't get this. Even when teenager boys come to my door "Trick or Treating" I think "haven't you guys heard of girls"? The guys on "Big Bang Theory" can get away with it. They are still hanging out at the comic book store. Plus knowing university science and math full of these extremely bright and eccentric guys, well, I get that.

What seems different is that without a sudden change in weather, we are headed for a very warm and pleasant Halloween this year. I don't mind because I enjoy seeing the kids at my door in full costume. Seeing an adult couple headed to a neighborhood house dressed as Tarzan and Jane not so much.

But for each person at an adult party that is one household that doesn't have their porch lights on. Now that is a shame! Come on now, buy a few bags of treats and enjoy the children.

Just thinkin' but it seems to me that "Dress up" is a game created by children for children. Our job is to applaud their efforts and make them feel like a princess or a zombie. "Brag on them, hug them and tell them they look wonderful".

Despite my annual whining, Halloween continues to become increasing adult. Adult enough that I look for AAA to announce that their "tipsy tow" program will be available any year now.

Hold on man. We don't go anywhere with "scary", "spooky", "haunted" or "forbidden" in the title. – From Scooby Doo

THE ONSET OF SEASONAL PSYCHOSIS
October 2016

I received two pieces of mail this morning, the Stigler News Sentinel and "The Holiday Toy Spectacular" from a national retail chain. Just by looking at the News Sentinel I could identify the current season. From looking at a catalog filled with toys, well, not so much.

Now the News Sentinel had a full back page ad dedicated to "ghost and goblins" and filled with trick or treat safety tips. By looking at the articles and spreads of photographs I could tell high school football regular season was well underway and that the homecoming season with Queens and Kings and their courts was concluding.

When I read an article of the pending basketball season at McCurtain. I knew the football playing schools in the county were really deep into their football seasons.

It is an even numbered year so there was a detailed sample ballot inside the paper. I find the News Sentinel sample ballot to be most useful when we are going to vote on several State Questions. I don't know about you but I've reached a point in life that taking a "cheat sheet" with me to polls is really helpful.

From the News Sentinel, I knew the first Tuesday of the first full week of November, Halloween and the football playoffs are upon us. Each was arriving at its appointed time.

However, receiving a Christmas toy catalog before Halloween has even passed, just somehow doesn't seem right. Now I'm as much for budgeting and planning ahead as the next fellow but this seems to be pushing the line a bit. I supposed this steady advance should not be a complete surprise since a day designated from Christmas shopping intruded on the Thanksgiving weekend several years ago. "Black Friday" is now just a part of the Thanksgiving lexicon.

For traditionalist or maybe curmudgeons like me, there was a glimmer of hope recently when several major businesses announced they would no longer be open on Thanksgiving Day. These retail giants stated it was their desire that their employs full enjoy their Thanksgiving Day with their families. Good for them!

In so many ways Thanksgiving is my favorite holiday. With its focus on Church, family and food, it seems everything settles in its correct place. As our other holidays have become increasingly boisterous, Thanksgiving retains an appropriate calm.

This year I plan on giving thanks for just surviving this presidential season – and for living in the United States.

Personally, I hope to enjoy the ghost and goblins of Halloween. I want to vote and preserve my right to complain. I want Thanksgiving to leisurely make its approach to us. Christmas seems so far off.

I am sure seasonal boundaries still exist. I just can't find them. Maybe the craziness is thinkin' too much about them. I don't know but I intend to keep looking.

Halloween starts earlier and earlier, just like Christmas. – Robert Englund

WHAT DAY IS TODAY?

December 2016

For my generation today is an anniversary that we are unlikely to forget. How could we forget December 7, 1941? The day that President Franklin Roosevelt called a "day that would forever live in infamy" now seems to be sliding beyond the recollection of so many.

My generation will not forget but for later generations the personal and emotional significance of the day seems to be diminishing. As my generation diminishes the question becomes, "Does an event have to have occurred in our lifetime to merit a lasting place in our social construct?" It is sure beginning to seem that way.

Exactly 75 years ago on December 7, 1941, the Empire of Japan launched an aerial attack on the fleet of the United States Navy at Pearl Harbor, Hawaii. This unforeseen attack pressed the United States to join into World War II. Our country had adeptly avoided entering the War since Nazi Germany invaded Poland in 1939. My father said he was hardly aware that Japan had invaded Manchuria even earlier.

The typical American on the street struggling in the depths the Great Depression was taken by surprise. The events of December 7, 1941 so profoundly impacted our lives that almost everyone remembered where they were when they heard the news.

I was almost 5 years old on that December Sunday. My generation remembers because our parents told us where we were. I heard I was enjoying a pleasant December afternoon with a picnic on my grandparent's lawn under the large ash tree that once stood along "A" Street. A man in pickup stopped and told us of the attack. It is said my mother grabbed my baby brother, James, took my hand and hustled us inside like the bombing had been at the City Lake.

Everyone clustered around the radio as information trickled in. It was the first of many evenings I would spend with my Grandfather listening to the war news on the radio and learning how to understand the war maps in the Tulsa World.

I don't believe my experiences were unique. In fact, I think they were commonplace. My father was in service. I came to understand rationing stamps for everything from sugar to shoes to gasoline. Many of us were "Tom Sawyered" into believing busting the orange coloring packet in the center of the white margarine packet and then squeezing it until it became yellow was an honor. It came to look okay but it never tasted like butter.

I have watched other events occur and fade. I suspect that endurance of a date in our collective conscious is related to the personal impact it had upon us. We will remember the date in November that President Kennedy was killed. It also changed us as a society. Our history will endure only if we share it.

Was President Lincoln shot in the spring or fall? Someone said, "I don't know, the movie didn't say."

The wisdom from the mystical fizz of my coke suggested we should read history. We should study history. We should learn the lessons only history can teach us.

Those who cannot remember the past are condemned to repeat it. – George Santayana

Prepare for the unknown by studying how others in the past have coped with the unforeseeable and the unpredictable. – George S. Patton

THINKIN' ON THE FOURTH
July 2017

When it comes to writing, I seem to be unable to anticipate a holiday. I seem to prone to contemplating it on the day and soon thereafter. It is like experiencing the holiday makes me think about the holiday. Or something like that.

When it comes to a holiday I benefit from the foresight of others.

Ah, food and fireworks! Fireworks have changed no matter where you live. Roman candles, sky rockets and black cat firecrackers evolved into community firework displays. Kids took a seat on in the bleachers or laying on a blanket gazing skyward rather than lighting and running. "Never, never light a firecracker in your hand!" "Hold that roman candle away from your body and point it skyward!" "Bottle rockets are meant to be launched from a coke bottle."

Remember those big red devils with the thick green fuse. They would blow a can at least 200 feet into the sky.

Don't misunderstand, I know fireworks displays are much safer even if they have made us into passive observers.

Food. What did the founding fathers eat during Independence Day celebrations? At a very early celebration of the John Adams family, Abigail is reported to have served green turtle soup, poached salmon with egg sauce, sweet peas and new potatoes with butter. Dessert was apple pandowdy.

Some authorities question the dessert stating that Abigail was far too practical a woman to have heated up her kitchen even for Independence Day.

Thomas Jefferson and George Washington, celebrating in Virginia, were more likely to have served ham or a summer favorite, roast beef. A true cynic observed that since the Washington's home and the Jefferson's home, being true Virginians, were not likely doing their own cooking. So, heating up the kitchen might not have been the issue it was in the more austere New England Adam's household.

It is suggested by many that Independence Day food moved from a summer feast to outdoor picnic during the Great Depression. Personally, as a boy, I remember fishing and swimming at the old strip pit. There was fried chicken, deviled eggs, potato salad and an ice-cold watermelon purchased at the Stigler Ice House. And my Grandmother Lane's cobblers. Dang, that all sounds good. Thinkin' on it now, somebody warmed up a kitchen.

As to fireworks, it was a neighborhood project. Jon Conard, Jimmy James and I pooled our fireworks. Under the supervision of Paul James, we produced an explosive celebration in the street in front of my grandparent's home.

Just thinkin', ever light a black cat in your hand and throw it? How many things did we do as children that are now considered extremely dangerous? Gosh, I don't think any piece of equipment on the old Boone School playground would pass modern muster.

I am well aware of the toil and blood and treasure it will cost us to maintain this declaration, and support and defend these states. Yet through all the gloom I see rays of ravishing light and glory. This is the day of our deliverance. – John Adams

We must all hang together or most assuredly, we will all hang separately. – Benjamin Franklin

THE ANNUAL SEARCH FOR GOOD FORTUNE

January 2017

The holiday season has past. I look back on the pleasures of the holidays. The sparkling joy of Christmas dims into the reflective calm of the New Year. This reflective experience can be interrupted by glitzy, alcohol-fueled New Year's Eve parties. Well, now that is a "once upon a time" deal for me.

Thinkin' about this, it seems that our holiday celebrations are filled with rituals that we often do not understand. We just know they are pleasurable or promise to bring us good luck. Maybe we just enjoy sustaining our family rituals. There is much to be said for that.

Each year, most often in their living rooms, folks gather to watch a lighted crystal ball gracefully slide down into Times Square, a silver slipper descend in Key West, a guitar drop in Nashville, or a large brilliantly lit pine cone come down 2 stories from the tip of the Weatherford Hotel in Flagstaff.

A number of our holiday traditions involve fine foods. As far back as I can remember come New Years, my family has adhered to the southern tradition of eating black-eyed peas with a touch of pork and cornbread. My Grandmother Lane was adamant about the good fortune associated with this dish. Reared in western Missouri and Arkansas, I suspect she grew up with the tradition. On the other hand, logic dictates that my Grandmother McBride, having hailed from Kilmarnock, Scotland, had to have adopted the tradition as she acclimated to the cultural traditions of the American south.

Odd, I can't hear discussions of the role of immigrants in our society and not be reminded of my Grandmother's heavy Scottish accent.

As to the origin of this custom, it seems that during his infamous march to the sea during the Civil War, General W.T.

Sherman is quoted as having said, "If a crow flies across the Shenandoah Valley let him carry his own rations". History records the Sherman's march as an efficient application of a "scorched earth policy".

At the time black eyed peas along with various greens such as collard greens, turnip greens, mustard greens, etc. were considered animal feed and not fit for consumption by the Union troops. When Sherman's march ended on December 21, 1864, the surviving southerners considered themselves fortunate to have been left a decent supply of blackeyed peas, salt pork and a variety of greens; enough foodstuffs to survive the winter. I do believe circumstances always determine what is considered good fortune.

I don't know about the luck element but I really enjoy black eyed peas with pork over cornbread. I enjoy this supper every time Billie cooks it. I believe most of us who were born into the depression and the food rationing of World War II have a special place for any form of beans and cornbread.

Understand there is cornbread and then there is cornbread and then there is Billie's cornbread. I have a marked preference for my wife's cornbread. Cornbread is versatile. Ever try cornbread with butter and sprinkled with sugar? Or cornbread crumbled into buttermilk? I grew up watching those variations. For those who are wondering, no, I have never tried cornbread and Coca-Cola.

The best comfort food will always be greens, cornbread and fried chicken.
– Maya Angelou

HOW WAS YOU HOGMANAY?

December 31, 2017

New Year's is such an odd holiday. Its style is clearly different from that of Christmas yet each, in its own unique fashion, is filled with hope. Many of the younger set enter the evening filled with optimism and resolutions of a more productive life in the new year only to awaken to a splitting headache and praying they did nothing too embarrassing during their celebration. Similar to those of my generation, their memory fails them.

Was there time I might have celebrated the arrival of the new year in such a robust fashion? I'm sure there must have been. Cocktails and a Midnight kiss followed by Champagne and verses of Auld Lang Syne.

Over the years, my wife has insightfully referred to it as "amateur night". A night to stay home, watch football, perhaps play cards and close it out by watching a huge glass ball descend toward a street filled with amateurs. Coffee was the preferred drink. Lordy, I'm thinking back to a time when the coffee pot was turned on before breakfast and turned off at bedtime. I used to enjoy blaming the coffee addiction on two of brothers-in-law who spent World War II in the Navy. From their tales I believe ships ran on oil and coffee.

But then again, I can go way back. My Grandmother McBride immigrated from Scotland when she was 16, old enough to have embraced the Scottish rituals and young enough to adopt new things.

The first New Year's celebrations I recall were in my grandparent's home. Although well prior to television, radio broadcast from Times Square were available. The wartime blackouts were in effect, so there were no "ball drops".

Auld Lang Syne was sung and as it came over the radio my grandmother would point out that it was written by a Scottish poet,

"Wee Bobbie Burns". The Scottish celebration that stuck with me was the "burning of the balls". Paper and other flammable materials were rolled into balls "double the size of a basketball", wrapped in chicken wire. A length of rope was attached to the ball by a bit of wire. The balls where doused with a touch of an alcohol-based accelerant and ignited.

With the blazing balls swinging over their heads, the celebrants marched and sang as they moved toward the nearest body of water. Arriving at the shore, the orbs would be given a mighty swing sending the blazing ball out over the water until "splash down" occurred. To a young boy it sounded like a lot more fun than listening to the description of a glowing ball being lowered in NYC.

My Grandmother McBride enjoyed telling me of celebrating Hogmanay, the word the Scots used for the celebration of final day of the year. Hum. Can you visualize a group of young revelers, twirling fire balls over their heads, charging down the slope toward Lake John Wells until they launched their burning sphere out over and into the lake? Wow!

It is still a hopeful holiday. We are hopeful no one gets injured. Even at that, I propose that it is considerable safer than driving under the influence.

"How did you get hurt?" "Oh, I was at a Hogmanay celebration out on the edge of the Southern Plains." Happy Hogmanay!

Be at war with your vices, at peace with your neighbors and let every new year find you a better man. – Benjamin Franklin

On Life

THE CURATIVE PROPERTIES OF FUN
March 18, 2013

It seems that recently I've been thinking too much about the confusing befuddlements of life. My family prescribed a temporary cure. Fun! Family fun!

It struck me that I have considerably more control over the fun factors of my life than I do over say Congressional sequestration or self-aggrandizing pseudo-ambassador's to North Korea.

As a cure to such morbid preoccupations, I renewed a commitment to fun, food and family – and basketball. I'm not talking about sitting in front of my big screen television set, I talking of taking my seat in the arena. As a birthday gift, my youngest son and his wife bought me three all session tickets to the Conference USA Tournament. It is a self-evident truth that my fanny can only occupy one seat at a time. My family willingly provided the essential company. Happily, for most sessions, three tickets weren't enough.

Here is the recipe. Get in your seat in the arena and enjoy a truly interactive experience. Watch the games intently and reacting to the events on the floor, applaud and laugh, fist bump. We coached from row F. It is astonishing how all the basketball wisdom is compiled in our seats and not on the benches of the competing. It is at your own peril that you underestimate the basketball knowledge of the female contingent of the family.

It is conversation that makes being in the arena the experience superior. Only politics and religion comprise the intellectual forbidden zone. Between games, halftimes, time outs and when the game is not really contested, these times bring first-rate family enjoyment.

The students in the bands are creative and entertaining to watch, blues from Memphis to a rendition of Marty Robbins' El Paso from UTEP to TU playing Take Me Back to Tulsa. Unlike concerts, plays, musicals and museums, the ticket holders are not required to hush. When you're traveling with a four-year-old, getting him up close and personal with the mascots becomes a priority.

Popcorn! Popcorn is subjected to a grading scale, C to A. Since there is no such thing as bad popcorn D and F are unnecessary. The BOK Center popcorn this week was a solid B+.

All these positive experiences can be duplicated at every high school or grade school basketball tournament. Set aside the time to have fun. Share a large bag of popcorn with the family, grab a handful and pass it on. I hold firmly to the hypothesis that germs ca not be transmitted through popcorn.

This week reaffirmed a conclusion I reached some years ago. It is more fun to have fun than to worry.

My Rx: Go have fun. And don't forget to grade the popcorn.

Trouble knocked at the door, but, hearing laughter, it turned away.
– Benjamin Franklin

A VIEW IS A VIEW AND IT'S ALL IN THE VIEW
December 18, 2013

A renowned medical journal pronounced that vitamins and other food supplements provide no benefit to the average American. It was clearly stated that all the necessary vitamins and supplements could be obtained through a healthy diet. Now remember we are talking about the "Average American".

Exactly which "Average American's Diet" is being discussed? Would it be the same ones whose diets, volume and content are so regularly criticized? I listened and decided it couldn't be. Those meals were entirely too healthy.

The more I listened, the more I wondered. I couldn't eat fish five times a week. Suggestions of broccoli and brussels sprouts and beans came frequently enough that my colon voiced an objection. Surprising, since I actually enjoy them.

Now, for many years, my wife has been a big believer in vitamins and food supplements. She is especially committed to good multivitamin and fish oil, no excesses but always the correct few. She holds firm to this view despite the fact that our typical diet is very healthy.

This matter was being discussed during a recent family gathering. I think it was family pizza night. Oops – well, a slice of pizza a week isn't too bad.

One of the boys chose to point out that our fidelity to what we consider "reasonable eating" hadn't done wonders for the "aches and pains of my bones and joints".

Being in the Christmas spirit, I sprung from my chair as all my joints gave a clatter. They creaked in unison if not in harmony. I offered with my cane to deliver a good thrashing.

Like a great many things in life, if I view it as being of benefit, it is. And I do. I do not view an occasional cut of beef as my enemy. So it isn't. Oh, palm sized portions only.

Just thinkin'. I realized that my dietary commitment is to variety, a little of this and a little of that and not too much of anything.

The more I think about it the more I come to believe we are defined by our views. Odd isn't it.

This morning, I was returning home after a very early morning errand. A bright full morning moon was sinking in the west. It turned such a rich red as it sank beneath the horizon. I realized I could focus on its beauty or upon the logic that air pollution accounted for much of the reddish color. My choice, so I choose beauty.

And a good multivitamin, fish oil and food.

Moderation in all things; especially moderation. – Ralph Waldo Emerson

INTENDED FOR MATURE AUDIENCES

January 21, 2014

For the purposes of this piece, just what is a mature audience? Well, do you have a Medicare Card? If you do, then you are clearly in the correct demographic. If you only possess an AARP card and you can remember when you got it, then you might be questionable. If you periodically forget you have such a card, then you are clearly "my people".

This morning as I was enjoying my second cup of coffee and making my way from the Tulsa World sports page to the comics, my wife ask, "Did you see "so and so" died?" The question is rhetorical. I have noted a lifecycle can be observed in the Transitions section of a newspaper. Originally you found your friends in the marriages section, and then you looked for the birth of their children. I think you can detect the flow of this stream of thought.

At some point a doughnut hole stopped being a mid-morning snack and became a point of concern on our Medicare medication program. We now strive not to reach the "doughnut hole". I think I'd still like to eat a doughnut hole, but there doesn't seem to be any lying around our kitchen.

It seems as "seniors" we have re-emerged as a target demographic for certain products, mostly medications. I see there are medications that mute the aches and pains in our bones and joint. So, we can walk on the beach and watch sunsets while playing Frisbee with our dogs. Now, the advertisers do need a visual to fill in while they tell us all the disgusting side effects the medication might produce. It appears that pharmaceutical companies are close to promising a restoration of all the pleasures of youth –with a pill and a profit.

Technology has made our lives better. When I bought my Nook, the young man made a point of showing me how to increase the size of the font so I could read more easily. He was right, but he didn't have to point it. It is much better than my Grandmother Lane reading her <u>True Detective</u> magazines and her Bible with a magnifying glass.

Think on this. I believe technology has made our life better than pills. There is much to be said for an E-reader and big screen television with more channels than a couple can ever watch. Of course, I'm not talking about the lifesaving stuff, I'm talking about the quality of life stuff. There is no reason that good healthy dose of fantasy should fade from our lives. I have to keep the emphasis on what I can do and not on what I can't do.

But just thinkin' – that can really be challenging some days. Still thinkin' – maybe it is what we can do that keeps us from dwelling on our challenges. Notes from friends help, conversations with your best friends – priceless.

I am grateful that I can write a bit. I'm not certain how this entire writing thing happened, but I'm glad it did. It is like talking to friends regardless of where they are.

Whatever poet, orator or sage may say of it, old age is still old age.
– Sinclair Lewis

THE NEW OLD-FASHIONED BARBER SHOP
2015

Like many men, the same barber had cut my hair for a number of years. Actually, while my barber remained a barber, the shop became a hair salon. What had once smelled of after-shave and tonic now smelled of chemicals for hair coloring and such. Some time when I wasn't looking about half of the clientele became ladies. The conversation in this shop had always been rather quiet, the focus of the talk on the oil business and the stock market. But now you no longer talked to the guy in the next chair; conversation was between you and your barber.

Life and vanity created even more diverse and changing circumstances. There came a time that I came in from the barber shop and my wife said, "He gave you another old man's haircut". I think I said something like, "Huh." I went into bathroom and looked in the mirror. I stared at the reflection and thought, "I have an old man's haircut." On ensuing trips to get my haircut I tried to explain to my barber what I wanted and what I didn't want.

That was harder to describe than I thought it would be. I wasn't looking to be 30 again, maybe I just didn't want to appear older than my age. I would try to explain it, fall short and return home with the same haircut. It brought me back to 1964 and United States Supreme Court Justice Stewart Potter's efforts to describe obscenity, hard-core pornography. He said he might not be capable of clearly defining it with words but, "I know it when I see it". I know an old man's haircut when I see it on my head.

So, I finally decided to try another barber shop. First a friend recommended a shop with a single barber, the owner was a man close to my age and the north wall was completely covered with golf balls. Several sets of old clubs were lying around. This looked promising. But I got home, looked in the mirror and I still had an "old man's haircut".

I contemplated my situation. Perhaps this was the only direction white hair would grow. Deciding to make one more effort, I got a recommendation from my grandson and one of my sons. I followed their suggestion.

The shop is small, clean and noisy, noisy in the right way. The Mayweather-Pacquiao fight was on the horizon. They were talking boxing and then put forth a prophecy on the NBA playoffs. The talk was inclusive, there was agreement, there was disagreement and there was laughter. Everyone talks and most everyone listens.

My next visit included my great-grandson. I was greeted with a "Hello, Mister Hal". My great-grandson just cackled, got his haircut and a sucker.

I now have a haircut very much to my taste. Maybe it is an adaptation of an "old man's haircut" but I don't see it. My wife doesn't see it. I'm satisfied.

I sat with my great-grandson watching "Scooby Doo" and sipping Coca Cola. There was nothing old about the smile on my face.

Do what you can, with what you have, where you are.
– Theodore Roosevelt

JUST DO THE RIGHT THING
July 8, 2015

There are times when life provides us genuine predicaments. In some of these circumstances the answer appears clear to us. We also know there is a well-reasoned but opposing point of view. Despite our understanding of the dichotomous positions we must propose a solution, we must choose.

I don't know about you but when such gnarly conditions arise, I seek advice. I don't seek "yes people" but rather men of wisdom and men of God and my wife. I know that I may or may not follow any part of their suggested solution, but I value this individual's viewpoint. After an even-sided presentation of my dilemma, I will ask, "What do you think?"

Often, I receive a thought or two which I appreciate and a response that can be distilled to "Just do the right thing". "Just do the right thing" sounds easy enough, but I have rarely found it to be.

I know that intelligent and reasonable people can disagree over the same set of facts. The past few weeks have provided us with a number of prime examples. Just ask The Supreme Court of the United States (SCOTUS). Don't you just love all the acronyms we now have for various people and institutions? The President of the United States is now POTUS. I'll tell you I didn't struggle with this dilemma. I don't find it a burden to refer to the President of the United States in a proper and respectful fashion.

Sorry, I got to thinkin' and I drifted. Despite the lapse in focus, I feel I "did the right thing" in expressing my opinion.

Back to the point, over the past few weeks, The Supreme Court of the United States gave us some classic examples of the manner in which well-educated and highly qualified people can hear the same arguments and yet disagree. I do think all nine Justices believe their decision represented "doing the right thing".

Now the Supreme Court of the United States had some exceptionally knotty cases. But given the aftermath of the events following the shooting in a South Carolina AME Church, the professional golfer Bubba Watson found himself in an unexpected conundrum. I am confident that Watson never anticipated this problem when he purchased the 1969 Dodge Charger used in the wildly popular 1980's television program, <u>The Dukes of Hazzard</u>. The roof of the car Watson purchased, the General Lee, was painted with the Confederate battle flag.

By the 1960's meaning of the Confederate battle flag was a far cry from the meaning of the 1860's flag, both unsavory to many but in quite different fashions. While diminishing in number, the battle flag still has its followers and defenders. Is its display freedom of speech like burning the American flag?

Back to that grand advice, "Just do the right thing". Bubba Watson saw doing the right thing as replacing the Confederate battle flag with the flag of the United States of America. I'll wager that the young man from Bagdad, Florida "sat on a porch and sipped a soda" while thinking about his decision. Then, Bubba just did his "right thing".

"Just do the right thing". How can advise so simple be so hard?

Let us go home and cultivate our virtues. – Robert E. Lee to his troops at Appomattox Court House.

AN EDUCATION IN COFFEE AND OTHER SUCH STAPLES

November 2015

I came across an article in a newspaper the other day that reported the results of a recent research study into the impact of coffee upon our health. It is not the first study on coffee I have read. Let's just say that the conclusions over the years have been quite diverse. This most recent study indicates 3 to 5 cups of coffee a day has a positive impact on our overall health.

I know that for years coffee was much more than just a breakfast beverage. The coffee pot was on from daybreak until bedtime. Many drank coffee after dinner while watching television. Some Social Scientist suggested this was influenced by the "coffee craving" of the veterans of World War II and Korea. Maybe.

Early workplace recesses were referred to as "Coffee breaks". The afternoon shot of caffeine was seen as a last shot of stimulation so the day could be finished on a high.

Personally, I suspect some crafty employee seeking a social break convinced an employer of the value of a final dose of liquid inspiration. My grandfather and my dad were old-fashioned, I guess. There were not coffee pots in Hays and Buchanan or McBride Radio and Electric. As a boy, it didn't bother me much. At dad's, the back door of Zenus Garland's domino parlor and its ice-cold Coca-Cola was only two paces across the alcove.

Regardless, remember when it was only Folgers, Cain's and Maxwell House. Then came some study questioning in impact of caffeine on our health. The color of Folgers cans became red and green. Now that gets me thinkin' about Starbucks current Christmas cup dilemma. I guess snowflakes or elves could have been fun but the Christmas Star strikes me better. I'm not sure a green Starbucks corporate logo on a red cup gets it done for me.

I have come to believe such studies are akin to the Oklahoma weather. If you find it disagreeable just wait a bit and it'll change.

How many times have we been back and forth on the nutritional value of chocolate? Is milk chocolate real chocolate? Yes, kind of. Regardless, it is 85% of the solid chocolate consumed in the United States. But if I like butterfingers is it going to influence my post Halloween consumption? The answer to the latter is no.

I think as long people are fascinated with studies about health, heart, calories, weight; vegetables and fruits, high fructose corn syrup and cane sugar there will be studies. Oh, can red wine bring heart health? Now there is a study I'll read.

Have you seen that there are new studies on the makeup of makeup?

Anyway, I have one question. Will an apple a day still keep the Doctor away? Has anyone done a recent study on that?

Early to bed and early to rise makes a man healthy, wealthy and wise.
– Benjamin Franklin.

Happy Thanksgiving from Billie and Hal McBride and family.

A SALUTE TO NEIGHBORS AND SIDEWALKS

June 24, 2015

Neighborhoods, there are good neighborhoods and not so good neighborhoods. Now most of us want to live in a good neighborhood, a place that is a vibrant positive component of our social environment. Ever think about what makes one neighborhood thrive while another withers and sours?

Many will promptly say, "The people who live there". As I think on it that is not entirely wrong but it isn't completely correct either. One must concede that without people there would be no neighborhoods.

I suppose in so many ways our basic interaction with people away from work and worship is in our automobiles. I will wave to someone I recognize or they have waved at me and I don't have a clue who they are. Dependent upon the weather, people get outside out of their cars at home. In some I detect I certain uneasiness. How will they know I'm important if they can't see my Mercedes? Very troubling for the insecure.

Now I have come to believe there is a certain living, breathing quality to neighborhoods. In fact, there are arteries and veins that carry the flow of socialization. The most effective of these conductive channels is the sidewalk. A sidewalk entices you to come off your property; it encourages you to walk around a bit. Walking in a street by the curb is not so inviting. A sidewalk seductively invites you out into your neighborhood.

Sidewalks make their way past each front porch in the neighborhood. If fact, neighbors sitting on their porches engage you. They know your children's names and the name of your dog. For many our dog is a constant companion on such walks.

You know the name of a lady's caged parakeet sitting on the porch for fresh air and sunshine. Pets are important to a well-functioning neighborhood even if they bark at 2 each morning. I always take a pocket full of treats for the neighborhood dogs. Everyone should have a dog or two who is happy to see them coming.

When you bring your wife home from the hospital to find a lemon tree "growing" in your yard, a tree composed of a large dead limb with plastic squeeze "lemons" as the fruit you don't have to guess who the arborist was. The same guy who arranged a neat line of gallon milk jugs filled with brightly colored water. They served no purpose other than to spike people's curiosity. And they did! It is simple. Neighbors are fun.

With my sore back and my dog's arthritic hips, I have regressed. There is less sidewalk strolling and more porch sitting. Oddly, I value the quality of sidewalks even more. Baby-strollers are wonderful. Everyone is talkative.

Even in bad weather, the view out the window from my chair is rewarding. Sharing such observations with your spouse is pleasant and insightful. Between sightings of friends, you are left to your thoughts. Your thoughts are enriched because of your friends. I toast them all with an ice-cold Coca-Cola. I'll even share.

The impersonal hand of Government can never replace the helping hand of a neighbor. -- Hubert H. Humphrey

RATINGS, POLLS, AND OTHER STATISTICAL ILLUSIONS

September 10, 2015

As the Presidential season creeps over us, we are bombarded by a variety of polls conducted by a diversity of interested organizations, media groups and other such interested parties. Surely a group with a vested interest wouldn't statistically skew the numbers to support their point of view. A mind exposed to years of such polls can become skeptical.

If these types of rating systems were limited to politicians and their agendas, I would not care much. I have been told the most accurate campaign polls exist in the camps of the candidates. This rather says that the truth cannot be effectively used to sway the electorate. Maybe that is just me being cynical.

Let's talk about more important ratings, like NCAA football. Did anyone ever figure out the statistical algorithm for selecting the teams for the national championship games just a few years ago? The current formula is supposed to be more straightforward. I'm skeptical.

Did you see the movie <u>Moneyball</u>? There was an application of statistics to the grading and selection of baseball players that appeared to work. I guess just because there is a statistical basis it is not doomed to fail or mislead. Las Vegas bookmakers do win a lot more than they lose.

How about the measurement of educational performance in the public schools? Teachers have been assigning grades in their classrooms since schools were founded. Grades were to report to parents that academic skills had been obtained. Somewhere and somehow, they became a competitive and comparative measure of achievement to their peers. Grades moved from local concrete measures to statistical measures, from local classroom norms to national norms. However, statistical analysis has clearly demonstrated that high school GPA is the best indicator of college achievement. Statistics do not always get wrong.

Ratings and Polls sell. Have you ever noticed a magazine or television news program hyping a poll like the "Ten Safest Cities in America", the "Top Ten Beaches in America", the "Ten Best Places to Retire" or the "Twenty-Five Best Colleges Values"? Such topics entice readers to purchase magazines or watch a television news program. Have you ever watched one of these pieces and wondered where in the heck did, they get that? Do you use *Rotten Tomatoes* to help you choose a movie? I do even know how simple and unsound the statistics are.

However, as a society, we do love these competitive and comparative ratings.

We had a window jarring rain storm move through during the early hours of morning. The day has begun with the air both cleaner and cooler. It is a coffee morning on the porch and not a Coca-Cola morning. I thought back to my first graduate statistics class. I thought "creative math". Five stat classes later I still felt the same way. I hear of a new study and I wonder. I know the benefits of good statistics and solid study design.

Back to elections and politicians, polls can make the erroneous appear to be truth. But they can also be statistically well-designed and quite correct. I am unable to ward off the temptation to tell you – "Trust your gut" and "If it sounds too good to be true, it probably is".

Facts are stubborn, but statistics are more pliable. – Mark Twain

AS THE SEASONS TURN

2015

Read the newspapers and listen to CNN, ESPN or such, it will not take long to conclude that the season of the soap operas is under way. Not literally the old-fashioned soap opera but close enough that it regularly fools.

Consider that a soap opera is the result of the practice of taking a plot, then dramatically exaggerating the intensity of life's common events and punctuating them with the most unlikely of occurrences. Additionally, there should an adequate amount of uncertainty to keep you hanging.

On the Monday following the ending of the NFL season many coaches and general managers are dismissed. This year several teams jumped the gun, firing their coaches before the season's end. Still there was enough left in limbo that conjecture and exaggeration could create uncertainty during the concluding weeks of the season, just like a soap opera. To stir the mix, some prognosticator will throw in the name of a coach who logic dictates he will be "safe" and suggest that his job is at risk.

Black Monday came and a number of NFL coaches and general managers were fired. Sportscaster spread a pall over each dismissal as if North Korean had tested a hydrogen bomb. Oh, I think North Korea claimed they did. However, there is considerable doubt by those who are authorities on such things.

If this is not enough, election season continues to cast a dark spell over us. The accusations are flying about. The "birther" debate has appeared for yet another candidate. Is a candidate born in Canada to an American mother a natural born citizen as required? I only know we grant such a child full and immediate citizenship. Words are flying about the lack of moral restraint of the spouse of a candidate while the individual was President of the United States. It will not be long until many of the presidential hopefuls will vanish from the landscape. Perhaps we can create a conspiracy theory or two. Ahh, we have the murkiness and sex needed to start a good nighttime soap. Make the necessary adjustments and you could have program similar to The Good Wife.

Back to athletics, basketball is moving into full swing as football moves toward its super climax. Did you see the Oklahoma-Kansas basketball game, all three overtimes? What an incredibly perfect basketball game! You will see very few in your life that will match the excellence of play and coaching that we were privileged to witness. I have seen a lot of basketball games and I cannot recall it's equal.

The basketball commentators (and critics) are in ready and in full throat.

This is also the season that new television programs are released for our approval. Some will make it, some will not. Just like coaches. Let's not forget that Award season is breaking out. From the Golden Globes to the Academy Awards or you might win a Tony or a Grammy. But most won't.

Are you uncomfortable with this uncertain season? It is only 6 weeks until pitchers and catchers report.

There are things known and things unknown, and in between are the doors of perception. — Aldous Huxley

YET ANOTHER MONTAGE
2016

Yet another annual winter ritual is upon us. Magazines and various television networks formulate a montage of significant people who have passed away over the past year. Each year we seem to lose several well know people who in some way touched our lives. Last year, each time a photo of Robin Williams appeared upon the screen, the assembled crowd emitted an audible gasp followed by murmurs about what a talent lost.

I will not deny that I enjoy such remembrances. I find the Academy Awards, the Tony Awards and the Baseball Hall of Fame to be especially well done. As I listen to these rosters, I am touched by many, even those I had forgotten had left us.

However, I confess these more formal exercises lead to me create my own less formal montage. Some well-know and some not so much. But I certainly will miss them more often because I'm reminded.

From the celebrity standpoint – well, I'm not sure the exact extent he'd consider himself a celebrity, but this year Yogi Berra tops my list of the "well-known" personalities we lost. Yogi's quotes are classic examples of commonsense wisdom, misspoken. The spring training directive, "Pair up in threes" or his political observation, "Even Napoleon had his Watergate."

There was his response to physical attractiveness, "So I'm ugly. I never saw anyone hit with his face". On observational learning, he said, "You can observe a lot just by watching".

In summary, he noted, "I never said most of the things I said".

While I enjoy his quips, I suspect I will always have two vivid memories of his playing days with the Yankees. I can still Yogi leaping up on Don Larsen after his perfect game in the World Series. Jackie Robinson's World Series steal of home with Yogi vehemently protesting the call of safe. To an interview not long before his death he insisted Robinson was out. Even with modern replay technology applied to old footage it is impossible to find any conclusive evidence, so safe it stays. But to use one of Yogi's more famous retorts, "It ain't over until it's over".

One of the unique characteristics of my list is that I don't require you to have died in the past year's list. It helps but it is not a requirement. So, David Letterman makes this years listing. Letterman left us after 33 years on late night television. Not gone yet not forgotten. I am still wondering the night with my lantern seeking "an honest talk show host".

We lost Gerald Kirk (Monk or Dr. Kirk as you prefer) with his dynamic memory of everything Stigler. He knew who lived in each residence and who operated businesses that existed long before our time. Monk was my most reliable source of Stigler gossip. Joe Robertson, who moved to Stigler and found himself a place, left us. Mott (Jim Thomas) is longer gone but I put him on my list each year.

Warm December afternoons keep a back-porch Coca Cola in fashion. After writing this column it is easy to image them in the fizzes of my Coke meeting the ice. Monk could list the soda jerks who poured our fountain cokes behind the counter at Head's. As we finish celebrating our holidays, let us toast them each and all.

They are only lost when no one remembers them. -- Anonymous Veteran

PUFF, PUFF, PUFF, WHEEZE

February 3, 2016

A notice from the Tulsa World popped up on the screen of my phone. It seems our Health Commissioner, Terry Cline, wants to increase Oklahoma's cigarette tax by $1.50 a pack. Now that is a lot milder than the typical topic of such notices; at least no one was shot. My first thought was that no one was killed but then I realized that would open up another closet of worms.

There was a time smoking might have been considered a sign of virility and masculinity. Now most agree that smoking is not grand for your health.

I had smoked for a few years, for me it was that period between serious athletics and true adulthood. Before that there was experimentation, mostly the occasional shared pack of cigarettes from Bell's Pharmacy (Head's Drug Store). We would wait until Doctor Head had returned to his pharmacy area in the rear of the store and we would buy a pack from the teenage soda fountain employee.

I found that a good bout of the flu combined with needing a cigarette was a nasty set of circumstances. It was a naturally occurring Aversion Therapy for me. I didn't know how to label it at the time, but I do now.

These feelings were inconsistent with the magazine ads and with Bogart smoking his cigarettes in *Casablanca*, *The African Queen* or *The Treasure of the Sierra Madre*. From my prospective, real men smoked.

Come Christmas or birthdays, the suggestion was that a boy should purchase his father a carton of Camels or Lucky Strikes, short and unfiltered, as a gift.

My grandfather, who I admired greatly, did not smoke. I never ask him why, he just didn't smoke. My father smoked over two packs of Camels a day. I know now how fortunate I was to have my grandfather's counter-cultural role model. I had two very small sons who actively discouraged me from smoking, another stroke of good fortunate.

Smoking causes cancer. The research began to become clearer despite adamant denials by the tobacco companies. It seems that recognizing half of the population didn't smoke, the female half, the cigarette companies latched to the Woman's Movement and started selling. Filtered cigarettes such as Virginia Slims with their slogan, "You've come a long way baby." Many in the almost tobacco free female population began to smoke and carried the cigarette companies for several decades – or so it seems to me.

Now, there are fewer smokers. There is more evidence that there is a firm link between tobacco and cancer. Seems we are trying to tax people into behaving in their own self-interest. As we have often discovered, it is difficult to save someone from themselves. Ah, but how we try.

Doug Cox (R-Grove) has proposed the bill Commissioner Cline desires. It would increase the cigarette tax by $1.50. Our present state tax is $1.03 cents. The large part of the tax increase is for teacher salaries, certainly a worthy cause.

We are going to fund our best thing with a tax on one of our worst things. Anything that seems that good on the surface I've got to think about – think about it a lot. Maybe some TSET commercials will bring clarity. Maybe but I'm betting on this warm weather and coke on my porch to help a lot. I'm just thinkin'.

When I was young, I kissed my first woman and smoked my first cigarette on the same day. Believe me, never since have I wasted any more time on tobacco.
—Arturo Toscanini

PUT IT ON MY TICKET

2016

Before World War II took him off in another direction, my father's ambition was to become a butcher, then open his own grocery and market. Dad would assert that he wanted to sell the kind of meat he'd like to buy. Now that seems a noble aspiration for a man who beyond doubt loved beef. I would think the business would be in grave danger of Dad eating up his profits. He loved T-Bone steaks.

Coming out of the Great Depression, a career as a butcher must have been quite appealing. The small market and grocery were dominant. The idea of Super Markets was emerging. Frix was the original larger grocery and my dad's first place of employment. Dick and Loraine Shelton would later provide Haskell County with a supermarket worthy of the name. But it is the small markets that delivered your groceries daily, at lunch would slice you a chunk of cheese or baloney and throw in a few crackers to boot. Each provided a line of credit that would get you through until pay day.

Do you recall the names? Sam Haddock and Harvey Pogue, they sold groceries and service. I know there were a number of other stores but my grandmother McBride seemed to buy from these two stores. Now these stores generally carried only one brand of a product. A discriminating shopper knew the brand they liked. With the fresh vegetable supply often quite erratic. When ask, "How is the lettuce?" An honest response best served both parties, just because the lettuce wasn't the top of the crop didn't mean she wouldn't buy it but she did want to know what to expect. My grandmother considered knowing the quality of a brand of canned vegetables is required skill. It seems Del Monte was a magical label.

Shelves were stocked with TenderKrust bread, baked by the Gulley's in downtown Stigler.

With a husband and a family to feed, the question concerning the meat became vitally important. If the round steak needed to run through a few extra times so be it, but do it. These ladies put great effort into preparing the food they put on the table. Compliments on the tastiness of a meal were never words misspent.

An order was called in almost daily. Seems Pogue and Haddock were the most common frequently used. I can recall being sent to secure circulars with weeks special from the stores after school. A pickup truck arrived on schedule, groceries brought in boxes, emptied onto the table and checked.

I have no idea why she said it but the delivery was concluded with "Just put it on my ticket". My grandfather paid the bills monthly. He did some shopping at Frix, then Shelton's Supermarket. In a Scottish-Irish household, potatoes were a staple of each meal. As the home grown supply diminished, selecting potatoes became his chief task.

I couldn't get off on a nostalgic tale without something jogging my mind. A grocery in our neighborhood unexpected closed. This store was an anomaly rarely encountered today. Located in a nice shopping area, it still delivered groceries and carried monthly charge tickets for qualified families. Like "Cheers", everybody knew your name. The business was entrenched and profitable.

However, the owners of the Square had another plan for the space and the space of a recently closed women's shop that abutted it. Both businesses were over 75 years old.

Another vestige of our past slipped away. I'll miss Petty's meat. The primary butcher was originally from Warner. We had great confidence in his counsel. But heck, I still miss Haddock's and Pogue's and Shelton's markets.

This morning the windows are all covered with Square's paper, obstructing the view in and out of the space. It doesn't seem right.

Dad would have approved of their T-Bone steaks.

Don't take a butcher's advice on how to cook meat. If he knew, he'd be a chef. — Andy Rooney

THE GREASY BURGER ISN'T GONE
2016

On occasion, I pick up my friend for lunch.

"Where do you want to go?"

After a very brief pause, I say, "How about a good greasy hamburger?" I know my friend holds the same fondness for a 'good greasy hamburgers" that I do. For some, an old-fashioned burger is a comfort food.

We certainly know that other fine dining establishments serving healthier options are plentiful. A great diversity of soups, smoothies, salads, chicken and fish can be found. Three cheese and avocado sandwiches are quite good. Mexican bowl from a national chain noted for it fresh local ingredients was high on my healthy dining list until a recent Listeria outbreak pointed out the challenges of keeping fresh things fresh and germ free for even the most conscientious of restaurants.

A wide variety of garden burgers cannot be ignored although I try. Billie somehow manages to create a tasty garden burger, another of her many kitchen miracles.

I'm certain that "good greasy cheeseburgers" and a blue plate special of chicken fried steak, mashed potatoes and gravy soothe the soul of many a man. Interestingly, these are comfort foods that do not take me back to my wife or my mother's kitchen. That award goes to "Sunday fried chicken".

The cheeseburger goes back to the cafes of the Stigler of my youth. I know every café in town served a cheeseburger. I once noted an early affinity for Mrs. Clements's burgers sold from a very small white wooden building outside the sale barn. Cheeseburger, coke and a shade tree were all an 8-year-old boy needed for a perfect summer lunch, an every Wednesday lunch.

The Malt Shop and the Stigler Café served very good burgers. Then, Johnny and Ruth Gulley came back to Stigler to assist with the family bakery located on South Broadway in downtown Stigler. They moved into the rent house behind my parents' home.

After a time, Ruth opened a small café just to the east of Sam Keith's barber shop. On my Saturday lunch break from Hays and Buchanan, I would have a double chili cheeseburger. Believe me you weren't picking that burger up. Bring a fork and a fist full of napkins. Now I don't know that reddish grease floated to the surface of the chili pot but it must have. An ice-cold bottle of Coke was the ideal beverage with which to follow each bite. It cut through the chili preparing the palate for the next bite of burger swimming in chili.

The Coke was ice cold and wet. The Coke was bottled at the Stigler Bottling Company. "Do business with Stigler merchants".

The truth is, as a boy, I ate few meals out. Thinkin' on it I have concluded comfort food is generated from emotionally satisfying experiences. The feeling results from company and conversation. Breakfasts create the most gratifying times; pleasant memories and warm conversations.

Just think about it bit.

If you're afraid of butter, use cream. – Julia Child

THE PROPHESIES OF EXPERT
PROGNOSTICATORS
2016

Exactly when did our world become so complex that we require panels of practiced authorities to explain matters to us? What were once just hobbies from sporting events to the arts and entertainment has become increasingly serious. Politics, a long-favored pastime never short of opinions, has taken on a humorist flare. Except that it is not funny anymore.

What I did find in all of these arenas now are numerous panels of "experts". The "opinions pundits" analyze every element of a contest. With so many networks airing coverage of elections by sheer volume the number of "political experts" grows and grows. There are times I believe that knowledge is trumped by opinion. If you have a view and can assertively express it, you're an expert. Functional comprehension of the topic is not always a requirement. Can you bellow your positions louder than your peers?

Oh no, wait, that is the candidates.

Some panels of experts are simply better than others. The Fox NFL crew is superior. As they offer their projections, they teach you the game. They are "experts" who played and coached the game. Terry Bradshaw, Howie Long, Michael Strahan, Jimmy Johnson and Curt Menefee are respectful and yet their wit is entertaining.

Fall Saturday's many folks ask, "Where is College Game Day this week?" I believe no ESPN expert is more closely followed this time of year that Joe Lunardi and his projections of the NCAA Basketball bracket, Bracketology.

You might be asking, where are the ladies?" I don't know. I do know there are women who know more football and basketball than my most men. I'm married to one of them. Oh, wait. I turned to CNN and found the women. They purport to know as much politics as men do. Wait, I believe I detected some doubt from the balcony. Ah, what do the balconites know?

Did you catch the "expert judgment" that determined the Oscars and the Grammys? Ah, the mysteries of subjective opinion in the world of art.

I do not believe that all experts reside in television events. It is just that they have blossomed and bloomed there, these pundits of opinion, these grand analysts.

I have been thinking even more about those with real expertise. May I suggest that teachers are the real experts? Opal Calhoun taught me the value of all knowledge. Lillian Riley and Ruby Sewell taught me to love literature and writing. John Harmon introduced me to a lifetime of history.

After an encounter with a true expert, you will have acquired knowledge you did not previously possess. You learn something.

The more I think about it, the more I believe it to be true. Still television is an interactive experience for me. If I learn I just nod my head in agreement. If I disagree or know it to be incorrect, well, I talk back to my television.

I don't know if the television learns anything or not.

A fool and his money are soon elected. — Will Rogers

HOW LONG DOES THE PARTY LAST?
2016

In referencing the time one should step away from his profession, my wife always admonished me, "Don't stay at the party too long". She did know that I greatly enjoyed what I did. She also knew that job performance was dependent upon mental acuity. A perceptible keenness of mind as to the evaluation of individuals in high conflict child custody matters. One once observed that it was akin to swimming in a sea of sharks and maybe it was.

A few years back an accident forced me to acknowledge that my time at the party was drawing to an end. When the sound of the crunching rear began fade in my ears, I'll swear I heard Dandy Don (Meredith) begin singing "Turn Out the Lights, the Party's Over". It was his way of letting Howard (Cosell) and Frank (Gifford) know he considered the Monday Night NFL game they were broadcasting was no longer in doubt, the end was inevitable. I don't know that he ever called a game prematurely.

There were times I tried to fool myself. I believed I had stockpiled plenty of Coca Cola and Ward's Ice Cream to keep the party going for a while. I was wrong. There are contingencies I didn't plan for. I don't think I chose to leave the party – but maybe I did.

Why think about it now? Our long-time family physician, Robert L. Cossman, M.D., is retiring. He says that it is time. I do not doubt his professional opinion, never have and never will. He did not simply care for Billie and me. He cared for other members of our family. We will miss his skills. We will miss his kindness. We will miss his friendship.

I always believed when my time came, I'd live on the golf course. Well, that was not included in God's plan. The good doctor is as passionate about fly fishing as I was about golf. I hope he finds a life on a trout stream to be fulfilling.

I hope this passage from Norman Maclean describes my friend's life some twenty years from now.

Now I am too old to be much of a fisherman, and now of course I usually fish the big waters alone, although some friends think I shouldn't. Like many fly fishermen in western Montana where the summer days are almost Arctic in length, I often do not start fishing until the cool of the evening. Then in the Arctic half-light of the canyon, all existence fades to a being with my soul and memories and the sounds of the Big Blackfoot River and a four-count rhythm and the hope that a fish will rise. – Norman Maclean, A River Runs Through It.

When I think of him retiring, I think back to Tom Conklin and Kenneth Conklin. Dr. Tom delivered me at home, at 605 NW A Street in Stigler, and in that same house he oversaw the death of my grandfather. They were faithful physicians to generations of Haskell County residents.

Dr. C, I wish you well. May the trout always find your favorite fly. I will raise a pint to a retirement well earned.

When a man retires, his wife gets twice the husband and only half the income. – Chi Chi Rodriguez

STUDYING AT THE ACADEMY OF COUNTRY MUSIC

2016

I have confessed that on the whole I am not a fan of the musical award shows. Now there are some you watch because you wife enjoys them. Any husband will tell you these are perfectly valid reasons to watch a television program. An exchange that allows you view "cops and robbers" and many ballgames is a very positive swap.

The ACM Awards are an exception. We both enjoy this programming. The best performers in country music place their talent on display and duets provide a previously unheard harmony. The acceptance speeches are humble, giving credit to the writers and arrangers, their family and the Lord. It is certainly not the arrogant presumptive entitlement I have heard on similar shows. No one tried to use their vantage to impose a political or social viewpoint on us.

In the late 1940's, Stigler had a building where the talents of country musicians where placed on display via jukebox. The physical structure wasn't much. It had the look of white temporary wooden shanty located about where Dr. Thomas' office is now. It seems it was up on blocks. On a good day the southern breeze carried the smell of hamburgers with grilled onions and Eddie Arnold. It was mostly male voices until Kitty Wells cut the air with "Honky Tonk Angels".

Had you been there and looked closely you'd have seen an 11-year-old boy sitting on a cement block behind the café drinking a coke and soaking it all in. I still enjoy most country music and folk music. From that vantage point, in Stigler, it was easy to discover the Grand Ole Opera, Little Jimmy Dickens to Minnie Pearl. Minnie Pearl was funny before television let you actually see the price tag on her hat. The lady was funny.

Later, straight from Austin, Texas, would come Merle, Waylon and Willie and the boys.

Just thinkin' – Is there an annual award to new operas? Is there something for classical music? Best performance by a Symphony Orchestra or by a soprano in a feature role? Since I didn't know I googled it. Do you count the International Opera Awards which began in London in 2011? It just strikes me that there must be recognition for such immensely talented musicians. I just can't find it.

I grabbed a coke from the frig and went to back porch. Often if I take a break like that, I'll find a random thought passing through. I did but it didn't pertain to music.

"How about those Panama Papers?" "Do you think anything will come from them?" Heads of State and other such folks are accused of sheltering money in through questionable bank transactions. Is it a question of international law leaving us to wait for Russia to explore Putin? Well, I guess we'll see.

Let's get back to Country Music. Even if it is about trains, trucks and love affairs it is much more soothing than thinking about an international monetary fraud.

I learned from a long-time farmer that pigs enjoy soothing music. – Jamie Wyeth

LIFE IN THE POSITIVE LANE
2016

I have long professed my ambivalent intellectual infatuation with television commercials. It is a true "love-hate" relationship. As with most things in life, it is easier to find fault and to criticize than to praise. It is quite unlike my involvement with ice cream. There is no bad ice cream. I find it to simply be varying degrees of good.

There are good and bad television commercials. I admire the good ones but it little effort to poke fun at the bad ones. Today I want to write about the positive and upbeat commercials.

After all commercials, good or bad, are the lifeblood of "free" television.

I think everyone has their favorite commercials. Here is my list of what I believe to be the best commercials. Check your list and we will compare notes.

There is the commercial about a young boy whose father is deployed. In an effort to contact his father, the boy wrote notes to his father with Crayons on sheets of papers. He then folds each sheet into a paper airplane and flies the plane across his neighbor's fence. The neighbor, an older gentleman, collects the planes and reads them. Touched, he decides to box them and forward them to the boy's father. Upon reading the "airmail" messages, the father writes, folds his responses into paper planes and returns them to neighbor. When the young man returns to play, he is greeted by paper airplanes sailing over his fence. He finds a message from his father written on each airplane.

How could you possibly not find hope in such notes?

Hope. The Johnson & Johnson commercials encouraging specialty nursing careers are first class. I especially like the one that is focused on Pediatric Nursing. The young male nurse is preparing to give what appears to be a painful injection to a girl. They begin to sing the "Hannah, banana, fofana" song together. They make it sound like a classic duet ideal for making the injection more palatable. It is so well done you have to ask yourself, "Who paid for that commercial?"

There is a commercial that begins with a very, very small horse walking out of a large carrier. He walks into a lush green and shaded pasture only to be rejected by his much larger and stronger cousins. His owner sees his dilemma and as she attempts to measure his sadness at the rejection, a strong empathy results. On her smart phone, she orders a small horse door or a large dog door, depending upon your point of view, from Amazon. The music that has quickly become affiliated with this story announces his arrival through the "horse door". He comes into the room and lays his head on his protector's knee. If you can buy the idea of a small horse in your living room it is an affectionate scene.

Next, there is the "tree hugging" commercial. Grandmother is showing Granddaughter the tree under which she met her Grandfather. In series of quite tender scenes the pair hugs the tree and hugs each other. Then they joined by the Grandmother's children, all now hugging the tree. The hook is as they are driving away a sign identifies the place as Woodstock. Ya gotta love it!

Maybe these commercials aren't great but they please me. How about you?

I think we all have empathy. We may not have enough courage to display it. – Maya Angelou

IN PRAISE OF DIRT, ROCKS AND STICKS
2016

Spring is arriving, plants and children emerge from their winter enclosures. As with the tulips, children spring forward from their winter nest with sound and color and curiosity.

This season brings childhood inquisitiveness into full bloom. They are free to pry and snoop into the ways of nature. From warm afternoons to thunderstorms, kiddies can create, experiment and fail.

While we must guard against adult intrusion into child's play, this can be a golden opportunity for parents and grandparents and such to come out of their staid protective shell of adulthood and just play a while. I believe there is no greater adult activity than playing with children. There is dirt to put your hands in. Do you remember how much fun it is just to dig in the dirt with your hands? Once we knew but sometimes, we forget.

It doesn't require too much; you just use what is there. Take a 5-year-old to any nearby gravel pile. With as much construction as is going on right now such piles are never in short supply. Now you can start hunting fossils. You will find seashells, ferns and other impressions intrigue us all. If they don't, they darn well should.

The outline of a fern or a seashell can electrify a curious 5-year-old. Then one of the great questions gets ask. "Why?" "Why?" That is the most insightful question a child can ask. "Why?"

Just because we don't always have the answer does not make it a bad question.

Kids love to be able to identify the type of tree they are sitting under by the shape of its leaves. Most neighborhoods have no shortage of specimens close at hand. This can make talking about acorns and helicopter seeds even more fun. Don't forget how much fun sticks can be.

Dig a little and all sorts of worms and other little critters emerge. You want to see scholarly snooping take place just show a kid a bug. I highly recommend relocating worms with a little boy or girl. There is nothing like a worm farm.

If you must yield to the adult imperative to teach structure and order, try a more conventional gardening activity with a child. Actually, just planting a few seeds in some Dixie Cups will do the job. Be patient and watch. A child will check each day for progress, sometimes it grows and sometimes it doesn't.

Playing with Mother Nature is based on experimentation, there are successes and there are failures. Here every child can learn one of life's fundamental truths, "Failure is not fatal." All you have to do is try again a different way. Add a little something, subtract a little something – but just keep messing with it.

You might say, "Experimentation and failure light the pathway to success". "Why?"

A flower is an educated weed. – Luther Burbank
In the woods we return to reason and faith. – Ralph Waldo Emerson
I was determined to know beans. – Henry David Thoreau

THE CLARITY OF A CHILD'S VIEW
2016

It is my opinion that as a child ages they begin to draw conclusions about the nature of the world. The most candid and direct observational insights emerge. Though often overly simplistic, they view the world in a most unvarnished fashion. They can see events or possibilities in a fashion that most of cannot.

As adults we often skew the true importance of circumstances, God forbid that we allow ourselves to appear even moderately ridiculous. After all we are the adults in the room. A child's view is not clouded by a volume of self-protective mechanisms.

Over the years I have come to genuinely admire the simplicity of children's logic. If ask, a child will answer your question in a straightforward fashion.

Sharing favorite stories about children brings back the experience itself even if it was years ago or days ago. Direct and honest insight is priceless, children are so genuine.

Once upon a time, I knew a boy who was about 8 or 9 at the time. In contrast with my suit and tie, he would dress in a western shirt and blue jeans, both starched and creased. A cowboy belt was woven through the loops and cinched with oversized polished belt buckle. His boots were polished to high shine.

With very little conversation you discovered this boy knew his way around horse and cattle. Only his slender body and his glasses with "coke bottle" lenses belied the otherwise "John Wayne" image. I think from my dress he judged me not to be a part of his world.

I got confirmation when at the conclusion of a talk, I asked if he felt there was anything else, I might need to know, something that would "help me". Now I was referring to the matter at hand but he didn't take that way.

He did not give a hurried answer. He thought, surveyed me and said, "If you live on a dirt road don't buy a black pickup truck".

Based on the evidence, he made a solid judgment of a perceived deficit in my knowledge base.

A few years later, a young girl of similar age, would wonder about how hair got completely gray. She asked, "Why is your hair gray?" I wish I had had a wise answer to give her. I over-answered her query with something rather silly. I know I included God's plan for aging hair in the explanation.

She looked at me and said, "Well, you know it doesn't have to be that way. You can go to Walmart and they will make it red or green or blue. They'll ever make it a "rainboo" for you". Once again, the simplicity of a child's logic prevailed.

No, I did not get the recommended rainbow hair style. Maybe I considered it. No, I didn't.

Recently my 7-year-old great-grandson and a friend were visiting. I was working on the final words of a column. They were exploring the section of junky work space that is behind my chair. His friend lifted out an adjustable blue metal cane the style of which can be found in most Walmart Stores and pharmacies.

Comparing it to the nice wooden cane I enjoy as much as one can enjoy a cane, he asked, "What is this?" I told him it was the cane I used in the salt-water when I went to the beach. My answer was true and he accepted it as reasonable.

Shortly, two young boys, each with a cane, paraded through the living room in front of my wife. She asked, "What are you doing?" It sounded like a logical enough question. The response came, "We playing old man".

My first thought was, "Guys, this it isn't as much fun as you think". Then, I realized kids can make anything fun.

Kids can be quite persuasive. They are about to convince me to give up Coca Cola in favor of Josh's Snow Cone Stand by the Golden Driller. It even has one of those "frames" that you take their photo in front of the Golden Driller. Kids of all ages enjoy illusions.

A person who never made a mistake never tried anything new. – Albert Einstein

Today was a difficult day. Tomorrow will be better. – Kevin Henkes, Lilly's Purple Plastic Purse

DEFINING A MAN'S TREASURE
2016

For me, Independence Day celebrations are often acknowledgements of our National Treasures. Each year I gain some new insight into the precious places and artifacts others have preserved for us. On July 4, these mark our progression toward becoming the nation that we so genuinely value. Among these are monuments built to mark the valor and the humanity of those whose life helped march us toward liberty and freedom.

I wonder. Do I understand what it meant for a man to pledge his personal honor and treasure to cause? Imagine after having argued, disagreed and struggled for almost a year, you find yourself in a hot sticky poorly ventilated room in the Pennsylvania State House in Philadelphia, working to find common cause with men whom we virulently disagree about many principles, the role of slavery in a society not the least of these. It is likely true that we disagreed about most things except the necessity of modifying our relationship with Great Britain.

Some found more progress to be made in the City Tavern than in State House. In due course, these men found a compromise to secure an intangible concept they valued as they valued Richmond and Boston. Liberty. They had so much to lose in the pursuit of this abstraction. Yet they stated, **"We mutually pledge to each other our lives, our fortunes and our sacred honor."**

Yes, some did lose all those things and more. Wait, I think they all saved their sacred honor. I can barely imagine such a promise. Fifty-six men signed an agreement containing that oath. A profound and meaningful agreement was obtained despite their disagreements. Such men are rightly deemed treasures.

It was at about this point that some sports reporter cited Kevin Durant as a State Treasure. Then, one used the term traitor citing his disloyalty to our state. Oklahoma was said to have been so good

203

to KD. Well, KD was more than generous to Oklahoma City. Ah, forget that and let's go have a jersey burning party.

By this point I lost my focus. I had intended to move this column toward our National Parks. Now those are true National Treasures, not artifacts but living breathing ecosystems. I'll write on those another time soon. I don't believe the Grand Canyon is leaving Arizona soon.

Huh. It seems to me that Durant is a businessman. NBA basketball is both a game and a business. In a few years when his talents begin to wane, do you think he'd maybe be told, "We have decided to move in another direction and we aren't renewing your contract". Don't believe it? Just ask anyone who ever agreed to play a game for money. There is money as long as you can play the game.

I wonder how many losing seasons with half-full arenas it would take before the team would be "on the block". I don't know. Let me call Seattle and ask.

What if Williams Companies had merged and left Oklahoma, taking all those jobs with them? Traitors! Or do I say, "Well shucks. It is just business."

Do you think a Coca Cola on the porch will clear this up for me?

The public cannot be too curious concerning the character of public men.
— Samuel Adams

THE UNIQUENESS OF LIFE LOST
(Up on the Death of a Sister-In-Law)
2016

My wife's eldest sister, Lou, died. I wanted to write a few personal recollections of her, an adequate number to preserve her essence for my family.

My initial attempts felt awkward. Most often I try to find some humor in my writing. This time the concept just sounded absurd. Death, grief and mourning don't lend themselves to any sort of humor. I was stymied.

Then, I attended her services. I anticipated the worst and discovered the best.

The services were held under a small shelter in the Sallisaw City Cemetery. It is a very nice setting given pleasant weather.

The service was conducted by a long-time family friend, Minerva and her son, Charles. They conducted the services consistent with their faith. They read from scripture and recalled Lou's life.

I listened and learned. Humor rested in the recollections of life. While many of us were taking ourselves far too seriously, Lou merrily went about being Lou. Her approach to problem-solving was unique. In Minerva's retelling of stories, I found an understandable relationship between humanity and humor. Lou wasn't Mother Theresa but she helped folks. A lot of us are better off just because she was here.

A life can contain absurdity, yet be filled with profound meaning.

Minerva chose not to speak of the latter times that where lost to the oblivion of some form of dementia. She spoke of "Miss Lou" backing her car up to the loading dock of the Oklahoma Nursing Home Supply, opening the trunk and filling it with towels, wash clothes, blankets, and the variety of foods that might ease someone's current situation.

For dramatic effect, Minerva suggested these visits took place under the dark of night, but they didn't.

"Now, Lou Elba, you shouldn't be stealing."

"No it's okay, Brent doesn't mind."

Brent, Lou's youngest son, owned the Nursing Home Supply at the time.

Now Lou enjoyed those deliveries. Brent, from a business standpoint maybe not so much, but he did say Lou and Minerva taught him about inventory adjustment.

About half way though, Minerva ask, "Where is that Emily Ann? That tree climber here?" Emily Ann was in attendance but she was walking Evelyn Belle, her 19-month daughter. Found and acknowledged, Minerva continued, "Now Emily Ann came to Sallisaw with Hal and Billie Jean. Lou kept Emily Ann while they went to the races. It seems Emily climbed a 40-foot to 50-foot Oak tree behind Lou's condominium. Unable to lure her down, Lou called Minerva. Hence forth Minerva would contend that little girl was the only person who ever "treed" Lou.

I was having trouble finding what I was looking for because I was looking in the wrong place. The humor is cradled in life's recounting.

Time has its own thief. It is named dementia. We are robbed of the knowledge another has gained through experience. One's final years can have richness in which we come to understand each other in extraordinary manners.

Remember when a person's final words were so valued?

I am a great admirer of our founding fathers, of their courage and their wisdom. John Adams final words were, "Jefferson survives". He believed his adversity, his ally and intimate friend in their later years had survived him. In fact, Jefferson had died a few hours before. Both died on July 4, 1826.

However, for whatever reason I believe Lou's passing words would have been more akin to Citizen Kane's word leaving us to wonder.

"Rosebud"

I really hate dementia.

I know so many last words. But I will never know hers. – John Green, <u>Looking for Alaska</u>

MAPPING THE HEALTH HIGHWAY
2016

There are weeks that I get so engrossed in other things in life that I wonder if there will be a column this week. It happened this week and I place responsibility at the feet of modern medicine. If today's medicine didn't have the technology to photograph seemingly every crevice in our body this would not have been a concern. Oh, I know that except for this technology graver concerns might appear later.

Having previously had these experiences, I want to attest that the mental and physical preparation for such examinations has become much more user friendly. I know it is unlikely that I will ever be provided a comprehensive road map as to what unexpected events might be encountered my life. However, when it comes to post-procedure explanations medical technology has outdone itself. Who else is going to provide you with color photographs as proof of health and with illustrations depicting the exact location at which the photograph was snapped? It is a lot like some of the National Forest Service's very best topographical maps.

I suspect these preventive procedures are going to get better (or worse depending upon your prospective). There are cameras now that can be placed anywhere. Well, almost anywhere.

Anyway, it is over and done. I passed.

On the subject of health, I received a number of questions about the health of my cousin, Boots. First the 97 was not a misprint. He is 97 years-old. He plays golf at Canyon Mesa Country Club, a short but challenging course 5 days a week. Oh, he doesn't see well anymore but every time he hits from a Par 3 he listens for the sound of the ball hitting the bottom of the cup. He has about 14 or 15 of those aces now. That would be about 14 or 15 more than me. It doesn't bother him a lick that his playing companions tee up his ball or that he now plays from the women's tees.

He plays hearts at the Club for a few hours every day. He keeps up with every dime he wins (or loses) on the course or at the card table. My youngest son will always ask him if he went to work today.

I think Boots' health is just fine. I'll tell him people ask.

You're in pretty good shape for the shape you are in. — Dr. Seuss

NICE TIMES IN SALLISAW
2016

During the past Christmas season, I wrote a column based upon the Christmas tradition of two Sallisaw brothers. The ritual was both family and business. Family and business – that is often a blend most difficult to sustain. I don't know that their views were always simpatico but they sustained at least two small businesses in Sallisaw over number of years. They operated DX station and the Western Auto. It was as if they came home to Sallisaw from World War II and had no intention of leaving.

I married into Sallisaw. Comparing it with my hometown, I felt Sallisaw was blessed with several World War II veterans who returned to Sallisaw with the intention of building their hometown into a thriving community. They saw the future in Sallisaw rather than Tulsa or Oklahoma City or such. I believe that at least for a time they succeeded.

Beyond the Farmer brothers, there was Alton Gean who owned Oklahoma Tire and Supply and was their honorable competitor. It is hard to even get started and not remember the contributions of their wives. Nelle Gean was a renowned teacher in the Sallisaw Public schools. Leila Jean (Reynolds) Farmer, well, she ramrodded Southwestern Bell until "progress" changed the nature of an operator in the phone company. All of today's conveniences aside, getting an operator who answered, "Central", was a luxury in its own way. If the line was busy they'd tell you who was on the line. The fire siren blew and you could call and ask where the fire was. If it looked stormy the operator knew if it was storming in Tahlequah or across the river in Stigler.

Stanley Tubbs ran Sallisaw Hardware and got a Library named for him. Palace Drug operated by a young Larry Hoffman and had a soda fountain best entered from the alley. Out the alley door and to the left, you found Ivey's Drug and E.B. Sanders. Beyond all else, E.B. was just a good guy. I trusted E.B.

Thinking of trust, a guy must trust his jeweler. Blanche and Barney Cheek crafted fine pieces, sold nice stones and wisely consulted many a man about their wife's desires.

Boss Green after teaching at Sallisaw Central operated a Farmers Insurance Agency across the street.

Just down the block, I was part of a family enterprise with Jay Reynolds in the Sequoyah Theatre. To the west was Malloy Orndorff's Furniture. Next door was the Sequoyah County Times. Jim Mayo had recently returned to Sallisaw to assume management of the newspaper. Now his son Jeff operates this Sequoyah County institution.

Anyway, I wrote a Christmas story about my wife's family for my family. My niece's boy, David Martin, was kind enough to send me a copy of the Sequoyah County Times that contained the essay on the paper's editorial page. I was impressed. I found editorial opinions that I believed at first blush could not have pleased everyone in the County. I judged it to be a courageous editorial page. Every thinking citizen of Sequoyah should be proud of their paper.

I am an avid fan of newspapers. I enjoy the feeling of the paper and the scent of the newsprint. The sports page, the comics and the editorial page read by our family over the breakfast table has long been a ritual. A real newspaper is meant to be shared. "Oh, you need to read this story." Ever try to share an E-Edition with your wife? Oh well, that is for another generation.

I hate the way the physical size of the Tulsa World has shrunk. The photos are larger and the words are fewer. I guess I just miss the days when there were two sheets of comics. The time when I could read the Oaklawn Park entries and results on cold winter mornings and hope I could make a trip soon. The line scores from the high school basketball games could occupy a full page. Not anymore.

It seems that in finding a cluster of well written editorials I got the pleasant Christmas surprise. I think the guys from the Greatest Generation would be pleased.

A Bible and a newspaper in every house, a good school in every district — all studied and appreciated as they merit — are the principle support of virtue, morality and civil liberty. — Benjamin Franklin

AS THE WORLD TURNS
2016

Recently, it has been hard not to spend some time thinking about change. A lot of things are changing.

Some changes seem to be larger than perhaps they are. Take the alterations to the Tulsa World over the past many months. Not only is the paper physically smaller, it appears to be reducing its geographic appeal. The changes seem significant because the information in the daily newspaper is important to me. I suppose the paper is meeting the needs of most of their subscribers.

I know my parents and grandparents believed the Tulsa World was a regional newspaper not just a paper for Tulsa. I grew up with that logic. It was our daily paper. Like my family, many families fashioned a daily ritual that included this newspaper. Considerable communication occurred with conversations that began, "Have you read this or that?" The paper provided the informational base for discussion. Well, sometimes it wasn't discussion, it was guidance toward what my parents or grandparents believed should be necessary reading.

In my parent's household, the morning paper was divided into 3 sections, the sports, the comics known then as the funny pages and the opinion page. Oh, if there was some headline story on the front page it would read early.

Do you remember when there 2 full pages of comics? 2 full pages on the larger sheets of paper that existed then. That was a lot of comics. I still love them to this day although I now have sought and found many of the comics on line. The change to a smaller sheet of paper hasn't been long enough ago for me to forget what that large full page felt like.

E Editions aren't for me yet. I need the feel of paper in my hand and that special smell. And I can't share it with my spouse. "I think you'll like this article." Sometimes I read a couple of paragraphs to her. She will do the same for me. You get to know folks that way.

To really read a newspaper you have to share.

I begin learning this in 1943 at a table in my grandfather's den. On the front page the Tulsa World had maps of current campaigns in Europe and in the Pacific with arrows pointing the movements of our military. Each evening after we listened to the news on the radio, my grandfather would spread out the newspaper and then retrieve a small and tattered world atlas. We poured over them. I know it was my grandfather's company and undivided attention that was important to me. I believed he was the source of all credible information. Huh, I still love newspapers and atlases.

Now, if I reach for my atlas someone will say, "Oh God, Doc is after his GPS again".

Now, over breakfast, my wife and I share the contemporary version of the Tulsa World. Smaller pages, large photographs and few words. There is clearly less to read. There fewer scoring lines from the high school games. You would never know the horses are running at Oaklawn Park or Remington Park. Don't waste your time looking for an obituary outside Metro Tulsa. I once depended on the newspaper for news, for details. Now I only glance at the editorial page. If it were not for Bruce Plante's world class editorial cartoons I might not do that. Now I can get about the same information on the evening television news. It is still a conversation starter but we often conclude with "I don't know, the article didn't say."

Incredibility we now have a television set in our kitchen. Who would have believed it?

I want to say some weekly or bi-weekly papers serve their communities well. Without saying I enjoy the News-Sentinel. The Sequoyah County Times in Sallisaw has team of excellent writers and offers a courageous editorial page. Quality work is still being done in the newspaper business. I guess it could be that television doesn't cover much Haskell County or Sequoyah County news.

I'm just going to have think about this for a bit.

Newspaper readership is declining like crazy. In fact, there is a good chance nobody is reading my column. – Dave Barry

All I know is what I read in the papers, and that's an alibi for my ignorance. – Will Rogers.

IMAGINATION AND OTHER FAVORITE TOYS
2016

Inspiration and imagination spark our childhood play. Match sticks can become soldiers guarding sand pile forts. I always thought that my play environment was filled with soldiers because World War II filled my childhood. Any boy worth his salt could view a sand pile through his mind's eye and visualize the battle site drawn on the maps of the newspapers. On a frayed map of the world, my grandfather would give me a larger prospective of the place the fights were taking place.

I could take this knowledge and use my imagination to construct a replica of the battlefields. My mother cultivated my creativity. She fashioned really fine stories filled with "what if" or "how else".

Imagination, creativity and inspiration were encouraged.

Matches, sticks, and stone collected from the gravel street provided a boy and his friends all the raw material needed for a day of enriched play. Any world could be created in a large sand pile. How it would do in today's world of video games, I'm not certain. Images projected on screens require little imagination. Can a sand pile compete?

Then, we age. Reality begins to guide our imagination. In our consciousness, imagination gives way to the concrete reality of preparation for work. We discover the unique gender differences. We find that to be just dandy.

As we try to emulate adult behaviors, then age overtakes us. We move into a more concrete and the repetitive lifestyle.

Adulthood emerges and the imaginative games of our young life fade away. Our competitive but cooperative team sports fade under the guise "growing up". We become more spectators than participants in many of our competitions, from basketball to debate.

We feel we are comparatively judged in our jobs and our professions. The first question any man is asked is, "What do you do?"

All we have to do is keep right on aging. It is our Grand Children and the Great Grandchildren who begin to guide us toward the rediscovery of fun. Yes, just the plain old fun of a younger time. Now, it is back to the Lincoln Logs. With my great grandson we built a log fort and a variety of plastic figures from bears to soldiers engage in battles. A box lid easily becomes a boat. Imagination is super magnificent.

The pleasure of playing catch with a medium sized rubber ball is easily rediscovered. Heck, you can even get pretty good at it again with a little practice. Did you know you could play catch while sitting in your chair?

Oh, I know age will ultimately win, but how it does doesn't seem to matter as much. What does matter is that and when you play, play like a child. Play with child when you get the chance, with a ball you coach, with a book you teach; have fun with both.

Don't forget to always share your Coke. Just thinkin'. Would you like to play?

Men do not quit playing because they grow old; they grow old because they quit playing. – Oliver Wendell Holmes

It is a happy talent to know how to play. – Ralph Waldo Emerson

THE IMPACT OF EXCESSIVE THINKIKNG
2016

Have you ever found yourself in a position that you had so many different things on your mind that you just couldn't focus? Well, that describes this week.

I had to stop and ask myself, "Am I thinking too much about too much?" The answer was yes. I tried to rationalization my situation, saying there has been a lot to think about. But truth is, things I don't need to think about keep me thinking about what I do need to think about. That is a conundrum.

Perhaps the clear indicator of this condition is that I start to confuse myself.

I believe the simultaneous appearance of personal, professional and political questions can turn the most logical of thought into a cloud of confusion. Have you ever noticed how changes and a loss of predictability seem to be involved? I know I like consistency. Or maybe I'm just not thrilled about surprises these days. Oh, wait. It was surprising others that I found to be fun.

I still consult on high conflict divorce cases. I thought this was limited enough I could remove any professional element from the mix. Well, this week reminded me now naïve that thought was. It still astonishes me how divorcing couples can lose sight of the impact it is having on their children. The most flawed logic says, "What is good for mommy/daddy is good for the kiddies". Oops, I feel a lecture coming on. Nothing like a good encounter with the legal system to muddled the mind.

Personal. If you have a family, there will be those days. Just enjoy them.

There is no shortage of political surprises these days. President Donald Trump has produced a stream of executive orders, early morning tweets and telephone calls to leaders of other nations. These alone are adequate to keep a guy thinking for a while. Have you noticed he has a pleased expression on his face as he opens the leather binder and displays the signed document for all to see?

I knew the expression reminded of someone. I just couldn't quite place it. Then Billie and I picked up Bud, our great-grandson, after school Friday. As soon as he was secure in the backseat, he pulled his spelling test with a perfect score from his backpack. He held it up for us to see. With a wry smile, he said, "We can put it on your refrigerator". I thought "Yes Sir, President Trump". I found it when I wasn't thinking about it.

I really do believe anything can be overthought. I know because I'm guilty of it. But there is no creativity without thought. After World War I, President Woodrow Wilson tried to sell an increasingly isolationistic country on the League of Nations. He said, "Sometimes people call me an idealist. Well that is the way I know I am an American. America is the only idealistic nation in the world".

His health robbed him of a final sales drive. We moved into isolationism and remained there until World War II. Oh Lordy, I'm not only guilty of over-thinking today, I'm dragging yesterday into this thing.

I'm going to get me Coke, a few peanuts and go to the back porch. I'm a big advocate of the clarity coke fizz and squirrel watching can bring to life. See if I can get my head out of these clouds.

Terrorism is psychological warfare. Terrorist try to manipulate us and change our behavior by creating fear, uncertainty and division in society.
– Patrick J. Kennedy.

If you want to make enemies, try to change something. – Woodrow Wilson

EMERGING FROM HIBERNATION
2017

Been thinking about Spring a lot lately. I suppose because it is Spring. The flowers are blooming, grass is greening, trees budding, the time has leaped forward and the prolonged interruptions of favored television programing by local weather forecasters has occurred. Of course, in today's television world, most of the under 50 group aren't watching the traditional "Big 4" channels anyway. And Channel 6 has an alternative channel you can go to and watch the "regularly scheduled programming".

Anyway, I've noticed there is another life form emerging from hibernation. They are making a predictable appearance as winter departs and spring emerges. Neighbors! I just looked outside and there they were. I hadn't seen many of them since fall. Now here they are, breathing life into the neighborhood. It is neighbors that enrich and fertilize our "neck of the town", to paraphrase Al Roker.

They both add and subtract. I noticed the subtractions first. The Notre Dame banner across the way has finally been taken in for the season. I wish they would take in the University of Alabama flag still blowing in the Spring wind inside – you know just give it a rest.

Neighbors! Don't you love watching kids fly down the sidewalk on bicycles or tricycles. Mothers pulling wagons filled with little ones. Four boys shooting baskets in the hammerhead. Two or three folks gathered at the corner, just visiting. You're welcome to join in if you like.

We miss a unique neighbor who inhibited the house catty-corner from us. He left us a few years ago. Mac was an engineer not long retired from a major oil company. He stalked his lot like he was checking a property line on 160 acres of West Texas. He grew up there, was educated there and flew his Texas Tech colors proudly. A recent Pickles cartoon involving attempts to repair a

217

sprinkler system could have been photographed in his lawn. It wasn't broken but it needed repaired. I know, go figure.

Mac adopted us, especially Billie.

When he tired of his wood work, he was talented but often he'd become enthralled with building novelties like say "exploding outhouses". Built around a mousetrap, he set one here and there. When some curious soul opened the outhouse door, to Mac's delight, it exploded in their hand.

His garage workshop was filled with chemicals no longer generally available such as DDT. Mac kept the entire neighborhood free from all sorts of pests for years. After his death, we feared it might be declared a toxic waste site.

We'd come home and he'd have planted something in our yard. He was fond of clematis which would eventually climb over the lattice on our porch. No, he didn't ask first, he just did it.

Every neighborhood needs a resident who will line gallon milk jugs filled with brightly colored water across his lawn and let folks imagine the purpose. Perking up people's curiosity just pleased him. Mac is still missed.

I'll bet this is the first thing you've read in a while that hasn't mentioned health care. Oops, there I did it. Guess I'll go to the porch, have a coke and watch the squirrels dig up the flower beds.

They claim this mother of ours, the Earth, for their own use, and fence their neighbors away from her and deface her with their buildings and their refuse. – Sitting Bull

NO THRU TRAFFIC
2017

There are times that a sign says exactly what it means. A "No Thru Traffic" sign has adorned the entry to our street for some months now. There is no mistaking that the barrier at the end of the street is serious.

If you have any question about the sincerity of the symbol just stroll the 50 yards to the principal street that is having larger storm sewers installed beneath it. I knew the gash in the street was deep. However, there are times that the value of a visual aid is unmatched.

As we turned into our driveway, the grandchild we had just picked up at school said, "Look at that man!" Given the tone of his voice, I had no doubt that I should look. There, at street level, bobbed the head of man in a yellow hard hat. Trust a me a first grader can be enthralled with the view of worker's head seeming to be bobbing along like a cork in a creek. After following the man's movements, logic dictated he was walking in a very long deep hole. As with a photo, a real-life visual image is worth a thousand words. Especially when viewed with a bright first grader!

Such stories can sound like exaggerations but I swear this is true. And I realize everyone's first grader is like the children living in Garrison Keller's Lake Woebegone, they are "well above average". I'm as guilty as any other parent or grandparent.

In fact, Jim Franks always considered me to be an authority on partiality. I would joke that I simply introduced him to nepotism. All of that simply because my grandfather paid me 10 cents an hour more than "Dr. Head" was paying him for doing the same job. If I could employ my grandson at a store in Stigler, I'd do the same thing. The point is I'm not opposed to a reasonable degree of nepotism.

On the other hand, I think there can be too much of a good thing. Just thinkin' about it, well, it seems to me our President has taken this nepotism thing out beyond a reasonable level. I'm sure, if I was the President, I'd want the best possible advice I could get, Lord knows I'd need it. Ah, no doubt!

I don't believe family is always the best source of a differential opinion. Maybe you only need so much of a good thing.

There is just a whole lot going on in Washington, D.C. these days that I'm confused about. But I listen to some of my friends and I don't feel lonely in my confusion. Of course, it is like nepotism. They are my friends and I'm past the point of wanting to hang out with people who chronically disagree with me.

You know what I'm going to do. It's a beautiful day. I'm putting my can of Coca-Cola in my hip pocket, grabbing a handful of "Planters" and heading to the back porch. Won't be long till the Final Four tips off. And then it's baseball season. That'll keep me from thinkin' so much.

I'm a product of nepotism. I don't think I would have had the profession I am in currently ... if it hadn't been for my dad. – Jeff Bridges (aka The Dude)

BANKER'S HOURS

2017

Do you remember "bankers' hours"? I really hadn't thought about them in some time. During recent years, banks seem to have had expansive hours to accommodate their customers. But it wasn't always that way. However, it does seem that many banks are reverting to the limited hours of old.

It seems to me that at the maximum the bank was open to the public from 10 AM to 2 PM. Now for folks working 7 to 6 those had to appear to be attractive hours.

"Are you keeping banker's hours?" This was the question that was teasingly ask of person who might be leaving work early – or arriving late. It referred to the hours a bank was opened to the public to transact business. In the Stigler I grew up in, it meant Mr. Stumbaugh would take you deposit. A.C. "Bo" Stumbaugh but for me he was only Mr. Stumbaugh. I don't remember the First National Bank of Stigler without him. I don't know if he was officially the chief teller but I thought he was.

I believe every successful business has a person, that vital cog, that makes it run. I always believed that to be Mr. Stumbaugh at the First National Bank.

During the summer months, my final task of the morning would be to take the store (Hays and Buchanan) deposit to the bank and return with the receipt. Just as my instruction concerning the barber shop was to always get in Mr. Lewis' chair, at the bank I was to go to Mr. Stumbaugh's window. If he was at his desk, I was to stand by the empty window until he saw me and returned.

BUT those guys and gals were doing all the entries by hand with pen and ink. Transactions were calculated in their head and transferred to paper with a pencil. Widespread availability of the mechanical adding machine was a relatively new assist.

If you want to see an old upright adding machine, take a visit to the Haskell County Historical Society Museum. The one that served Topsy Williams in Lloyd Sigmon's office is on display. As an aside, Topsy was Bo Stumbaugh's sister-in-law and she was the longtime Haskell County Tag Agent just preceding my mother.

Anyway, the people at the Bank in Stigler were looking at your eyes and not at a computer screen. I could see in Mr. Stumbaugh's eyes if he understood my request or if I had relayed my grandfather's instructions correctly. If I was a little off, he explained to me how to do it correctly.

You know, a small town contained so many teachers that never taught a day in a classroom. I was so fortunate to have come across so many of them.

I've got to hustle to make the bank before it closes. It is only open 10 AM to 4 PM now.

I truly believe that banking establishments are more dangerous than standing armies, and that the principles of spending money to be paid by posterity, under the name of funding, is but swindling futurity on a large scale.
– Thomas Jefferson

JUST READ THE QUESTION!
2017

As some of you may have observed, for two weeks I have managed to over-think the question. The inquiry did not say, "Compare and contrast." It asked, "What was life like before the internet?" I managed to take a simple question and make it into an intellectual inquisition.

I responded to a one-sided question with two sides. I felt I need to present both sides of a one-sided coin.

I can construct a rationalization. I spent my professional life evaluating people and then attempting to provide plausible, understandable explanations for their behavior. Behavior that had often occurred under the most distressing of circumstances. I felt compelled to find equity in inequitable situations. No. Well, there are nuggets of truth but I don't buy that either. If there was any hangover from my work life it should have been the guiding principle of an expert on the witness stand. "Just answer the question."

How about this? "At times, do humans, by overthinking the matter, make the easiest of situations more difficult?"

Anyway, maybe the old cliché is true and the third time will be the charm.

Before the internet, we communicated in a slower more thoughtful fashion. We talked with each other. As a boy, I recall sitting on my Grandparents front porch attentively listening to the adult conversations. As an adult, I remember sitting on the deck in our backyard talking with my wife and my family. And not just on special occasions but most evenings. We learned to listen and to speak. Conversation was an art form. Were there times the ladies were carrying on one conversation while the males talked about another? Absolutely.

Before television we listened to the radio. Do you remember when we sat and looked at the radio as we listened to it? I liked radio. Radio encouraged you to create images in your mind. I watched as my parents envisioned a collection of clutter fall from Fibber McGee's closet. As for me, I saw many baseball games on the radio. Each character appeared as my mind created them. The radio brought music. Now that I think about it, the radio let us hear everything.

Which came first, the radio or the movie theatre?

Movies at the Time Theatre or the Meadow Drive-In gave face and form to our admired characters. Then, television came. The technological miracle of our time. Stick an antenna thirty feet above your roof, point it in the right direction and there was Sgt. Friday in your living room saying, "Just the facts, Ma'am, just the facts".

Before the internet, the arrival of the mail was a big deal. We wrote letters. We shared letters. There was something organized about the way family letters were read aloud in my grandparent's home. You came to know family your never met. Their voices wove the threads into the fabric of family.

Books! Books were hard to find but we read. Stigler had no public library but the State of Oklahoma did. I ordered and returned books by mail from the State Library. The Boston Store in Fort Smith had a for fee lending library. Racks of paperbacks adored the Palace Drug Store. My Aunt and Uncle had a set of encyclopedias, World Book, I think. I spent hours alone with those white bound books. We read what we had.

Newspapers and magazines flourished. The Saturday Evening Post to Colliers to Time and Life, magazines were purchased, read, shared and traded.

Telephones were attached to a wall. You made your call, conducted your business and hung up. A daytime long-distance call could cost you "an arm and a leg", we waited until evening or even better until the weekend to place a quick family call. The rate structure tells you telephones were for business.

With gasoline reasonable, the "Sunday drive" became a more frequent evening activity. Your head out the car window in the breeze was fun until you got hit by a large flying insect.

Games were many. They were played on card tables and in the grass. Games were not played alone on a computer screen.

A thirty something just asks me if there really was life before the internet. Huh!!

If Al Gore invented the internet, then I invented spell check.
– Dan Quayle

READING INSTRUCTIONS BRING GREAT BEGINNINGS

2017

Charles Dickens began one of his great works writing, "It was the best of times, it was the worst of times, it was the age of wisdom, it was the age of foolishness – it was the spring of hope, it was the winter of despair – authorities insisted on being received in the superlative degree of comparison only."

Are you thinking thoughts evolve? I will begin in one place and end up in another. Have you ever been there? I'm not talking about forgetting what I went into the room to get. I guess I really get distracted by my own thoughts.

"It was the best of time and worst of times". I was originally considering the assembly of toys. Have you heard the standing jokes about instructions which say "Some assembly required"? For me these are more than jokes, they reflect personal experiences and frustrations. With the number of online purchases growing, "assembly-required" is increasing familiar direction. Now, later in life, I have discovered reading the instructions prior to beginning the assembly process can be very helpful.

I suspect most of us have found ourselves well into the night sitting in the living room floor prior to Christmas or a birthday or some holiday trying to put together a wagon, an electric train set, a tricycle or some such toy. Having recently purchased a new PC and attentively tried to follow the directions of a young technician, I quickly became convinced that Dickens must have had similar experiences. It makes sense that he encountered the "best of times and the worst of times" in his daily life just like the rest of us.

No, let me think. I'm certain toys and furniture came assembled in Dickens time. Word processing involved an inkwell and a pen, spell check was a dictionary. Just thinkin'.

In 1853, Dickens was describing the period surrounding the French Revolution. Since he penned those words people have viewed them of being descriptive of so many times and situations. As I read what I had written I realized how easily these comparative images could be used to describe the conflicting opinions so easily found in our present political climate. 1853. He could have just as easily been describing life in the pre-civil war United States. But he wasn't.

Maybe the world hasn't changed all that much since 1853. Or at least the world of politics and human motivation Best of times or worst, wisdom and foolishness, hope and despair. There is no shortage of authorities speaking in superlatives while belittling others. "Tremendous, Greatest ever, huge, fake or phony news. There are "Lightweights, Morons and Really Bad People". Some things don't change. "I'm really smart. I went to the Wharton School of Finance." That is an Ivy League education! An education just like that of George W. Bush, Barack Obama, Bill Clinton, George H.W. Bush, John Fitzgerald Kennedy and so on.

Do you believe those schools provide some special knowledge in government? I don't know. They do provide an education to an abundance of bright and privileged students.

I hope someone is reading the instructions. Oh well, think I'll have a root beer. It will be a change.

Good directors give short and specific instructions to their actors. – Bill Hader

HOME DELIVERY'S NOTHING NEW
2017

What did you think when you heard Amazon had purchased Whole Foods? I'll confess that at first, I didn't quite know what to make of it. I read somewhere that Amazon was going to be to retail what Walmart was 40 years ago. The hypothesis was that Amazon was going to do to Walmart what Walmart did to the small local store, put them out of business. Now that just seemed unlikely to me but like all good hypothesis this one will be tested.

Our neighbors across the street are a couple of young professionals with two very small children. My wife and I noticed that a UPS truck made a seemingly daily delivery. Our first thoughts involved some type of addiction to one of those shopping channels. Truth be told we enjoyed this guessing game for about a month.

The husband is a young man we have known since he was a small boy. So, one day when we were both out I just ask. He explained that given the demands of their lifestyle they ordered almost everything except food from Amazon. Now, we are talking diapers to toilet paper to toothpaste to clothing and even the occasional book. How about that?

Is Amazon's recent purchase a harbinger of home food delivery? Some authorities say yes, others no. It certainly seems that with Amazon Prime anything you want can be delivered in a most timely fashion.

But a couple of things come to mind. One, there is a socialization element to pushing a cart down the aisle of a store. Informal, casual conversations are fun. Kids hanging from shopping baskets are a delight.

Second, home delivery of groceries really isn't new. At least it isn't new if you are old enough to remember. In Stigler. I can think back to Pogue's, Poe's and Haddock's groceries. I know there were more but I can't recall them. My mother and my grandmothers would call their orders in almost every morning. Shortly before noon a pickup truck would park on the street behind the house. A young man would hop from the truck. He would retrieve a box of groceries from the truck bed and deposit it where the lady of the house desired.

On an especially rainy day, I remember seeing the box of groceries retrieved from under a tarp that covered the truck bed. The box was covered as he carried it through the rain into the house. I thought getting to work in the rain like that must be the coolest job ever. It had to rank right up there with splashing through mud puddles.

Now I wonder how the proprietors of these community institutions felt as Shelton's and other supermarkets appeared on the grocery landscape. By the way, I still don't know quite what to think of Amazon purchasing Whole Foods. You have any thoughts? The baby bird has flown from the nest so my back porch is available to me again. I got a lot of pleasure from that little bird. I think I'll go sit on the porch, drink a coke and think about it a bit.

I learned that life will go through changes — up and down and up again. That is what life does. — Ben Okri

THE SOUND OF SURVIVAL
September 15, 2017

Have you driven through a small community in rural Oklahoma and noticed how few commercial enterprises existed? You'll notice it has a couple of gas stations, a small grocery and a café or two. There is a garage that will repair anything and will sturdily weld two pieces together. Concrete curbs, now breaking down, boarder the streets from the sidewalks. They suggest that once upon a time a larger and more prosperous town existed.

On one end of town you notice an aging "rodeo" grounds. The wooden structures, pens and some seating, had been in place long enough that the wood was a weathered grey, some boards were no longer as secure as you would hope. Perhaps at the other end of town was a baseball field. The pipe and wire backstop, likely constructed by local men, appears sturdy even if the wire was starting to turn up in a few places. A railroad tie now seals an opening in the fence behind home plate. Sometime in the spring the field had been mowed, a weed eater had edged along the fence and under about three rows of wooden seats. They serve the purpose since most folks sit in lightweight, inexpensive lawn chairs along the fence. A better view can be secured by backing up a pickup truck and placing the aluminum framed lawn chairs in the bed of the truck. If you pass through on a summer Sunday you might catch a double header in progress.

If you took the time to count you would find at least a half-dozen Churches of various religious denominations.

As you exit the town and start to pick up a little speed you ask yourself, "What the heck keeps this place on the map?"

I have a theory about this that I will share. In your initial drive through town you missed the singular thing that draws a small community together. You didn't see the school. The school is the life-blood of the small farming community. The campus is likely a blend of buildings of all vintages. The structures will range from a WPA building to a relatively new gym.

Close examination will allow you to see many of interior structures ranging from lockers to lab tables to seating was built by local labor, from skilled finish carpenters to solid rough carpenters. You know that is a high-level of community involvement when a person walks into their children's school and you briefly look at you work. "I built that."

The common goals of the public school can bring a community together as nothing else can. Parents are seeking an education for their children. School activities draw the community together. The spectator seating at school auditoriums, gyms and athletic fields are true community gathering places.

A quick look around the seats at an activity and a child knows they do have a village supporting them. People who are interested in them and their team. They do represent the people who talk to them in the grocery, sell them gasoline or hamburgers or such.

The citizenry talks about the school activities. The Junior Play, the Senior Play, a concert, a variety of "seasonal programs" draw interest even from individuals who have long since graduated. The school is the forum that binds the community together.

Many worthy projects were first discussed during the halftime of a ball game. "You know if we just all got together it wouldn't take a lot of money."

In most small towns, the school district is the largest single employer.

When you are at the game Friday night, home or away, look to see what school group receives the profits from the concession stand. After you get your popcorn and Coke, you might just leave a little extra change if you can. Maybe just say "Thank you" to the volunteer sacking your popcorn.

Intellectual growth should commence at birth and cease only at death – Albert Einstein.

TIMES THAT TRY MEN'S SOULS
2017

There are times that try men's souls. Most often these are frustrating times associated with circumstances that involve perplexing moral issues or seemingly inconsistent secular stances. Most of often our opponent is ourselves. We seek to impose clear solutions on to blurred circumstances. We are convinced there must be a correct resolution to some mystifying intellectual struggle filled with options.

After considerable thought, we remind convinced that a correct answer exists. All of our applied logic convinces us no clear, correct answer exist. But such logic does not sway us. It is at this point we find ourselves most troubled by this absence of clarity.

Regardless of logic, pressed to the wall, we will determine a "correct" answer. We will then defend our chosen path against all other options. We can even come up with a rationale to defend the illogical, an amazing intellectual feat.

I think much of the time we are wrestling with spiritual or governmental issues then we find ourselves so conflicted. Ken Burns recent documentary aired on PBS and took us back to such a time. Americans with violently opposing points of view found themselves locked eyeball to eyeball, defending their ideologies. If you watched Mr. Burns' work with a semi-objective eye, you likely still have passionate but mixed feelings about those days in our lives, a hard time with many residual feelings. I was surprised watching this documentary how many emotions were aroused and revived.

I hate to confess that such noble ideological causes were not what I had in mind when I begin to write this piece. What is currently "trying my soul" is trying to decide what game to watch tonight.

Game 3 of the World Series is going to be telecast while at the same time the University of Tulsa-Southern Methodist game will be on ESPN. I hate to abandon a team on a losing streak.

Further, there is high school football game across the street, so close I can clearly hear the public-address system from my porch. From previous columns you know how strongly I feel about "butts in the seats" at high school events, from athletics to concerts to stage plays.

As I look ahead at the weekend, a serious of similar but distinct crisis loom on the horizon.

What about the OKC Thunder? I put them aside. We have a whole season of them remaining.

Okay, one day at a time. I recall how blessed I am to have a wife who loves football and the World Series. I am happy I get to choose between positive alternatives, not a negative choice in the bunch.

You know for my grandfather it would have been a simple choice. The World Series was the only event for which he'd take a half-day off from the store. But for many of us now, these are the times that try men's souls!

I hope you read this and remember that sometime the world is a quite serious place. At other times not so much.

"Ya still out!" – Yogi Berra on Jackie Robinson's steal of home base in Game 1 of the 1955 World Series.

UPON CONSIDERING THE PRICE OF PERMANENCE

November 14, 2017

Recently, I have been pondering the concept of permanence. Are there tangible or intangible entities that evolve into an irremovable position in our life? I think I began to consider the possibility it was a process of assigning considerable significance to people, possessions and ideas that somehow come to have meaning to us.

Now that sounds higher minded that what I had in mind. I accept that there are certain people and ideologies I want to keep. I want a permanent place for those I have lost. I try to record their history and their essence for others to read and recall.

I was thinking about the silly stuff that we somehow overvalue. I believe we all recognize it in ourselves even if we don't want to admit it.

Most often these mental and emotional attachments make little sense. Ask any wife how many times her husband has watched <u>The Godfather.</u> "Only every time he stumbles on it while channel surfing." Channel surfing during a commercial while watching a perfectly acceptable episode of <u>Law and Order: SVU.</u>

With the new programing guides that keep the audio of the program playing while you're exploring the visually displayed guide. "Well you never know when there might be some great option on." "No, I can't think of a program I'd leave SVU for."

Permanence: The state of being permanent; durable. Permanent: Enduring without fundamental or marked change; stable. Permanence promises a predictable environment. I resist change. I really like predictability and stability. Both just frequently elude me. My wise wife says I spend much time "chasing my tail".

Why do I have favored books? Why do I keep them by my chair? Why do I have preferred passages marked and margins filled with notes? Why do I read them and re-read them? I do find comfort believing I'm not alone in these practices.

Those that nurture our theological life seem the easiest to understand. In others I discover philosophical and behavioral directives that chafe me with guidelines that seem to pat. I struggle to understand them. I sense a rigid conformity in exchange for free will. I am reassured by those with moral imperatives that challenge me to ponder the human condition. How can I find the reassuring permanence I seek in such a conundrum of variables?

With that said does anyone else keep a copy of <u>Brown Bear</u> nearby. Tell me reading that book to child on your lap is not true sustenance for the soul. The hug of a small child feels pretty darn permanent to me.

But why do I so enjoy the drawings or the school work of my great-grandchildren attached by magnetics to our refrigerator – oh, I know it is really an ice box and it is somewhat uppity to refer to it otherwise. Neither the etchings or the ice box are permanent but I don't know why they feel that way.

Obviously, this topic is on my mind and isn't going away quickly. There is so much inconsistency and unpredictability in our world today. There is an unsettling danger in the air.

Wisdom is found in the fine bubble mist of cold Coke pour over ice. I don't know why. It passes my mind that our children must be wiser than we are. I don't know why.

It is those we live with and love and should know who elude us.
We can love completely what we cannot completely understand.
– Quotes from Norman MacLean, <u>A River Runs Through It</u>

HOW TO FIND A HERO

November 20, 2017

Where does one find a true hero today? I guess it depends on who you are and what you're looking for. From café to barber shop to lecture hall to church group to sports broadcaster, I hear the question raised. "Who do my kids admire?" and for Lord's sake, "Why?"

Most often these discussions stumbled as we tried to agree upon what constitutes a hero. Or a heroine. I recently expressed the opinion that in this day and age gender differentiation was outdated, that a hero was a hero. The replies I got left me acutely aware my opinion was not universally held.

I prefer to use the word hero to indicate both male and female. For very different reasons, I admire both Elenora and Franklin Roosevelt. Then, after the aristocratic Roosevelts came the plebeian Harry Truman. For me, all three are heroes. Heroes don't come in one flavor.

Harry Truman, a World War I Hero and a failed Independence, Kansas dry goods store operator, he rose to the U.S. Senate by learning how to coexist with Tom "Boss" Pendergast and his Kansas City political machine. Truman advanced to the Vice-Presidency at the whim of FDR and Pendergast went to Federal prison over tax issues.

Pendergast died shortly after Truman was sworn in as Vice-President. Truman against considerable advice to the contrary attended the funeral. He said, "He was always my friend and I have always been his."

Truman had given early notice of his capacity for independent thought and decision-making. During World War I, he rose to notice by making a command decision in the field. A decision that while not totally consistent with his orders saved a neighboring infantry division from an intense and lethal shelling. After receiving a "royal eating out", his artillery battery was reassigned to provide covering fire for a young George Patton's tank brigade.

Is it necessary to admire the totality of an individual to consider them a hero? I don't think so but that's me. Perfection is just too hard to find.

As a younger man, it seemed easy to find champions. But I don't think I was looking for my heroes "to high and to far away". I was just looking around me, people I could reach and touch. People I knew.

I saw how my grandfather's commitment to Hays and Buchanan. He was genuine. I never knew a kinder man than my barber, Walter Lewis. Mr. Lewis was a gentleman.

Paul James of Oklahoma Tire had a deferment from World War II that many people criticized. Mr. James conducted himself with dignity though faced with "righteous criticism". He knew his truth. I know that while our parents were away, he took many of us to the "old pits" and taught us to swim. He helped many of us with baseball although his son wasn't interested in the game. I saw Mr. James bite his tongue and I learned from him.

Baseball. Remember local Sunday afternoon heroes like Pete and Bud Faulkner? I do.

My Uncle, Herbert Claunts, knew how to deftly give a child more candy that their penny would have bought. I sat on a stack of boxes and eavesdropped while "Dad" Bankhead patiently listened to someone lobby him to print a story reflecting their point of view. He listened closely, he thanked them and then told them he'd print truth.

There were so many. My hometown was filled with heroes, true role models. Perfect people? I don't know. I believe most of them to be honorable men and women. They had a sense of purpose, felt committed to a righteous cause. I clearly remember their sense of purpose and a belief that self-sacrifice was required to obtain a goal.

There was an obligation to community. They seemed moral and principled people. I wanted to be like them.

I don't believe heroes are just in books or in times long past. I believe we are surrounded by heroes if we just take the time to look. Each of us needs to remember little eyes are watching.

A hero is no braver than the ordinary man, he is just braver five minutes longer. – Ralph Waldo Emerson.

NEARBY CHAMPIONS

December 3, 2017

Last week's musings left me still seeking some clarity about the nature of the people we admire or even idolize. I tried to understand the idea that in finding our role models, our heroes, we failed to recognize how close they were to us and how young we were when we first knew them. It is like many of those who ultimately influence so much of our character and our lives we knew when we were very young. They might have been our family, our friends or our neighbors. I just had to stop and think about it.

Hometown athletic heroes, I'm not certain when we first acquire a hero. I know we get them and we admire them. I recall Jimmy Curtis stopping to talk to me as his girl-friend walked him from the football field, a tradition in those days, after a big win in the fall of 1948. Jerrell Beller lived catty-corner and would shake my hand and briefly talk after a game. I was a small boy, they were hometown heroes. Those are acknowledgements a youngster never forgets.

Do you recall Gene Keith, the Wigington twins, Paul and Cecil Wise and Paul Wyers?

I so admired the business men of Stigler.

I'll bet today's women can remember back to the older girls and the women they admired. Often role models just aren't very far from any of us. With good fortune and wholesome parenting, once upon a time, we got to be someone's role model. We didn't volunteer, it wasn't a goal we pursued, it just happened.

A couple of Saturday afternoons ago at a football game in Kansas, two children were honored by being a part of the pre-game coin flip. Can you imagine their excitement? What do you suppose they thought when they were told not to shake hands with the captains of the opposing team? To decline to grasp a hand extended with the best of intentions, it seems contrary to what we try to teach our children. But their home team heroes did the same, so it must be okay.

Now the measure of each of us becomes "how do we respond to adversity"? The problematic nature of life repeatedly asked this question of us. I suppose we could make a gesture that had its birth in music videos and performance and mouthing obscene phrases that have been with us for generations. But we don't have to, we choose to. Even in the heat of competition our response remains our choice.

Do you want to explain it to an 8-year-old boy? I didn't but I did. We just talked about how we treat each other. He looked through the lens of his current religious development and answered, "So what would God do." Well, yes.

What do we teach our children to do when they make a mistake? I'm not suggesting an answer because I'll bet you know. Sometimes that is just the best we can do. Personally, I just hope others get it.

I propose role models are only offering suggestions. It is up to each of us, as we mature, to choose to follow them... or not.

Heroes are not limited to our youth. We discover new ones among us all the time. How about the old gentleman who emerged from his home on recent Sunday morning and with his rifle saved many lives outside a small Texas church house? Not bad for an old guy.

Although it might feel that way at times, we are never alone. You never know when little eyes are watching.

A hero is commonly the simplest and obscurest of men. – Henry David Thoreau

Tell me your heroes and I'll tell you how your life will end up. – Warren Buffett.

The Weather
and the Seasons

WEATHER AND MEN OF A CERTAIN AGE

January 6, 2014

The temperature here last night dropped to one degree below zero. Now that was the real temperature not the wind chill. Now that is cold enough to get folks talking. It seemed to bring up the question are men of a certain age really preoccupied with the extremes Oklahoma weather can achieve.

In listening, I have concluded many of us do speak of such weather like it is a common enemy. I heard the weather described in many colorful fashions, but the most intriguing was the seeming contradiction, "It is cold as hell out there". Now, I always understood that Satan maintained an awfully hot climate. I suppose there is some logic to blaming any uncomfortable extreme on the Devil himself. I'm okay with that.

How do you know you're in that man of certain age category? I believe a clear indicator is when you wife says, "If you go there and fall, don't expect any sympathy in here." And she clearly means it. A friend suggested that maybe it was when we had few of our youthful preoccupations left to amuse us. In a fashion, he might be right. Perhaps challenging the cold weather offers a vague testimony that a fading virility persist. My wife just says I'm nuts and she has always been quite perceptive about such things. Still, there was a time we didn't get weathered in.

I perversely admire the Packer fan sitting in below zero weather, rooting the Packers home. I say I understand it, but I don't. And I'm sure not going to do it. If Stigler or Cascia were playing for an Oklahoma state football championship, then I would consider that to be extenuating circumstances. As I think on it I did sit the freezing fog on the night the 2007 Ice Storm came to watch just such an event. The more I think about it, I believe I now enjoy saying I did it as much as I did watching it. Would I do it again?

That is an indecisive maybe! If we do it, take all the warmers you can buy and a thermos of a potent coffee based elixir.

Then again, I can watch the Packer's play on a big screen in a big warm chair.

I still don't know why men of a certain age are fascinated by the weather. We sure do talk about it a lot. I'll just have to think on it a little more. Not much else to do, it's really bitter cold outside.

Being soaked alone is cold. Being soaked with your best friend is an adventure.
– Emily Wing Smith

THE SHIRKING WORLD OF WEATHER

January 27, 2015

This morning I got on an elevator with a tall, slender and well-conditioned young physician still in his exercise gear. We spoke. Then, making conversation, he said, "That is brutal weather." I looked at him and said, "I thought it was really pleasant out." He responded, "Oh, I meant the weather in New England." I nodded and considered the possibility he had been so involved in the New England weather playing on the televisions at the health club – well, he forgot where he was. I don't know but the sheepish expression on his face suggested that might be the case.

I suspect few remember when the most reliable weather forecast was found by calling the telephone operator or the Sheriff's Office and asking what they knew about the weather in Eufaula. Dark clouds that way would bring about a discussion as to whether the rain was going to follow the river or perhaps stay south of the mountains, raining in Lequire. The household AM radio would be so static filled that you could not have heard a weather report even had a station been predisposed to provide one. Anyway, the only weather that really mattered was in Haskell County.

As I recall it weather was mostly a surprise. We didn't expect it but we knew it when it arrived. Did you ever comfortably walk to school in shirt sleeves and freeze on your walk home? I wondered how bare legged girls in their dresses didn't really freeze to death.

Then, the technologies of war became the extravagances of peace. Television first began to have a weather man on their 15-minute evening news cast. He told us what had happened and took an educated stab at the future. Do you remember Don Woods and Gusty? Then, increasingly affordable radar replaced the pen and a large sheet of paper on an easel. Meteorology became a science and meteorologist replaced the weatherman.

Now, helping feed our 24-hour news cycle, the forecasting of weather on television has become a national pastime. We are told about low pressure systems off the west coast of Africa. We watch intently as hurricanes are tracked and landfall projections are made. Just recently the news provided us with repeated projection of a horrific nor'easter would produce a crippling snowfall from Philadelphia to Maine shores. Based upon the meteorological projections, all public transportation was closed in most of the region.

Well, New York and Philadelphia only got a moderate snowfall. Boston and northeast got much of what was forecast. A meteorologist apologized.

What puzzles me now is why did we care? The weather report was that we had perfectly lovely weather here. If a blizzard had been headed our way, then I would care. A wild line of thunderstorms filled with rowdily rotating clouds, I want to know about that. But I'm still "iffy" when dramatic meteorologists take over the screen in my home. I sat in my chair grouchily missing the latest episode of some "blood and body, cops and robbers" program.

Perhaps I am just skeptical. Perhaps I just miss Gusty.

One cannot predict the weather, more than a few days in advance.
– Stephen Hawking

LOVING THE CLIMATE YA GOT

February 1, 2015

Sometimes I get to thinking about topic and I can't let shake it from my mind. Most often I'm just over-thinking one piece of trivia or another. It seems to be an Oklahoma ritual to grouch about our weather. There are days I have had grouching down to a fine art and I'm not just talking about my opinions on our weather.

Like many I've said, "No one lives in Oklahoma because of the weather!" But you know there is a great deal to be said for diversity. Take Phoenix as an example; on a recent Sunday, they hosted both the Super Bowl and the final round of the Phoenix Open. Routinely a boring arid 80 and 55, they awakened to fog. How did Phoenix get a dew point high enough for fog? The long-time residents were thrilled to see such a weather phenomenon. After all most of them are just like us in that their pockets aren't deep enough to contain the cost of Super Bowl tickets, so they intended watch at home. After all you can buy a wall to wall LED television for the cost of one Super Bowl ticket on Stub Hub.

Monday they were back to their boring repetitive season of "Early Summer". Now Phoenix only has two seasons; early summer and summer. You know for sure it is summer when the asphalt in the parking lots begins to stick to your shoes. In my mind the Valley of the Sun is not the only place with two seasons. Two seasons, those are either hot and hotter or cold and colder.

We are blessed with 4 full seasons. Each designed so that we appreciate the next. Each season is strong and unique. Each enriches our life in a different manner. Coming out of a harsh cold night and warming over a stove or fireplace has to be one of life's satisfying experiences. Conversation and laughter add the proper spices.

Spring! It is warmth, color and smell. I think the harsher the winter has been, the more we enjoy the warm weather of spring.

Spring weather, with early evening rain storms that carry superb feels and smells onto porches and through open windows, bring pleasant temperatures and gorgeous green meadows and hillsides. Ponds are full. Tree lined creeks are running agreeably toward the rivers, unless they are flooding.

Forgive those thunderstorms that get out of hand and twist up very unpleasant and destructive winds.

Our summers are hot and humid. Waters are cool and pleasing. Sounds on starry summer nights are mesmerizing. Forget mosquitoes, ticks and chiggers. But don't forget the bug spray. Lie on a quilt and watch the evening stars, it is the same feel as the first winter night your wife has put the flannel sheets on the bed.

Our falls bring welcome cooler nights and the leaves turn. On a good fall the leaves turn, leaving hillsides looking as if they had been painted by brilliant artist. On Friday nights in our towns just look for the lights. You should be able to see them from the hiway. Hope springs eternal on these Friday night playgrounds. Teams and followers dream of being able to practice in the depths of December.

We are blessed with the diversity of seasons. I relish four seasons. There is a great deal to enjoy and a good deal to grouch about. Both important human activities, I think. We focus where we will. If the greens aren't frozen it is a fine day for golf.

All seasons have something to offer. – Jeanette Walls in <u>*Half-Broke Horses*</u>

OKLAHOMA SPRINGTIME: BLOSSOMS AND CELLARS

April 4, 2015

There are many things to like about Oklahoma springtime. The jonquils shove their rich green leaves above the winter ground and then place dazzling yellow blooms at their tips. Driving the back roads of rural Haskell County, you occasionally come upon some these brilliant blossoms in an open field.

The arrangement of the jonquils suggests they are the remnants of an old home site. Today all other indications of the home site might be gone unless you get out of your car for a closer look. Sometimes a small pile of stone suggests the scant remains of a fireplace or vestiges of a stone walk. Such traces of the past remind me that families committed to living on their land once dotted every forty acres or so of our county. Such a demanding lifestyle is difficult to even visualize today. Yet there was time for flowers and blossoming shrubs.

Look more closely and you might see a pattern to nearby trees. In late spring, I can note elms and mimosas, but the large flat leaves of a catalpa tree or the bright red spring flowers of a burning bush would further give away the location of a once loved home site.

I have great admiration for the sturdy folks whose arduous labor built the foundation of this county. Interestingly, what has endured are the flowers the wives and mothers carefully planted, the trees to shade their playing children and allow tree swings to be hung.

On a few of the identifiable home sites, evidence of another staple of Oklahoma spring can be seen, a reinforced concrete storm cellar. I understand it had uses far beyond providing a shelter from a storm, but to me these mounds of concrete and soil will always be storm cellars. Some cellars would be surrounded by beds of jonquils. My mother said it made them easier to see when the skies darkened or after nightfall.

Today television stations with their advanced radar systems have adequately terrified the populace long before any storm has actually thought about forming. There is one channel I prefer because they switch their regular programming to another channel they operate. I appreciate being given the choice.

Recently there was storm containing several tornados. The storm sirens became a steady wail. I decided the basement was the better part of valor. My wife pointed out any other alternative was stupidity. Although I have been known to opt for stupidity in the past, our six-year-old great-grandson was with us that evening. He carefully supervised my cane and handrail descent down the steep steps into our basement. And who else would consider playing catch with a whiffle ball in your basement during a storm.

The storms have passed. The morning sky is a bright and clear, the air seems cleansed. The coffee smells crisper. We have a burning bush in full bloom just off our front porch. I believe it is beautiful. The man who thinks it in the fall hates the long thorns. But I'm not removing my flowering bush. It is springtime in Oklahoma.

How fair is a flower garden amid the trials and passions of existence.
-- Benjamin Disraeli

MEMORIAL DAY AND MAY WEATHER TALES
May 21, 2015

While watching the storms move through Haskell County throughout this past week, I found it impossible not to recall my own encounters with our complicated May weather, "Memorial Day storms". Now tracking and evading May rainstorms is a skill every Oklahoman is wise to acquire. All of us have our "May weather tales", many as we made our way to and from Stigler, anxious to spend Memorial Day with our family members residing there.

To recall our most memorable, I didn't have to think long. Memorial Day of 1976 was the clear winner. May of that year had been a good month for our family. Our eldest son had graduated from high school and I had completed my doctorial program. Graduations are future orientated, family achievements that leave everyone a little full of themselves.

As we were returning from a Stigler visit in the late afternoon of May 30. I don't recall where we first saw the dark clouds building to the west, but I do remember commenting on not having to fight the sun on the Muskogee Turnpike.

By the time coins were tossed in the basket to pay our toll, the sky was black and rain had begun to fall. Just outside Broken Arrow, the heavy rain push by a stiff wind dropped the visibility close to zero. Then what appeared to me to be galvanized metal trash cans begin to strike the car. I discovered siding, peeled and rolled, from mobile homes and flying through the air resembled trash cans.

The tornado we drove into was small. The rain storm was not. It was a record. Measurement centered in SE Tulsa indicated that seven to ten inches of rain fell in a three- hour period.

At the outer edge of Broken Arrow, I was enticed by the lights of a QT that punched through the disturbingly pitch-black night. I pulled off on to what appeared to be a level road. I drove into a flooded intersection. The car first seemed to float, then sank to a level just below the windows. With some assistance, we safely but not dryly abandoned the car.

Intently looking back through the pouring rain from the under the canopy of the QT it was evident that the deceptively disguised water had already trapped at least four other cars. Several more would quickly follow.

An elderly lady who had been attending evening church services down the way drove into the water. Several of us hustled out into the rain to help her, but she exited her vehicle unassisted. She stood erect in the stream. She popped up her small black umbrella, tucked her bible under her arm and waded out of the mid-thigh water. Her long dress was soaked from the waist down. Her gaze challenged anyone to comment upon her predicament. Her hair, her Bible and her dignity all stayed dry. The lady was impressive.

I believe she called on a higher power. I called AAA. I am confident she got better service than I did.

From my back porch it is beginning to look rather dark to southwest. Oh well, May is only half done.

In the Spring, I have counted 136 different kinds of weather inside of 24 hours. -- Mark Twain

OH, PLEASE NO MORE WEATHER
2015

I did not intend to write another column on the weather so soon. Then I spent a couple of nights watching television weather forecasters bask in the sound of their own voices until I became lost. I'd try to flip back and fourth to the Rangers game, then a glare from my wife unmistakably communicated that if I touched that remote control again, she had plans it.

The screen became covered with multiple warning and watch boxes. The crawler crept across the bottom of the screen with a variety of warnings and watches. Sirens periodically blared until the sound begins to grate on the nerves.

Storm chasers voice their observations adding to the confusion. "It's dark out here. I think I saw a rotation. The lightening gives us some light. But it's night and if there is a tornado it is rain-wrapped and I couldn't see it." Spotters out looking for something that they couldn't see even it was there. I'm convinced driving out into bad weather looking for a storm makes no sense.

I do recall hearing that one of the ways to detect an Oklahoma native is that when the storm siren sounds, he will go outside to see if he can spot the storm. Maybe it is simply genetic. If I figure it out, I'll let you know.

I must confess that despite its truly gnarly side, the diversity of our Oklahoma weather does provide an awfully lot to think about.

Storms can enlarge and transform in a most impressive fashion. The new technology is almost as remarkable. A recent weekend tornado seemed to emerge over Broken Arrow as the television meteorologist watched on one radar screen or another. They didn't forecast its formation but saw it in real time, leaving them stammering.

A storm tracker turned back and drove into the storm. In a panic he announced that he seeking shelter beneath an overpass, a quite iffy decision. Then he compounded his miscalculated decision by announcing he was abandoning his vehicle to seek refuge under the metal framework of the overpass. With what sounded to be genuine fright, he proclaimed he was "clinging to a girder" as the wind tossed him around. He precariously clung to his steel beam, jostled by the wind and dodging debris, until the storm passed.

I know the television stations hype the high level of training their spotters receive but that does make a fellow wonder doesn't it.

We are all left to seek our weather guidance where we have confidence. Personally, I just look and see what Josh has to say. Josh is from rural Oklahoma and just completed his freshman year at a major Oklahoma public university and possesses a sincere passion for the weather. He posts his forecast, watches and warnings on Twitter. His words are uncomplicated. His maps are clear and his directional arrows are straight. Unlike a local station, he doesn't claim to be "Certified Most Accurate". He is "uncertified by the unqualified". Josh is just understandable, straightforward and correct a more that acceptable amount of the time. He makes the weather a whole lot more fun.

Weather forecast for tonight: Dark. – George Carlin

THE WEATHER BEING THE WEATHER
July 13, 2015

This morning I awaken and my wife was watching the Today Show. Through my early morning fog, I saw the cast standing under bright orange umbrellas. The crowd standing outside was covered with vivid orange plastic ponchos, thin but serviceable.

I heard one of the ladies say, "It is not supposed to rain in July". Another of the cast noted that it wasn't raining but rather the air was so humid that the water was simply dripping from it.

Now I am not an authority on New York weather. From years of late-night television watching I have been given the impression that July in New York City was a time marked by its heat. From the most unreliable of sources, David Letterman, I would expect a hot and humid environment filled with the fragrance of over-ripe garbage left too long for pick up. I don't think he was talking hot and humid compared to Oklahoma standards but still hot and humid.

I was shaving when the thunder and lightning arrived. By the time I had finished, a driving rain storm had rolled in. I stepped out back. It felt and smelled of a spring rain.

Oklahoma July, well, I don't know where it has gone either. I see four inches of rain fell in Stigler the other night. I'll bet the bar ditches are full and some creeks out of their banks. It does seem that during July and August we were most often praying for rain and not reciting "Rain, rain go away, come again another day" with house bound children.

A friend called and we talked a little golf. I realized my favorite but now stale story about carrying a tack hammer to place tees into drought hardened tee boxes was no longer relevant. A golfer now sloshes their way to the tee box. My wife suggested discussing the fashion in which "root rot" had affected flowers planted at the correct time was appropriate.

I have been given to understand this to will pass and we will hit the century mark next week. Now that sounds darn near tropical to me. Do you think we will be able to grow palm trees soon? Do oak trees thrive in a rain forest?

Wait, it has only been a few years ago that I was setting timers to water our shrubs and lawn at 4AM while we were away on vacation. The yard was bone dry and arid. It was so dry that it seemed unusual to me. Were we headed for another dust bowl and was it moving to the east? Well that is obviously a big "No".

Thinking of the dust bowl, today it seems that California has inherited it. There is severe drought, the fields are parched and Magnum, PI is "stealing" water by the truck load.

I went to the back porch, sat down in my chair and opened a Coca-Cola. I wondered if this was what the experts meant by climate change. I don't think so but I don't know. I think it just the weather being the weather. I think I hear the sound of thunder and rain rolling my way.

Some people walk in the rain; others just get wet. – Roger Miller

LAZY HAZY CRAZY DAYS OF SUMMER
2015

A friend recently asked me, "How did we get by in this heat and humidity before air conditioning?" I told him, "We didn't know anything else. We couldn't even dream of refrigerated air."

A few Stigler homes tried "swamp coolers". These evaporation units did not experience the same success in Stigler that they experienced in the extremely dry heat of Phoenix or Albuquerque. An evaporative cooler mostly just made the furniture close to the window damp. Some like my Grandfather and Grandmother McBride had an attic fan. Sleep close to the window and you had a luxuriously cooling breeze. Yes, I know it was just rapidly moving hot air but it really felt good about midnight. As a boy, I thought it was a true wonder. At my home, mother would first sprinkle the sheets. She would then direct the fan from on top the chest of draws so both my brother and I got something of a breeze.

I just don't remember much talk about an actual temperature until television weathermen weaseled their way into my life. Now I can get preoccupied with it.

I think mostly summer comfort was a matter of expectation, acceptance and acclimation. We expected the evening to very warm. The radio broadcast of the Muskogee Reds baseball games distracted my focus from the heat. I now choose to believe a person cannot create visions of a baseball game being played and be hot at the same time. I know in truth we all just acclimated to the heat and knew a complaint had no cooling effect.

There came a time, I believed a song sung by Nat King Cole captured the essence of summer time. It changed my hopes and expectations. His voice softened summer. Remember it?

Those lazy hazy crazy days of summer.
Those days of soda, pretzels and beer.

The days were better only because my grandfather upgraded the air conditioning unit in Hays and Buchanan. It dropped the temperature about fifteen degrees below the outside air temperature. Now it didn't help the heat on the second floor to which I rolled boxes up the steps and unpacked the fall and winter merchandise. My break sitting in the "cooler air" on the third step, the drinking a bottle of Coca-Cola seemed marvelous.

I could now anticipate evenings. Old mellow Nat would sing our illusions.

Don't hafta to tell a girl and a fella about a drive-in
You'll see more kissin' in the cars than on the screen.

The Meadow Drive-In sat on open ground to the west of town. At the Meadow the summer heat became tolerable, I don't think many really thought of it. I know it was July and August hot, it just didn't matter.

Now the Meadow is gone. It was probably killed as much by air conditioning as by television. Television seems to mostly reruns blended with a few original summer offerings, mostly on premium channels. Oh, did I mention the Cardinals or the Royals or the Rangers are on most nights? I most likely did. Have you noticed how many Oklahoma kids are doing well in MLB? Did you see Dallas Keuchel from Bishop Kelley (and a Razorback) was the starting pitcher for the AL in the All-Star game?

Baseball is our constant.

It ain't the heat, it is the humility. --- Yogi Berra

CONSIDERING THE SHADE OF FALL GRASSES

2015

There are those among us who when they think of fall only consider the chilly mornings and the colors of turning leaves. I also enjoy these invigorating indicators of the arrival of fall.

The color of the leaves on Talimena Scenic Drive seems dependable. However, the brilliance of much of our eastern Oklahoma countryside seems to depend upon so many weather variables, rain to days of sunshine. I have heard many theories over the years and I am certain some are correct. I just don't know which ones are correct. Worse, come the next fall, I will have forgotten which theory I thought to be reasonable the previous year.

I have found there are other dependable indicators of the arrival of fall. The "heating and air conditioning" arrives to service the heating unit. Billie runs our electrostatic filters through the dishwasher so they are cleaned to her satisfaction prior to his arrival. Do you notice that distinctive aroma of dust and heat the first few times you turn your heating system on? While not as pleasant as viewing lovely leaves, the aroma is still a sure sign that fall mornings have arrived. Moving the thermostat from heat to cool in the same day, I suppose that could be an indicator of fall or spring. But I vote that it is a clear sign climate control technology has spoiled me rotten.

Sitting on our back porch, I watch the squirrels scurrying about and burying their winter storage beside Billie's pansies. Our terrier makes every effort to chase them from the yard. These interactions are as dependable as the leaves turning and perhaps more entertaining. As my dog has aged it has become a sprint the squirrels inevitably win.

As the wild life predictably moves inside the exterminator reliably appears.

257

With this fall came a new entertainment. We have a new neighbor who takes his lawn and landscaping even more seriously than Billie now takes ours. A landscape architect carefully placed each tree and shrub. They hauled in huge stones and built the most beautiful fire pit I have seen. I have begun to call it "Stonehenge". I know you're not supposed to covet anything of your neighbors, but I really like that fire pit.

Our lawn is now mature. But shade grass must be planted each fall. The pace of our life dictated that we skipped a planting cycle last fall, so this season seed was sown into the patches of bare dirt under our large lacebark elms. Across Zunis seed was spread into still green bermuda and sprinkler heads leaped from the ground four times daily to water the seed and refresh the bermuda. The fall grass emerged a lush green winter lawn. Ours not so much, it just laid dormant.

Last week nature displayed her sense of humor. Our neglected grass sprang to life. Our neighbor's grass fell victim to the curbside parking of a large construction crew. The crew digging very deep holes along 21st Street and filling them back up or so it seemed. Their lovely grass was trampled. I have found considerable entertainment value in the condition of his grass. Neighbors with a sense of humor become treasures.

I do have to be cautious or he might suspend my visitation to "Stonehenge".

> There is not a sprig of grass that shoots uninteresting to me.
> – Thomas Jefferson.

IT IS A GOOD DAY FOR A GAME

2016

Sitting out back when the early March temperature was headed for 93 degrees, I was reminded old men should periodically write about the weather. It is just what we do. Like a badge of recognition, old men discuss the weather. Only a senior citizen could recall that over 60 years ago there was a similar March day in 1954, high school baseball season was just under way, and it was scorching by first pitch. Bob Burge's pitches were sizzling like the afternoon heat. I thought it was a good day for a game.

I wasn't distracted by thoughts of being at home under the air conditioner. The few whose family had a unit did not play baseball. Now that I think about it I can only recall two families who did have window units. My grandfather had an attic fan. Stick you head in the window and it was wonderful in the late evenings.

This day it was humid and the increasingly damp flannel uniforms stuck to you. The occasional breeze was quite cooling. I'm sure many of you could guess that by nightfall the sky was lit by explosions of lightening and followed by loud roars of thunder. It was a real gully-washer that went on well into the night. It sounded and smelled really good out my window. Then, a large limb crashed from the ash tree in our front yard. Have you ever tried to saw dense ash wood with a bow saw?

If weather is a beef steak such recollections are the heavy marbling. Old men can talk about weather in both the past and present tense. If you think about it, we have more to talk about. But truth be told we are no better at predicting the future weather now than we were at 17. It is just that weather happens around as we create memories. Memories slow, we talk about the weather like it was the most important thing – but it's not.

Anyway, sitting on the back porch, I realized that I was obligated to write a little more about the weather. I understand if I don't, I'll be required to turn in my AARP card.

As a very unusual winter draws to a close, this March has produced some very unique days. All in all March of 2016 has been composed of warm days and some rainy nights. Weather is now inside the house as well as outside. Today we had to set the heat to knock the morning chill from the house and turn it to air conditioning in the afternoon. Alas, efforts to stabilize the household temperature are doomed to failure. Ah, maybe it is the temperature of my body that vacillates. Who knows?

I could point out that my back porch is always comfortable. Or is it that I only sit out there when it is comfortable. I'm pretty sure that is it. If it is a tad uneven a good ice- cold Coca Cola will take care of that.

If you have a 6-year-old boy around you can get up a game of whiffle ball. It is a good day for a game.

Climate is what we expect. Weather is what we get. – Mark Twain

SPRING STORMS
2016

A few days ago, Oklahoma springtime officially arrived. The heralds of its arrival were two long track EF-2 storms passing just north of the Tulsa Zoo. While this might appear as "gibberish" others, Oklahoma natives know exactly what it is.

Said in jest, several years ago I heard there was a way to identify of Oklahoman on a stormy afternoon. When the tornado sirens sound an Oklahoman will go to their front porch to see if they could see the storm. Judging by the number of camera phone videos shown on the local news cast, it is a practice that has not vanished. Rather it is enhanced in that now you take your phone with you hoping for a Facebook/twitter worthy photo.

Now I will acknowledge that I have stepped onto a porch or two during a thunderstorm. I enjoy watching the rain falling, feeling the moist cool breeze on my face, and seeing the lightening. The muscle of a routine spring rain storm is impressive and invigorating. They have a clear vitality to them; they rinse the pollen and dust from the air. At the same time, the intense spring rains cleanse and purify us.

Stepping out to check if I see a tornado is a different matter. I know many who claim that is exactly what they do. I am doubtful. I think that is why God built basements. But then again, my father would see a thunderstorm he judged to be north of the Canadian River. He would gather up my mother, across the bridge at Whitefield and try to drive into the heavy rainstorm.

Whatever his logic, he had no desire to drive into a storm south of the San Bois. Dad judged those storms to be more erratic and unpredictable. At times such as these I have been curious as the validity of his hypothesis. The inquisitiveness never sustains itself long enough for me to check into it. Sometimes the not knowing is more enjoyable anyway. It really doesn't matter if he was right or wrong, as with most Oklahoma men he enjoyed being an authority on the weather.

Still and all, it was my mother and my Grandmother Lane who really seemed better at forecasting the weather. When the porch "sweated", they called it "Weather brewing weather". Between these natural signs and the Farmer's Almanac, they were most always right

They did not have the technology that our modern television weather forecasters have. In fact, much of that time they didn't even have television. If it had been around, I suspect Dad would have had a better location of those rainstorms. But maybe not, my wife is pretty accurate using my Grandmother Lane's meteorological methodology.

The next day will often bring a lush high blue sky with an occasional puffy white cloud aimlessly wandering the sky. Nice isn't it.

Conversation about weather is the last refuge of the unimaginative.
– Oscar Wilde

HARBINGERS OF SPRING

2017

Clear signs of another spring are here. Harbingers. Harbingers is a 2-dollar word meaning there are signs spring is almost here. When you say the word aloud it does have a ring to it, it sounds like birds and spring. It is a pleasing word.

Just go into the job tomorrow, look at your co-workers in the eye and say, "Harbinger" – three times as fast as you can. They will look at as if you've lost a marble or two but you'll feel all refreshed. It is fun to just confuse people along, keeps them guessing. Just like spring. Nothing can keep you guessing more than springtime in Oklahoma.

The redbuds and bridal wreath are blooming. My neighbor's tulip trees have blossomed and faded. The dogwoods are close and the shade grass is greening. However, plants are not the only clear signs of spring.

We are again on Daylight Standard Time. Our clocks are reset, fresh batteries are in the smoke alarms. Give me 2 weeks and I will be adjusted. I have never been fond of this "time changing ritual". I have expressed my opinion of this mutilation of Greenwich Mean Time to the extent some consider me a little annoying. I don't care if it is Standard Time or Daylight Time, just leave it alone.

Conference basketball tournaments, the final vestiges of basketball winter, are done. Selection Sunday was the harbinger of "office brackets". Hope springs eternal. This might be my year to win or Gonzaga's year or can a Big 12 team cut the nets while "One Shining Moment" plays over the television. It is spring so all is possible.

Oh, that first weekend in April and the Master's Golf Championship will be played on the most visually beautiful course in America. Will this be the year I decide if the bird sounds that are such a staple of CBS television coverage are fake? Allegations of "fake news" fill the media, please no "fake birds".

The other night, I was sitting in a lawn chair watching a youth baseball practice. As twilight set in the air started to chill, then I went to the car to retrieve a jacket. The practice continued. These first-grade boys were having a fine old time. Some understood the goal was to throw a ball so that another player could catch it. Others not much. A ball would sail over a boy's head and the other would chase after it.

Have you ever just sat back, relaxed and watched a little boy (or girl) chase after a ball? It is pursuit of pure joy. They still understand how to have fun, how to really play. They pick up the ball and head bad toward the infield with one arm wind milling, racing back close enough to throw the ball over the head of the friend they are playing catch with.

I conclude that laughter makes you immune to the chill in the air. Some of the boys are still in their shirt sleeves. Others were cornered by their mother and have a sweat shirt on. Me, oh, I still have a boy's sweat shirt in my lap. He is just having too much fun.

Then, a young couple strolls past on the walking path, holding hands. I eat a couple of peanuts and take a sip of my coke. Spring has so many blossoms.

Life is what happens to you while you're busy making other plans.
— John Lennon

REMEMBERING AUGUST

August 30, 2017

The most common question overheard in any cafe in the area goes something like this, "Can you ever remember so much rain in August?" The answer is no, not in my lifetime. Springs were green, August were brown. You could look at a green lawn and guess with your spouse as to how high that neighbors water bill was going to be. The Augusts I recall involved hard cracked dusty ground, go back far enough and I can reminiscence about bare feet on hot sidewalks. Now I do have to go back a while to stir that memory.

The August air would be so dry that sprinkling the sheets before climbing in bed brought some effective evaporative cooling, for a little bit. Then, you would lay and wait for the oscillating fan to make its way back to you.

I know all about the "April showers, May flowers" concept but this "August deluge phenomenon" that brings lush lawns and beautiful blooms befuddles me a bit. That and August floods. This is a kind of August with which I am not familiar. Dust devils (Whirlwinds) I recall but floods and tornadoes, well, it just doesn't seem right.

Then again, I suppose I should look at all those wonderful July days, their afternoon highs only ranging into the mid-80's. Was July supposed to be that way? Or maybe this non-traditional August weather can be blamed upon the full lunar eclipse that passed all the way across our nation, from the Pacific Northwest to the Atlantic coast. If that is the case then hold on, in 7 years another full lunar eclipse is coming out of Mexico through Dallas-Fort Worth and skirting very close to us. Now this is a weather hypothesis that we can test. Well, at least test it a tad.

Other August things do seem quite familiar. August always heralds the approaching school year. Friends begin to send and posting "first day of school photos". I don't completely understand the appeal but I really enjoy the photos. Education has any number of landmarks. Formally, we seem preoccupied with the conclusions, now having all varieties of graduations from kindergarten to professional degrees. I believe beginnings are more exciting. No cap and gown photo will ever challenge a first grader's smile in the sheer joy and excitement category.

This morning, I was drinking a little coffee and listening to the national news. The weather forecast gave me a glimpse of now Hurricane Harvey. It is easy to forget that the Texas gulf coast has some nasty August weather inclinations. They are talking about so much rain on the Texas gulf coast that it is going to make our storms look like a passing summer shower. Guess if you're always braggin' yours is "bigger and better", sometimes it is.

I hope our friends living on South Padre stocked up on water and coke. Or better, as my wife says, "I'll beat the seagulls off this island".

Anybody who says they are not afraid at the time of a hurricane is either a fool or a liar, or a little bit of both. – Anderson Cooper

Books, Newspapers
and Entertainment

MAKING A MOVIE IN OSAGE COUNTY
March 4, 2014

The front-page headline in the Tulsa World recently gave voice to some of our state legislators' concerns about subsidies provided to the film industry, enticing them to make movies in our state. The focus was upon the recent film <u>August: Osage County.</u> I had seen in the News Sentinel that the film recently played at the Time Theatre.

I have yet to see the movie. I likely will but I remain hesitant. I know the play well.

Unquestionably, the film is an ideal platform for those opposed to the film subsidies. The plot is centered on a dark and dysfunctional family; the language is very rough and distasteful. The play's realism can overwhelm the unprepared viewer. It's transformation into a motion picture received state incentives to be filmed in Oklahoma. A more completely Oklahoma play could not have been chosen, its Oklahoma roots could not be deeper.

This Pulitzer Prize and Tony Award winning play was written by a native Oklahoman, Tracy Letts. His parents were long time Oklahoma educators and his mother, Billie Letts, is a well-known author in her own right. His father, Dennis Letts, taught English at Southeastern Oklahoma State University for 30 years. At the insistence of his playwright son, Professor Letts played the role of the alcoholic poet father whose disappearance keys the family gathering at the core of the play. He played the role in Chicago and on Broadway until shortly before his death. His obituary in the New York Times quotes him as stating, "You're talking to the fellow who went from the Tishomingo Community Theatre to Broadway. That's quite a step."

This tale of a dysfunctional kin could have been set in any state in our union, but it is set in Oklahoma. The plot is unpalatable for most. I have seen the stage play and purchased a copy of the script from the now sadly departed Steve's Sundries.

My wife and I purchased tickets to the Tulsa Performance with many of the Broadway cast in place for all our family. Our family reviews were split but all agreed the play was exceptional. It was the intensity of the theme and sizzling language that was off-putting.

I had reservations when I heard an intricate 4-hour play had been made into a 3 hour movie. Something had to be lost and nothing could be gained.

Back to subsidies, no one in a decision-making position should have been ignorant as to the nature and content of the play. Were they seduced by the names of the monstrously talented actresses chosen for the cast? Who knows?

Award winning stage plays and books do not always become fine movies.

Is it cost-effective to pay a movie production to come film in our state? I don't know. I do remember the howl when the movie <u>Oklahoma</u> was filmed in Arizona.

Just thinkin'. How much does our state benefit from paying folks to come here and make their movies. I don't see permanent jobs. I'll bet there is a state department in charge of motion picture production. I think I can tell you this, somebody is making money. It reminds me of when a circus would come to Stigler.

"Don't worry about avoiding temptation. As you grow older, it will avoid you." – Winston Churchill

AN ULTIMATE LITERARY PRIZE
February 4, 2015

From critic to casual reader there has been a common question floating about, "How about Harper Lee?" The question is asked with a distinct tone of admiration.

I think most of us, readers from the avid to the relaxed, believed that Harper Lee was headed in the direction of J.D. Salinger. One extraordinary book never to write another, rather "one and done" so to speak. Nonetheless each gave us a masterpiece of American literature.

There was always the rumor that she feared she could not match "To Kill a Mockingbird". Of course, there was also the rumor about the extent of her contribution to the writing of Truman Capote's "In Cold Blood". She never seemed to comment on either. In the time-honored custom of the true southern lady, she chose to stoically keep her dignified silence in the face of such controversy.

But there in a secure box belonging to her recently deceased sister was a manuscript. It was for a novel, "Go Set a Watchman" and was written prior to "Mockingbird". The "Watchman" manuscript was discovered attached to the original typewritten manuscript of "Mockingbird".

It is difficult to get a truly enthusiastic response from a jaded group of individuals oriented toward pointing out the weaknesses in an otherwise strong literary offering. But for now they are energized. It takes a bit for the "doubters" to make their appearances. I have full conviction that the cynics will begin to raise their questions. Trust me, they will make their appearances.

For Miss Harper Lee, to find a manuscript she thought was lost long ago has to be exciting. At 88 and in very poor health, it had to be exhilarating. There was a manuscript that her editor sent her away to rewrite from the point of view of the child, Scout, Jean

Louise Finch. "Watchman" contained Scouts flashbacks to the childhood events. The editor saw that as the core of the story. I'd certainly not question the decision given the wonders of "Mockingbird".

But to visit Scout as adult female, coming home to visit her elderly father Atticus, is intriguing. Having been told it was inadequate and should be significantly rewritten, it is easy to see how one might lose such a manuscript or even destroy it.

I believe most who have written with considerable enthusiasm have a half finished manuscript or even two lying around. You lose your path or your keenness for the tale. You like it but it sits alone and rather lost. Miss Lee said "Watchman" was completed, submitted and rejected as requiring the tale be told from a different prospective. She had judged it to be a fine effort.

I don't expect a work the quality of "Mockingbird". It doesn't have to be to be excellent. I look forward to July and being able to read "Go Set a Watchman". You might know my drill: A glass with ice, Coca-Cola Classic and popcorn from the microwave; my chair and my heating pad. And a much-anticipated book, a gift to each of us from Miss Harper Lee of Monroeville, Alabama.

Miss Jean Louise, stand up. Your father's passing.
— Harper Lee (To Kill a Mockingbird)

GOING, GOING, NOT GONE
February 27, 2015

Periodically, I hear stories of the demise of magazines on the television. Oops – I think I might have just found something here. Technology does modify our behavior, the national news at five-thirty. Television news gives me topics, my newspaper the details and my magazines enrich me. It is not the way I started but it is where I find myself.

Magazines. I love my magazines; the Smithsonian, National Geographic, Sports Illustrated and Arizona Hiways along with a couple of American history quarterlies. My wife enjoys Real Simple, House Beautiful and Southern Living. We have the luxury of enjoying listening as the other reads a passage that interested them. I read my magazines and my wife provides the highlights of her reading. What a deal!

Beyond my personal gratification from reading magazines, I have found a secondary benefit for any parent, grandparent, etc. National Geographic and Arizona Hiways are filled with splendid photography. A 6-month-old child can be taken into your lap, become enthralled with the bright colors as you repeatedly create stories in a voice filled with excitement and with their name. Shazam!!! You have a young man or young lady who will find a lifetime of joy in the printed page.

Unfortunately, it appears that magazines will not remain constant. In my mind the quality of Sports Illustrated's writing is fading. Frank DeFord and Rick Reilly primarily are displaying their great talent in and on other venues. I hope SI finds its way back from the brink of tabloid, from such disasters as their flawed series on Oklahoma State University.

I know the number of newspapers is shrinking. Each that vanishes is an immeasurable loss. To my embarrassment, I forgive such losses slowly. I am still mourning the passing of the Tulsa

Tribune. When I was about 10 years old, I learned the value of the Tribune from a well-known Stigler businesswoman who received it by mail to guarantee of the final edition of the previous afternoon. Of course, I found that it doubled the opportunities for me to discover a point-of-view of which I approved.

This is the lady who convinced me a newspaper should provide facts for digestion while also providing us adequate opinion to fashion brisk discussions. After all, where is the fun in "preaching to the choir"?

I open my can of Coca-Cola; pour it over the ice, sip too soon and the fizz sprays on my upper lip. It is like a new point of view; it both exhilarates and makes you revisit your conclusions about the topic. I find I'm just not always right. I okay with that.

I'm not okay with losing good newspapers and magazines. I can buy them and read them. I have to believe that helps.

TIMES THEY BE A CHANGIN'
2016

I have taken advantage of opportunities such as this to mark the departure of an entertainer who has provided many of us with considerable pleasure. I realize that it is never long before someone will ask, "Who was that?" "You know the guy who used to have a late-night show. Saw a bit of him the other night. He's got a full beard now and I just couldn't think of his name." "Oh, Letterman, I remember."

Garrison Keillor will close out <u>A Prairie Home Companion</u> before the fireworks go off on Independence Day. For several generations he will be the last of the great radio show host. Unlike television entertainers, prospects don't seem to be forming a line outside Minnesota Public Radio to follow him.

To the contrary, it will not be long before someone asks, "What was that guy's name who used to live in Lake Wobegon?" Ah, "The News from Lake Wobegon", a fictional town where it is always "quiet out on the edge of the prairie, where all the women are strong, all the men good looking and all the children are above average". Keillor further described his imaginary home town by stating, "It was a Lutheran town. Everybody was Lutheran. Even the atheists are Lutherans. It was a Lutheran God they didn't believe in."

This was a throwback to the finest of radio with each character possessing a distinctive voice. The sound effects were pure genius.

Some years ago, at the Brady Theatre in Tulsa with my eldest son, I was fortunate enough to see a production of <u>Prairie Home Companion</u>. I took my Coca Cola and made my way to our seats, Keillor aimlessly ambled out onto the stage seeming to acknowledge no one in particular. He was a tall man in rumbled suit whose eyebrows matched his clothing and whose other body parts didn't seem to quite fit together. His head lowered he ambled toward the center of the stage. He made an awkward acknowledgment of the gathering and then as if upon some concealed cue, he began the program.

He was a caricature of the American Midwesterner, a living breathing piece of Americana.

He would acknowledge in a later interview with Jane Pauley that he would be considered a high functioning autistic. He beyond doubt possessed a great intellect perfectly configured for radio.

Drifting back to his characters, I loved "Guy Noir, Private Eye". With the start of each episode I could see Bacall entering Bogart's office in <u>The Big Sleep.</u>

It is true confession time. I know some wondered why I wouldn't start seeing morning patients/clients until 9:15 AM. The answer was never complicated. Each weekday on NPR Garrison Keillor voiced the brief program, <u>The Writer's Almanac</u>. For me it was a true cerebral jump-start to the day.

Mr. Garrison Keillor, my Mark Twain with a microphone, thank you.

Thank you, God, for this good life and forgive us if we do not love it enough.
– Garrison Keillor
A book is a gift you can open again and again. – Garrison Keillor

Social Issues

ON CONSIDERING LOVELY LADIES
April 17, 2013

President Obama during a recent address to a semi-private gathering, I believe unintentionally, shined a light on a fascinating topic. He acknowledged an old friend whose wisdom and legal skills had allowed her to rise in regional government. He observed that she was a quite attractive lady. He said she was "The prettiest Attorney General in the United States" or something akin to that.

You could argue that it is nice the President noticed. I don't believe the First Lady is sporting new bangs with the hope her husband will find them unattractive. All husbands know wives are very conscious of such responses. All husbands all know about the trick question, "Does this dress make me look ____?" No sane man responses, "Oh, I didn't notice."

Guys, you ever been asked, "Are you going to wear that?" Women notice.

In this day and age, some will find it reassuring that the President is heterosexual. Others, not so much.

This really got me thinking. It does seem that beauty products remain a major industry in the United States. From cosmetics to weight awareness, from zumba to spanxs, it seems ladies work really hard at looking nice. I for one appreciate the effort. If I ever work really hard at something I don't mind a tad of acknowledgement for the effort.

In this day and time when there is so little agreement in Washington, D.C., I find it refreshing that a majority might agree that a pretty woman is good. It seems the only topic we have any chance of securing majority approval in the Senate. Although there does seem to be a group espousing the position that telling a woman she is attractive is at least a misdemeanor.

This morning I heard a respected lady interviewer speak to "the elephant in the room" as being the fact that Adam Scott, the new Masters Champion, was an exceptionally handsome man. She further noted he must be considered a "most eligible bachelor". Although stating the comment made him blush, he did not seem excessively perplexed. I recall the word "hot" being used. I don't think this will be a national story by nightfall.

As gender variances are prone to do, I feel somewhat confused. I'm going to get the last of the coffee, go to the porch and watch the soft rain. Spring rain does have a distinctive smell. I don't have to think much on that, it is just there to be enjoyed.

I'm going to think on the purpose of lipstick.

That's okay for me, but don't you think Congress has some more important topics on their plate? Just thinkin'.

Everything has beauty, but not everyone sees it.
— Confucius

THE INTERVIEW AND "CYBER-WARFARE"
December 21, 2014

Did you hope to go to the Time Theatre and watch the movie, The Interview? I didn't either. I know Seth Rogan and James Franco have a large following in a younger demographic. They are said to be skilled at comic satire. I would tend to believe that they probably are. But it seems that the young dictator of North Korea doesn't appreciate satire or he was just offended by a movie whose primary plot is his assassination.

As I understand it, being rather immature, he chose to coordinate and launch a successful barrage of cyber-bullying on Sony Studios. It seems a batch of embarrassing emails was released with the threat of releasing even more. Now, it has been hard for me to determine exactly how much of it directly concerned The Interview. It seems there were threats made toward potential ticket buyers resulting in a number of the major theatre chains declining to exhibit the movie as scheduled. Now Sony Studios has cancelled the scheduled Christmas Day release, placing the movie in the cold storage of January or February.

There have been cyber-crimes before, just ask Target or Home Depot or Staples and any number of banks. But these were the old fashioned "I want to steal your money" crimes.

Not being one to pass up a conundrum like this, President Obama said he wished the President of Sony would have talked with him first, before making the decision to pull the movie. It was said that the United States clearly knows that North Korea was responsible for the cyber-attack. However, as a matter of national security, "We know but we cannot tell we know." Nothing as reassuring as a politician saying, "Just trust me."

How about sending Dennis Rodman to use his influence with the youthful bully? Now that is an unsettling thought?

I'm really glad we can identify the source of such cyber-terrorism. I just wish our technological skills could prevent such events from occurring in the first place.

It was chilly enough on our porch that my coffee was really steaming. There is little like hot coffee on a cool morning. I got to thinkin' more about the cyber-intrusions into our world, especially the financial world.

I did decide the money I've buried in the Folgers's Coffee can in my back yard is safe from cyber-terrorism. My stock market investments, not so much.

In thinkin', it seems like it is bad idea to give a child a country to play with.

And I don't believe this challenge is going to leave us soon.

Courage is fire. Bullying is smoke. – Benjamin Disraeli

MARRIAGE AT THE GRAMMY
January 27, 2014

Sunday evening, I made one of my annual capitulations to my wife, and to my eldest granddaughter and my daughter-in-law. I surrendered the remote control to the television and settled in to watch an awards show, this night it was the Grammy Award Show. For me, clearly, the most painful of the awards shows.

We have two other televisions in our home. So, I could have slinked away and watched, say <u>The Godfather</u> on AMC or there is always an NBA game on some channel or another. However, I'd have had to surrender my spot at the dining room table for the consistently outstanding meals the ladies prepare in anticipation of these awards show. Even if I don't understand this "red carpet" thing, I do understand a dinner plate. Even better, I understand a dessert plate.

And in complete candor, I enjoy watching television programs with my wife. I love the running conversations we have. The Lord only knows how many "cops and robbers" programs she has endured with me when she'd likely rather be on the food channel.

This year the show took an unexpected turn on me. In unison, a number of gay couples were married on the program. Huh!

For almost 35 years, I was a forensic evaluator with my practice limited to conducting high conflict child custody evaluations. So, I have a grasp of marriages spinning out of control and coming apart, bumping and bruising their children as parental emotions fly randomly about. As the years progressed, a clear trend emerged. More and more of the parents I was evaluating had never been married. Some resided together for several years and had multiple children. Whatever the reason, they weren't interested in what they viewed as the formality of marriage.

This thought has drifted through my mind on occasion over the past few years. Heterosexual couples who have full access to lawful marriage seem to be disinterested or a least cavalier about participating in a government sanctioned Rite of the Church. It is a Rite upon which I consider the very fabric of our society to be founded.

I must confess the alternate lifestyles do confuse me. But they are committed in their pursuit of legal marriage. Will their divorce rate be lower? 35 years leads me to say, "I doubt it".

I know I'm not going to figure it out right now, no matter how hard I think. Lots of thoughts come to me as I take a deep breath and watch a Coke fizz. So far I haven't even found the right questions on this one.

So, I'll just say marriage is greatest thing that ever happened to me.

Now when did you say the Oscars are? Is the menu out yet?

Just thinkin'.

Where there is love, there is life. —Mahatma Gandhi

A TIME IT IS RIGHT TO WRITE
May 6, 2015

At first blush I thought the "Baltimore unrest" was one of those events that while it grabbed my attention, I just didn't need to write about it. Some goings-on just don't need another person throwing in "their two cents worth".

As the unrest turned to street riots, then to looting, to burning stores and automobiles, to the Orioles playing a game in an empty stadium. Still, I tried to convince myself that just wasn't an Eastern Oklahoma matter, there would be no stones thrown at police officers in the streets of Stigler. I told myself to just let it go.

At first, I just couldn't find an understandable cause. Agree or disagree, we mostly understood a march across a bridge for voting rights, the anti-war protest during the Vietnam era, and the abortion demonstrations. All were controversial and contentious in their time. Each group represented a reasoned point of view. There was violence.

Initially I watched as an athletic shoe store was ransacked and it made no sense. President Obama declared, "The looters are not protesting, they are stealing". I agreed.

When I saw a looter carrying toilet tissue and what looked like laundry detergent it didn't feel quite so far away. A mother marched out into the madness and found her son. She yanked at his sweatshirt hood and grabbed him by the ear and physically guided him to the safety of home. I got that and I would have cheered if I thought she could have heard me.

Over recent months our cities and suburbs have provided incidents in which an African-American man has died in a conflict with local law enforcement. Some have lit a fuse that ignited local racial conflicts and economic inequality bringing uprisings to their streets. Other places not quite so much. Don't misunderstand me, I do not believe that racism has gone off into some corner and died.

If you mull it over Tulsa recently had incident that could have gone south in a hurry. A 73-year-old Reserve Deputy Sheriff, saying he had confused his taser and his weapon, shot and killed a man fleeing from the site of a weapons and drug sting being conducted by the Tulsa Sheriff's Office. There was some protest, followed by an initial review that revealed some responsibility of the part of the Sheriff's Office. The review appeared to be open with reasonable disclosure. There have been resignations but no riots.

I know everything is not "peaches and cream" and "sweetness and light" between the racial communities in Eastern Oklahoma. I also know that there is not burning, rioting and looting in the streets after a Deputy made a whooper of a mistake. I know there could have been but there was not.

I went to my porch chair and had a Coca-Cola. I realized that this was despite the fact that every night the television is filled with murders, robberies and drug bust that must make Tulsa seem like a scary place. I offer a toast to the voices of sanity.

I'm pleased I chose to write these thoughts. Just think on it.

It is not desirable to cultivate a respect for the law, so much as for the right
— Henry David Thoreau.

SUITS ME JUST FINE
2015

What type of dress lends itself to success in the workplace? Now let's get this straight right off the bat, if you think I'm going to examine the wily world of women's wear you'd better thing again. My grandfather suffered no fools.

Do you recall the old saying "The clothes make the man"? I heard a conversation on the topic of men's dress in the workplace. Since then I have become considerably more observant.

A couple of obvious facts must be stated. First, it depends on the job. Second, times have changed. A few years ago, no one ever heard of "casual Friday". Some corporations still have not heard of it. There is a subtle societal expectation to be met within each cooperate culture. I recently heard a wise man say if there is doubt, err on the side of over-dressing a notch rather than under-dressing. No man ever lost a business account by wearing a coat and tie to a meeting.

It is not news that I am a fan of television's late-night talk shows. The host is always in a very nice suit and tie. The guest can be another story.

Our news, national and local, seems to be delivered by a man in a suit. A suit and tie lends credibility. They reflect stature and authority. I am coming to believe that it also reflects the respect we have for others, their positions and their institutions. If a knowledgeable educator wishes to be as a respected authority, try a suit and tie. Dress like the professional you aspire to be considered.

Every government official dresses in suit and tie. President Obama paid us a visit. By the time he arrived in Durant he discovered the Oklahoma heat and humidity. He took off his coat and rolled up the sleeves of his starched white shirt. Now I saw video of him rolling up his sleeves, but I never saw him carrying around his coat. I wonder who takes care of the Presidential coat. His coat is always buttoned. That's class.

In the business world, a man's dress can be a direct reflection of status. Some enjoy pointing out Steve Jobs black tee shirt. I have a photo of Mr. Jobs standing behind three of the original Macintosh computers, floppy disk and all, wearing a suit and tie. His creative cohort, Steve Wozniak, was similarly dressed. Great success does bring certain privilege.

Certain places command respect. A suit and tie are a prerequisite before offering expert testimony in a courtroom.

That gets me thinkin'. I wonder what the Justices of the Supreme Court of the United States wear under their robes. I suspect quite formal attire. Nonetheless, I think my fanciful ideations are more fun that the real facts. The more I think about this the more fun it becomes. Now this is just way too much fun.

Oh, by the way, dress for your job. I'd be silly to show up in a suit and tie for job better done in a pair of overalls.

I buy expensive suits. They just look cheap on me. ---- *Warren Buffett*

ON WARS LONG PAST

June 4, 2015

Only after it passes each year do I seem to grasp the personal significance Memorial Day carries. This year was no different. I know it is a day intended for remembrances. It seems that somewhere among the headstones recollections that are hidden deep in my psyche are rekindled.

There are those I knew and who will forever reside in my memory. There are those who I know through legend and lore. But it is the stones of whose I never knew but bear familiar markings that arouse my curiosity and bring wonder. World War I, World War II, Korea, or Vietnam, Memorial Day is a day for remembering those who served. I have yet to note Iraq and Afghanistan. In their own time they will be there.

A child buried by parents whose stones now appear as guardians for a child lost far too soon. Those always touch me. Still I know this day is about our soldiers.

Memorial Day was established as a holiday in 1868 as Decoration Day. It was to honor those who died in the American Civil War, both those of the Army of the Republic and the Army of the Confederate States.

Most are unaware that there is Confederate Memorial and Section at Arlington National Cemetery. Since the construction of the memorial, the President of the United States has sent a wreath to be laid at the Confederate Memorial each Memorial Day. Only President Harry S. Truman for two years and President George H.W. Bush for his term did not follow the tradition. President Obama followed the tradition and added sending a wreath to the African American Civil War Memorial located in Washington, D.C.

As first-hand memories fade our knowledge of the men and the families who sacrifices are honored on Memorial Day grow fainter. Documentarian Ken Burns' PBS documentary on the Civil War regenerated our familiarity and interest in the men and the circumstances of the Civil War.

Tom Brokaw's writing <u>The Greatest Generation</u> along with the efforts of Steven Spielberg and Tom Hanks efforts with HBO series <u>Band of Brothers</u> and <u>The Pacific</u> were exceptional at introducing generations to World War II and the vast differences in the European Theater and the Pacific Theater. <u>The Pacific</u> was largely based upon magnificent memoirs by Eugene Sledge and Sid Phillips.

I appreciate those who fought Civil War and World War II. I know them better because these men cared. I fear World War I and Korea are slipping away. Vietnam, gosh I don't know. I wish a "Eugene Sledge" would step from among them and tell us their story.

I do know they deserve more appreciation than we have given. And what of the parents, the wives and children who sent a loved one to war. They merit a great gratitude.

Never forget your own but take the time to find a soldier's stone and leave a coin upon it.

Patriotism is supporting your country all the time and your government when it deserves it. – Mark Twain.

HOW MANY CHOICES DOES A PERSON NEED?

September 21, 2015

I must confess that it is only in recent months that I have become aware of how many choices a person can be faced with during a single visit to a supermarket. The cereal aisle alone can be terrifying. I thought I wanted Cheerios only to discover it was not that easy. I had no idea how varieties of Cheerios there could be. I found regular, honey nut, multi-grain, apple-cinnamon, frosted and honey nut crunch. I'm sure there must be more.

I was certain I wanted Cheerios and not Corn Flakes, not bite-size Shredded Wheat or Raisin Bran. Then my eye caught Honey Bunches of Oats. I had enjoyed them at an earlier time but I couldn't remember if it was the gold box, the red box or the blue box.

Many weekday mornings we eat oatmeal. I thought I'd just simplify this and buy some Quaker Rolled Oats. Nice round container with the Pilgrim on it. Wait! There are Irish Oats and steel cut oats. Where did they come from?

I was unprepared for so many decisions. A box of cereal isn't just a box of cereal any more.

My admiration for my wife grew. It really got embarrassing when I found that the cereal I'd been eating with sliced bananas and grapes was named Kashi Island Vanilla Shredded Wheat and some kind of Kashi oat flakes. When I write it here it sounds almost like "The Un-American Breakfast of Champions". It sure is not plain old Wheaties. Now who ever heard of Kashi Fruit Loops?

I evaluated my situation and decided it was time to move on to a product with which I had a clearer relationship, Coca Cola. Not Diet Coke but regular Coca Cola, my childhood friend.

Well, guess what? I found Coca Cola Classic, Cherry Coke, Vanilla Coke, and so on. There were multiple Diet Coke products but I'm not a fan. Today I saw large glass bottles of Coke with a white sticker indicating it was bottled in Mexico. Turns out Mexican Coke is made with pure cane sugar and not the high fructose corn syrup that sweetens Coca Cola Classic. Huh! Wonder if New Coke served a "darker" purpose? I don't know, just thinkin'.

I purchased my Coke Classic and headed for Braums'. God bless my wife. She possesses a body of knowledge about such things that leaves me intellectually embarrassed.

I was grateful to be home. I fixed a glass of tea and headed to my chair to watch a little golf on the Golf Channel. I joined the programming in the midst of a commercial. "Lord, do you know how many kinds of Bush's beans there are?" And the answer is, "A whole lot!"

Am I "grocery challenged" or what? My wife suggests "spoiled rotten".

I've reached a point in my life where going to the supermarket is a day out. – *Ashley Jensen.*

More die in the United States of too much food than of too little. -- *John Kenneth Galbraith.*

GUNS, OTHER GUNS AND STATES OF MIND

October 13, 2015

Several months ago, I wrote this opinion piece, then for whatever reason I do such things, I set it aside. The recent events at a small Oregon community college brought it back to the front of my mind. In reading the final paragraph of this piece, I feel our better angels will only find us if we actively look for them. So, I'm pressing send this time.

It is extraordinarily difficult not to be have lost substantial elements of our emotional equilibrium following the heartbreaking mass murders at Sandy Hook Elementary School. Our emotions of Aurora, of Columbine, of Oklahoma City, of so many other senseless tragedies are momentarily revived. Mystification and confusion consume our conscious mind. We seek to impose logic upon the illogical, we become displeased with our failure to make sense of the senseless.

I cannot even bring myself to imagine the throbbing pain of parents and of first responders who must live with the memory of the bodies of small children ripped unrecognizable by multiple gunshots. These events leave us all to hypothesize about the motives and the fragile mental state of the youthful mass murderer. Such times leave us with a profound but ill-focused anger.

Make no mistake, I recognize the role that the unspeakably profound tragedy in Connecticut has played in reigniting an intensely emotional discussion of our ambivalent relationship with firearms.

Immediately after this tragedy Bruce Plante, an editorial cartoonist and a man I consider to be my friend, drew a poignantly delicate and personally wrenching editorial cartoon of a father protectively hugging his daughter, her head buried in his shielding shoulder. I need to believe that we all understand this tender message.

A more recent editorial cartoon drawn by the same cartoonist depicted two duck hunters. One armed for his hunt with what I imagine to be my Remington Sweet Sixteen. His hunting companion came outfitted with a rocket launcher and ammunition so technologically advanced that it contained a QDS, a "quack detecting system".

As with any well-crafted cartoon (or column) designed to stimulate thought, multiple interpretations are possible. As an old duck hunter, I recognize my belief that if I shoot something there should be adequate remains to cook and consume. Others will and should take away distinctly different messages.

In this writing, I realize I have no point to make, no position to posture. I wish to tell no one what to think. Nor am I seeking another person to provide me with an answer. I simply want to share my confusion and concern. I will contemplate this moment for it will soon pass. May the good angels of our better nature find us.

A long habit of not thinking a thing wrong, gives it a superficial appearance of being right, and raises at first a formidable outcry in defense of custom. But the turmoil soon subsides. Time makes more converts than reason. - - Thomas Paine, Common Sense, January 1776

THE SAGA OF BATHROOM BILL
(NOT PUBLISHED IN SNS – OBJECTIONABLE CONTENT)
2016

I recently got an inquiry from a relative asking, "Who is this Bathroom Bill and what did he do?" I admit I was briefly stumped before it hit me. Old Bill wasn't a person, Bill was a thing. If I was inclined to cite a Will Rogers saying it is one of those jokes that legislative bodies play on us now and then. Hum -- the more I considered this point of view the more I believed Mr. Rogers might have been correct.

With very little research, I quickly discovered that Bathroom Bill wasn't some serial pervert. Instead I found that the legislation that is the focus of this conflict is an LGBT law. It seems that the City of Charlotte North Carolina passed an ordinance that would allow transgender people to use the bathroom of the gender they identify as. Well --- let's just think about it.

The State of North Carolina responded with House Bill 2 – know as the "bathroom bill". In summary, State law trumped local law, saying cities can't pass laws stricter than the State law. The State of North Carolina argues that it is a matter of safety for women and children in public restrooms. I think there are both privacy and safety issues here but how in the devil do you enforce such laws. Not every transgender individual is as identifiable as Kaitlin Jenner (previously known as Bruce Jenner). Now she has been on a magazine cover or two. Driver's Licenses for sure won't be dependable. What a gnarly, knotted mess has been woven.

Entertainers, from Bruce Springsteen to Pearl Jam, Cirque du Soleil to Ringo Starr began cancelling appearances in North Carolina. Again --- Huh --- entertainers are withdrawing from contracted appearances before avid fans with the intent of leveraging law.

Then someone somewhere leaped forward and "played the race card". "I remember when there were 4 restrooms everywhere, 2 white only and 2 colored." The statement is true. I guess there was some illogical fear associated with the shared use of public restrooms or locker rooms or drinking fountains or bus seats or God only knows what else.

Such reckless behavior will obviously require the intervention of the Federal Government. It was at this point that I stopped writing yesterday. I felt comfortable I had a pleasant column on an unpleasant matter. Then I woke this morning to the news that President Obama had spoken on the subject and stated the position of the Federal Government. That does seem to me to carry a little more weight than an intervention by a lower Federal Court.

Oh Well, Old Bill might be confused but I don't want to be. I do not have any confusion about what restroom I should use at Tulsa International Airport. After thinkin' a little more on it, I'm more concerned about my bags arriving at the same destination as my body. Did you see that line of bags outside Sky Harbor in Phoenix yesterday?

For right now I think I'll just let Old Bill be mystified about the he, she, it gender issue. I'm going to pop a coke on the back porch and listen to the fizz. I think as citizens we have some really important matters to consider. Just thinkin'.

Government's first duty is to protect the people, not run their lives.
— Ronald Reagan

AN ILLLUSION OF CHANGE
NOT PUBLISHED IN SNS – RACIAL THEME
March 11, 2015

I believe I rarely write from my somber side, but given recent events I feel trapped here. I find this happens sometimes when I am required to confront the possibility that something, I believed to be both true and significant might have been an illusion (Or God forbid "I was just flat wrong!"). I need to write about it and hope I find a pathway.

In recent months, there have been more violent occurrences in which race seemed to have been involved. However, it was a chant on a party bus at the University of Oklahoma that has truly concerned me. I have always been especially proud of Oklahoma and of my home town, Stigler. In listening to the chant, I could have tolerated the n word but the references to lynching are appalling. That the story leads the national news for four days was distressing to me. This bright, white hot light shined upon Oklahoma stings.

While I will confess, I have never been one of his leading fans, I found some emotional sanctuary in the vigorous and forceful statement of University President, David Boren.

In 1960 I genuinely believed that in my lifetime I would see racism vanish in our country. When I grew up in Stigler, there were no African-American families residing in our school district. Beyond the streets of Muskogee and a bit of commerce conducted in my grandfather's store, I had never had any real interactions African-Americans. Then, I found myself in a university with completely integrated athletic programs. It did not take along to discover that in a basketball practice, race didn't matter, teammates were teammates. And thus, for our lifetimes we remained, there are only two of us left now.

I was optimistic that my children and grandchildren would see an almost race neutral nation. I was naïve.

I had no agenda and was never active in any organized civil rights activities. I was quite busy making a living while my wife raised our boys. It just seemed all okay.

Time passed and we heard an increasing number of African-American success stories. Yet, I would hear disquieting tales about the deterioration of metropolitan school districts coupled with the rise of successful private schools. Large waiting list at the old established preparatory schools became the rule. I had to sense something wasn't as it should be. I fear I gave it nodding recognition and moved on.

I guess I just needed to believe it. A basic truth quietly discussed between close friends inside a married housing unit in 1960 may exist. Laws can be changed but attitudes are an absolutely different matter.

I wish the national perception of our state had not been even briefly defined by the behavior of a group of alcohol fueled post pubescent boys.

Oh well, this is a day where the fizz of Coca Cola as it falls on the ice is an elixir for my soul. It is as calming as the ideal Oklahoma spring day viewed from my back porch. I do love my home state. I know I take events that portray it an unfavorable light too personally. I talk to my Coke, it doesn't talk back. I get to keep my illusions.

Racism isn't born, folks, it's taught. I have a two-year-old son. You know what he hates? Naps! End of list. --- Denis Leary.

ENHANCED INTEROGATION AND CHRISTMAS

December 11, 2014

I am accustomed to our Congress providing me with a source of amusement, even on occasion fine performances of the ridiculous. Now we elected these folks, but they seemed to have been mired in inaction over recent years. So the least they could do is provide us with a good belly laugh along. They want to be disagreeable about healthcare. Well, I still believe a good laugh keeps the Doctor away.

I turned on the nightly news and discovered CIA had released a report. A fella could easily get the idea that a politically proper position for torture must exist. Excuse me, Enhanced Interrogation Techniques. Help me. Is this a part of the Democratic or Republican platform? Now for sure, Nancy Pelosi was railing against the failure of the Enhanced Interrogation Techniques.

The more I listen and the more I think about it does appear the big compliant is not on the morality of torture but that the techniques didn't work. It does seem I've heard this "End justifies the means" logic before. It seems just a bit ago that it was a method of "Keeping American Safe".

It seems another of the complaints is about hiring some behavioral scientists to design the program. Some eighty-one million dollars worth of design and now Congress and the CIA can't determine if this group was expert in Enhanced Interrogation Programs. Huh! I guess there are experts in Enhanced Interrogation. All I ever saw in graduate school was guys I thought took too much pleasure in shocking rats. I'll bet the robed men from the Spanish Inquisition would have worked cheaper if they were still around.

Wait. Let me rethink this. The CIA needs help with interrogation techniques. Huh! I would have deferred to the Central

Intelligence Agency on any and all forms of clandestine information gathering.

Should the CIA and the Congress have a relationship? Why do I have this feeling that the answer will be "yes and no"?

I know he has made some remarks but I'm waiting on John McCain to make some direct remarks on the matter. He is a POW who was tortured and confessed to some fabrications. Seems he will have first-hand insight the rest of us are gratefully lacking.

This has been great weather for a back porch and a sweater; coffee and contemplation; sipping coffee and just thinkin'. Seems there is some line between justified torture and unjustified torture. You talk about a troubling moral and ethical decision, this is a WOW!

All this in the Christmas Season, there just might be an answer or two here. I re-read a Christmas favorite, <u>A Christmas Memory</u> by Truman Capote. It is a simple tale of an eccentric aunt, a little boy and the preparation of a Christmas cake to be mailed to the President. If you need a gift for someone special purchase a copy and wrap it in the lovely paper it deserves. In its leaves you might find an answer to interrogation.

It might just answer the question of how a free and spiritual people came to be asking themselves about the righteousness of Enhanced Interrogation Techniques.

It is inexcusable for scientists to torture animals; Let them make their experiments on journalist and politicians. – Henrik Ibsen

IT IS ALL IN YOUR PROSPECIVE
2016

It has been a real challenge not to hear at least some of the variety of opinions floating around since an 11-year-old "Access Hollywood" video was released. There has been an attempt to explain away certain undeniable comments as being boyish "locker room banter".

Have you ever noticed how inexpensive opinions are? Maybe that is why there is so many of different kinds of them floating around.

It does seem to me that whatever prospective we are predisposed to believe, well, there is a view, with acceptable justification, that fits us just right. Of course, we have networks and political campaigns staffed with the worlds most skilled rationalizers on the job! They don't get paid the big bucks for second class work.

It is the locker room one that I'd like to share my prospective on. I have been fortunate enough to have spent considerable time over the years in men's athletic, country club, and exercise club locker rooms. In behalf of my gender I want to say the behaviors and the attitudes voiced in the "Access Hollywood" video is not "routine locker banter". While I have known athletes, who behaved poorly outside the locker room, I have never heard such degrading and aggressive attitudes expressed toward women.

An apology to teammates is the closest thing I've ever heard and that was only once.

Back to prospective, ladies, I've never spent much time in a lady's locker room. To me logic dictates that a woman's prospective must be different. The candidate didn't clearly indicate "male locker room banter". So, if you have something to say concerning the language in lady's locker rooms, please speak up.

ALSO, did you catch the no homework trend in education? What do you think about that?

Well, as with many such things I had a predisposition. I spent over 30 years teaching a few classes each semester just because it pleased me. It did not matter if was a class of high school juniors or of graduate school students. I never assigned homework.

I have always believed that students of that age benefited more from play and family time. I'm really about activities from music to athletics for grade school kids. I'm about being a kid. Those of you who know me really well are free to reserve your comments.

I always believed that high school students might benefit from homework in classes such as upper division math, not from psychology or statistics.

It does appear that parents need to be doing their research on the value of homework and arrive at an informed opinion. This choice seems to be coming.

These opinions were also inexpensive. I prefer the word inexpensive to cheap.

The greatest deception men suffer is from their own opinions. – Leonardo da Vinci

INTO HARM'S WAY EACH DAY
2017

Not everyone who receives their regional television news from a Tulsa station lives in Tulsa. Even if you live south of the Canadian River you will come to know people whose jobs bring them in the public eye. I'm not writing of the weather forecasters who can become local celebrities, not of the sportscasters nor the news anchors nor of politicians.

I have in mind those folks whose jobs thrust them before the camera. They disseminate information that interests us or concerns us. Today I have in mind a man from the Tulsa Police Department, Sergeant Dave Walker. Sgt. Walker is head of the Tulsa Police Department's homicide unit. I don't know about you but it seems to me that Tulsa has had more than its fair share of homicides, enough that Sgt. Walker has become a familiar face.

This most creditable man is both serious and solemn. My wife and I have watched him for several years now. We have questioned how any person could perform in a position that brings him in repeated and direct contact with the most brutal and sordid of crimes. And yet he does. He stands before the camera, somber and "tells it like it is". We have developed considerable admiration for this man we have never met.

There are times I listen to him and I am reminded of Jack Webb's Sgt. Friday saying, "Just the facts Ma'am, just the facts". It seems only a few years ago that Sgt. Walker's hair was black, now it is flecked with considerable grey. It sounds about like how President Obama came into office and how he left it. Such a man might be able to conceal much of the impact of the emotional trauma he had witnessed over a career. It can't just flow from his psyche like "water off a duck's back".

I know being a police officer has always been a very difficult and demanding profession. I remember watching George Cooper,

Stigler's first after World War II, manage some most awkward, even dangerous situations. Marshall Cooper made them seem controllable.

In today's world, peace officers are more frequently finding themselves in hazardous, unpredictable circumstances. "Harm to self or harm to others" decisions must be made in a heartbeat. Complicated situations hurl themselves toward them faster that any reasonable person can think.

More often, our police are called to the scene after the fact.

Imagine walking in after a young man had pointed a handgun at his palm and fired. The bullet pierced his hand, flying across the room fatally wounding a teenage girl. The second young man so rattled by the incident he stumbled, the gun in his pocket discharged striking him in his leg. It sounded like a horrifying scene from a tragic comedy. But it wasn't.

How do you remain composed and professional after observing the aftermath of such avoidable tragedies? I don't know, ask Sgt. Walker. He has seen this and far worse.

I think we all get it. Sgt. Dave Walker is never on the scene of good news. I hope the Stigler Police Department has no use for a Chief of the Homicide Unit. We are getting better about thanking those who serve in our military. They are not the only men and women who go into harm's way to serve us. A sincere thank you can go a long way.

People I wouldn't trust with a sharp pencil shouldn't be allowed to have guns. – Sgt. Dave Walker (Tulsa Homicide Division)

On Our History

BRIDGES, BUILDINGS AND ARTIFACTS
February 21, 2015

Not long ago, I read an article on the front page of the Stigler News Sentinel about the 1910 Iron Bridge. It helps us tread that dicey line between safety and historical or sentimental value. This line is not always as clear as one might think. There is a long standing social myth that proclaims new to be better. Just ask the folks recently lined up outside an Apple Store. Most often in a consumer society, there is some truth to the myth.

However, there is great value in the familiar; in the predictable. It is there we find meaning and comfort and self-awareness. The familiar relaxes the intellect.

Buildings and bridges, letters and artifacts have value because of our emotionally attachment to them. While the process is elusive, we find an emotional thread weaves its way to our past. A tangible yet indiscernible pathway that when walked can provide sensitivity, pride and security. An ambiguous sense of who we are. It excites us.

Just over a year ago, the George Washington Presidential Library was opened. Considerable emphasis was placed on a single surviving letter from President Washington to Martha Washington, from a husband to a wife. This letter survived because it was concealed in a desk drawer. It is a letter that strongly suggests a loving and passionate relationship between this man and this woman.

After his death, Martha burned all the letters he had sent her. That is all the letters except one. A single letter that so humanizes our first President and his wife.

I was recently given a gift far greater than its intent. My eldest granddaughter, Emily Ann, gave me a Friday with her at the new Woody Guthrie Center in Tulsa. She knew my interest in the man and in his work. The interactive exhibits were pleasing to senses.

The letters, original lyrics and poetry, artifacts and instruments satisfied the most discerning historian.

At the conclusion of our day, I gave her my original copy of Joe Klein's biography of Woody Guthrie. History is meant to be shared.

History is the oddest of ducks. It can define us, influence us and yet be brushed aside as trivia. "It's boring! Which ever we choose, it is our history. It seems so easy to loose sight of the simple fact that history was made by people. No family history is insignificant.

I am proud of the Haskell County Historical Society and Museum. It seems that so few other communities are fortunate enough to have this quality of historical displays. While it touches each of us a bit differently, Hubert Claunts' candy case has meaning for so many of my generation.

I often speak of the impact growing up in Stigler had on me. I know the impact wasn't made by brick and concrete, it was made by the people. However, it is in the preservation of artifacts that the essence of the people important to our lives is secured. If we fail, we are all the poorer for it.

I wish I had written more love letters to my wife.

Study the past if you would define the future. — Confucius

WHEN HISTORY BECOMES HISTORY
September 3, 2015

Over the past few years, an increasing interest in history has emerged, history of all sorts and shapes. Personally, I am pleased to see an increasing number of articles on Haskell County History appearing in the Stigler News Sentinel along with an acknowledgement of the efforts of Beverly Franks and Noretta Livesay at the museum of the Haskell County Historical Society. Our history merits preservation.

Clearly, history is not limited by the range of our recall. History is further influenced by the range of our personal interest. As I have strived to increase my knowledge of the history of Stigler and Haskell County, of the Indian Territory, the more I have come to grasp that such histories are ultimately about people and families.

For years I have been infatuated with the rows of daffodils, the earth covered cellars and various decorative arrangements of stones that can be found dotting the rural roads of Haskell County. It is not the flowers or the rocks themselves but that they are indications of the individuals who once resided there. Why does an abandoned shed remain erect long after the original home structure gave way to time and the elements?

Some wish to define history as everything that occurred before us. It certainly is not limited to our personal recall. But much history is dependent upon the written personal recollections of men and women. Consider the remarkable letters exchanged between John and Abigail Adams, between George and Martha Washington and the late in life correspondence between John Adams and Thomas Jefferson. Think how these have enriched our understanding of men and women of the American Revolution.

Will emails be preserved as letters written in ink upon good paper were? We could ask the opinions of some politicians. Ah, probably wiped clean with a cloth. Beyond the political fun, it is a great question.

How valuable are the journals of Lewis and Clark and the men who traveled with them? In researching my most recent book, although a historical novel, I found great understanding in the letters exchanged between many of the primary characters. They candidly wrote of marital matters and parenting, the difficulty of being apart and hardships of the desert frontier. More importantly, how fortunate are we that the University of Virginia retained them.

Our history is enriched as an individual chooses to record their personal recollections. Consider how privileged your successors will be to have your recorded memoirs. For years I have encouraged everyone to write a collection of their favorite family stories; then deposit a copy with the Historical Society Museum. That is all it takes. With each deposit the history of our city and our county will grow richer.

You do not have to read scholarly histories in which you have no interest. Do read books that interest you. Heck, just read the Stigler News Sentinel's articles on the history of the county.

Much is still there for the viewing, like the vault seeming to be oddly attached to back of a North Broadway building. Did you know that there was once a library in the existing Court House?

The farther backward you can look, the farther forward you are likely to see. – Winston Churchill

Dedicated to Gerald Ray Kirk, Ph.D. and his immense affection for all things Stigler.

ON CONSIDERING A CANNON BALL
October 8, 2015

I believe everyone's mind requires an occasional stirring. I know for certain that mine does. Recently Carl Green, the curator and owner of the <u>Taloka Valley Cultural Heritage Center Collection</u>, contacted me regarding cannon ball that had been offered to him. I was familiar with Carl's collection because the Stigler News Sentinel had recently done a fine article on the curator and his collection.

A gentleman is offering Carl a cannon ball that he discovered while working for the "railroad" in New Mexico and Arizona. He had uncovered the cannon ball about three feet deep in sand, rock, river sediment and whatever else might be covering an artifact in that arid landscape. Except for the intermittent short-cuts, the original rail road beds followed the established wagon routes which followed earlier game trails. Through life and research, I had become familiar with the geography and history of the area. My most recent book, <u>Gatewood</u>, was set in the Arizona and New Mexico Territories of the 1870's and filled of historical and geographical tidbits. Carl thought I might have some insights we could share.

A cannon ball about the size of baseball. Huh. Buried under three feet of whatever. I thought about it. It stimulated my imagination. In such a stirred psychological state if I see an animal galloping across the prairie, I enjoy first thinking zebra and then horse.

I thought of the Spanish Conquistadors and the small cannons they towed across that countryside. Consider the Battle of Acoma Pueblo or the Acoma Massacre depending upon your point of view. It occurred in 1598 and there are reasonable recordings of the events. Small cannons were used at the onset of the fights. Could they have left a stray ball lying around? I find that intriguing, unlikely but fascinating.

Now the U. S. Cavalry chased the Apaches all up and down the Animas River Valley of western New Mexico for a half century (1840-1890). These expeditions hauled rarely used small cannons with them. Still the thought of owning a cannon ball that was launched at Geronimo, missed and buried in the river bed is captivating. Wouldn't that be a fun piece of history to have? Just thinkin'.

I sip on my Coke and think on it. I become certain that there are many more simple, rational and levelheaded answers, more plausible explanations. It could be that 150 years ago someone got tired of lugging it around, just dropped it off. However today I prefer the more nonsensical. Such answers amuse my imagination.

Anyway, I hope The Taloka Valley Cultural Heritage Center Collection obtains the cannon ball. It will there, secure for others to research and hypothesize. I don't believe that from the Curator's prospective it will replace his pre-Civil War ox cart, his Atlas Steam Engine and Steam Boiler or even his wooden hand-cranked washing machine on his list of favorite pieces. Still what a fine curiosity piece, it is old and it is a cannon ball and it was found in a most interesting and unusual place. Like the Haskell County Historical Society, I'm just glad Carl's collection exists.

The sound of a kiss is not so loud as that of cannon but its echo lasts a lot longer. – Oliver Wendell Holmes, Sr.

THESE LANDS ARE OURS

2016

I realize that using a title referencing ownership of "lands" can be really ambiguous. I slept on it and decided that no other title fit this piece. Before I got distracted last week it was my intent to write about these lands, the rich and varied lands of our National Park System. What could we consider to be more ours than a National Park or a National Monument?

If I wanted to be argumentative, I'd say Stigler residents, with Roye Park and the "Partnering for the Park" community improvement project might fit even more neatly into the concept of "our park on our land". Volunteers and local funds make it yours in a most special way.

However much of what we see even today in our National Parks came from a form of joint labor born of the Great Depression. WPA structures still dot our parks and hiking trails or paths constructed by the CCC guide us to the top of mountains or to the bottom of canyons or to ancient dwellings in their sheer walls.

My first visit to a National Park was disillusioning. I was in the 5th grade traveling with my brother and my parents to Fort Worth for a family visit. We stopped to visit Platt National Park in Sulfur, Oklahoma.

It was noted for its healing waters and a swimming hole. However, the water had a distinctive but familiar aroma. Being the proud owner of nice chemistry set, remembering the chemicals inside a maroon case, one good whiff and I recognized the smell. It was the "rotten egg" scent that I could create by heating sulfur. Perhaps it wasn't quite as bad but it was close enough for me. Platt is no longer a National Park, it is still listed with National Park Service as the Chickasaw National Recreation Area. I'll bet it still smells of sulfur. I haven't been back to check.

Have you ever noticed how many of our parks are built around waters?

Long ago when we were very young, my wife and I lived in northern Arizona. I had a part-time job working for a wholesale grocery and a delivery took me to Bright Angel Lodge on the south rim of the Grand Canyon. I first saw it after a mid-April overnight snowfall. I will never forget the canyons snow-topped walls, blinding in early morning sunlight. I couldn't wait to drive Billie to see this marvel on the earliest possible weekend. It wasn't the big hole in the ground I expected.

The Grand Canyon still enthralls me. I will attest you can visit the Canyon over and over again and it always changes.

Billie was the first of our family to discover Yosemite. She raved about it until my anticipation was intense. We visited it together some 5 years later. Still all I can say is "Wow!" There are places that just leave you struggling for adjectives.

National Parks are magnificent! Go see one. Go see them all. Oh, just take the family to Lake John Wells or over to Robber's Cave State Park. The most important part – Take the family. I am convinced our sons and daughter-in-law could write a nice piece about taking our grandchildren on visits to the Grand Canyon.

Each of our parks is a gift from one generation to the next. Every stroke taken at Roye Park will become part of a generational gift if it is just valued as such. Parks, from nature preserves to playgrounds, nourish us.

The wilderness holds answers to questions that man has not yet learned to ask.
– Nancy Newhall
Laws change, people die, the land remains. -- Abraham Lincoln

A PICTURE CAN BE A PHOTOGRAPH
2016

What is the difference between a picture and photograph? For all practical purposes there likely isn't. Picture is the broader term meaning any image. If you have a pencil and a tad of talent you can draw a picture. A photograph requires a camera.

Although it makes little sense, I always felt there was some difference in quality. Mathew Brady took photographs of the Civil War, he did not draw pictures. I always notice when a courtroom does not allow cameras and drawings by talented individuals seem to fall short. A little snooty on my part, I guess. Maybe it is because I can point a camera and I am quite inept with the pencil.

There are times nothing will replace a drawing. Just take a look at an editorial cartoon by Bruce Plante and you'll see insights expressed that a camera cannot capture.

Do you want fun? On Throwback Thursday the Stigler News Sentinel's Facebook page has shown many old photographs. Now they are treasures to some of us because they revive memories. For many of us these are images of people and times long past that stir emotions in our psyche. For others, just pictures of people and places that we never knew. Do you remember the ad with the photo of the two brothers that only my 97-year- old cousin seemed to recall? Where you touched by the expression on their faces and how proud they seemed of their year-old business? I was.

It should not be a complete surprise, just take a Brady photograph, you look upon people and scenes you never could have known yet they retrieve something from deep in our collective unconscious.

I treasure a photograph of Grandmother, Anna Wood McBride, just before she departed Scotland for the United States. My wife, I cannot tell you the pleasure I find in photographs of her clicked before I knew her. Recorded images of a curly headed little Martin girl will always release an unfathomable smile.

Me, I've taken thousands of pictures but maybe a half dozen photographs. Like golf, I find the equipment makes only a moderate difference in the result. I snap away and hope for the best. I have boxes of pictures not selected for placement in a family album. There are those who encourage me to trash them. I'll mumble something but I never do it.

Here is my operating hypothesis, if I snap the shutter closed enough times, Shazam! –a blind pig finds an acorn.

From Ansell Adams to Arizona Hiways, it is landscapes that I believe reach us. We believe we are looking at the same photograph of a landscape yet we find different meanings, meanings similar but distinct. But the important thing is that we find significance in the image. Landscapes lend themselves to discovering diverse meanings.

Not sure where all this is headed. Think I'll take my camera, a glass of ice and cold Coke and go to the porch. Do you remember the line from Inherit the Wind that says, "We look for God to high up and to far away"? I'm going to see if I can find a photo in my backyard.

Sometimes I arrive just when God's ready to have someone click the shutter. – Ansel Adams

HOW FAR BACK CAN YOU THROW THURSDAY?
2016

From its raw beginnings a few years ago, I have enjoyed the Stigler News Sentinel online presence. The current Facebook page has news and fun features. Throwback Thursday is my favorite. It is a feature for the curious.

Recently a photograph of cowboys on a spree at the "D Ranch" west of Stigler appeared. I remembered the Duke family who lived on the north side of Number 9 highway. I concluded from the photo that a spree involved lounging and smoking sizable cigars. The tent suggested a temporary camp site. I saw no hint of permanence.

I made a comment asking if it was in fact the home place of Donald Duke, SHS Class of 1951. I remember Donald as fine quarterback. Then, someone at the News Sentinel found the name "Maud Duke" associated with the photo.

Now the name was familiar. I telephoned my Cousin Boots in Sedona, Arizona. Boots Claunts is the son of Hubert and Vivian Claunts of Stigler 5& Up fame, think of a candy counter and school books. Cousin Boots graduated from Stigler High School with both of my parents in the Class of 1936.

Anyway, Boots Claunts, at age 97, has a razor-sharp memory especially about the Stigler of his youth. Logic dictated that if I wanted information about a "Duke Ranch" or Maud Duke I should telephone Boots. So I did.

Boots remember the same property I did, just 20 years earlier. He recalled two children of the Duke family, Les and Maud. I remember Les Duke as Donald's father.

Maud Duke is another story. Boots said she married Claude Bell who owned the drug store "Dr. Head" eventually bought. That is how Dr. Head came to run Bell's Pharmacy and Claude's brother,

Arnold Bell, owned the Palace Drug. You have to be from Stigler to remember that kind of stuff.

If you wonder about the "Doctor" Head, I suppose it was technically a nickname likely derived from the fact Dr. Head would perform a variety of medical services not otherwise available in Stigler. There is no telling how many sore throats were cured by his notorious throat swabs. Or maybe not, but swabbing a sore throat sure seem logical and the way it burned you knew it had to be killing something.

Anyway, the rancher's daughter became the storekeeper's wife. Maud Duke became Maud Bell. That sounds like something straight out of a 10 cent Saturday western at the Time Theatre.

A nice benefit to calling Boots is that you always get a second story. This time it was an oldie but a goodie. He spoke of a young Choctaw boy who ran the 100-yard dash faster than the wind. George Scott was leaving every competitor in the region in his wake. Then George got invited to a meet in Chicago. He came home telling of his experiences. It seems that George broke quickly only to see the backside of a young black competitor quickly distancing him. Jesse Owens impressed George. Great story when Boots tells it.

When a society or a civilization perishes, one condition can always be found. They forgot where they came from. – Carl Sandburg

STATUES AND OTHER MONUMENTS

August 25, 2017

Confession time. This is about the third essay I have tried to write on this topic this week. Each time I would get about three paragraphs I was satisfied with, something changed. I would do the contemporary version of waddin' it up and tossin' it the trash.

Understand I have no desire to write about statues to the Confederacy or to Civil War heroes. The current conflict simply got me thinking about statues and other monuments. I have now concluded that these reflect where we were at a given place in our social history. These origins can national or regional, while others are quite local. Some are important, others not so much.

The War Memorial erected on the Haskell County Courthouse lawn is important to me. If for no other reason than the name W.D. Hargis, Jr. is engraved on it. W.D. Hargis, Sr. maintained his office above my father's radio and television repair shop and I came to know him well. His son's name on that stone monolith was quite important to him, so it became important to me. It is my strong suspicion that the monument is important to any number of Haskell County residents.

I want to note the observation of a family member. A monument can only be erected if it reflects something of importance to the people who have the money to build it. I think another good thing about our War Memorial is that it took a group effort. I wonder if the bench placed on the courthouse lawn by the SHS Class of 1955 would be considered a monument. I don't believe so but it is an awfully nice bench and I'm proud to have my name on it.

Still thinkin'. Do you believe the Pioneer Woman statue in Ponca City could be built today? Did you know President Herbert Hoover delivered a radio address from the White House and famed Oklahoma humorist Will Rogers spoke at the site during its unveiling? Do you think similar dignitaries would agree to speak for a similar event today? Maybe if we had another E. W. Marland.

It was dedicated on April 22, 1930, the 41st Anniversary of the Land Run of 1889. I'll bet that today there will be someone asking just whose land were we giving away? I suspect legally or otherwise there were folks living there. Oh well, that is another story for another day.

It is a beautiful statue. If you have never seen it, do.

On July 2, 1864, while our country was fragmented and engaged in a great Civil War, congress passed the law creating the National Statuary Hall Collection in the United States Capitol. I'm always a bit proud to see the statue of Will Rogers in the background of the site where so many interviews are done inside the United States Capitol. Each state can place a statue of two individuals the state views of great merit. We chose Will Rogers and Sequoyah.

I suspect you are going to learn some other states choices very soon.

Me? I'm going to the porch, pop open a Coke and contemplate the wild flowers freed by an incredibly wet August. Nothing controversial about lovely wild flowers. My wife and daughter-in-law know I like sun flowers and they planted some this year. I have just discovered the first bloom. I'll enjoy my sunflowers.

I saw the angel in the marble and carved until I set him free.
— Michelangelo

TALES OF OUR FOUNDING FOLKS
(Part One)
2017

Over recent months talk of our Constitution and the assurances it provides us has become a hot topic. As various laws and orders have been blocked at the district level by federal courts, appeals discussed, the exact nature of the power of the judiciary has come front and center. What will it permit? Settled Law suffers no fools until it is no longer settled law.

I recently listened, without interfering, to a companion describe how our Constitution would protect us any government we might elect. He spoke as if the Constitution was a document which if followed like a recipe, could allow no harm could come to the United States. There are just too many checks and balances. He expounded on the wisdom of Thomas Jefferson in his construction of the document. I am not a historical scholar but I am an admirer of Jefferson, John Adams, and James Madison. My patience with the spread of "fake knowledge" expired.

James Madison, not Jefferson, is commonly credited with writing the document. At the time of the Constitutional Convention, Jefferson was representing us in France. John Adams was similarly occupied in England. I do not wish to suggest that our Constitution does not reflect the philosophical beliefs of both men, it does. But they didn't write it.

Isn't this magnificent document constructed in a fashion that it can save us from ourselves? Well, yes and no. The brilliance of our Constitution is the fashion in which it allows for maturity and change. Unlike many politicians, it is adaptable.

Article III provides a foundation for the forming a Judiciary with Supreme and Inferior Courts. It was during this competitive peak of the acrimonious relationship of Jefferson and Adams that the Court would move toward functional definition.

Jefferson had defeated Adams in the Presidential election of 1800. As Adams presidency was grinding to a close, he discovered there were many appointments to judgeships available. One was the Chief Justice of the Supreme Court. It wasn't considered a big deal because the judiciary was not held in high regard at that time.

Adams appointed John Marshall to the position of Chief Justice. Now, Marshall was Jefferson's second cousin but Jefferson despised him. The story goes that many years before a close female relative of Marshall had spurned the serious advances of a young Jefferson. Whatever Marshall's actual involvement was, Jefferson had never forgiven him. Adams seemed to feel what better parting gift could he left President-elect Jefferson than the appointment of a man he despised as Chief Justice.

Not that the role of Chief Justice was all that important at the time, it wasn't. There were not even plans to construct a building for the Judiciary at the time.

In truth, Adams appointed so many new individuals to the judiciary that not all the signed appointments could be delivered before Jefferson's Inauguration. James Madison – yes, same Madison – was the incoming Secretary of State and he saw no reason to waste good time delivering of these documents. One such document appointed William Marbury to a position of Justice of the Peace in the District of Columbia. At first blush, this would no big deal one way or the other. It seems folks underestimated now bad William Marbury wanted to be a Justice of the Peace.

He sought to obtain his letter of appointment by going to the office of the Secretary of State. He left less than satisfied. So, as one could do at the time, he went down to the Supreme Court and filed suit against the United States.

Well, I bit off a bigger tale than I can chew in one setting. I'll finish it next week.

The Constitution doesn't guarantee happiness, only the pursuit of it. You'll have to catch up with it yourself. – Benjamin Franklin.

TALES OF OUR FOUNDING FOLKS
(Part 2)
2017

I think I left William Marbury on the steps of the Capitol preparing to file his petition with the Supreme Court to receive the signed document appointing him a Justice of the Peace in the District of Columbia. I have this vision of Marbury kicking the mud of an unpaved Washington street from his boots, stepping into the Capitol, asking for directions to the rooms in which the Supreme Court, newly moved from Philadelphia, was located.

It is an easy vision to conjure up since the Supreme Court did not move into a building of its own until 1935. Between 1801 to 1861, the Supreme Court convened in whatever space was available. It assembled in several Capitol office spaces as well as a few boarding houses and taverns.

Anyway, Marbury filed his petition and his case was heard. The result is often viewed as the most important decision in court history. Chief Justice Marshall penned an impeccable opinion for the unanimous Court. Marshall wrote that Secretary Madison, acting in behalf of President Jefferson, was wrong in withholding Mr. Marbury's appointment. HOWEVER, he wrote that court had no jurisdiction in such a case and could not compel Madison to honor Mr. Marbury's appointment.

Chief Justice Marshall skillfully presented the opinion that the role of Supreme Court was to determine if an act of Congress conflicted with the Constitution, that the primary duty of the Court was to uphold and protect the Constitution. The Constitution was the "law of the land" and the Supreme Court was the definitive authority on Constitutional matters.

Oh, for those of you who are curious, William Marbury never did get his job.

Now you'd think that pretty much settled matters. But politics can clutter the seemingly most simple of matters. Along comes a matter with which most residents of eastern Oklahoma are familiar, President Andrew Jackson and the Indian Removal Act of 1830. A missionary, Samuel Worcester, who was imprisoned for violation of Georgia's law forbidding Missionaries from living on Cherokee land without a state license filed suit. A suit against the State of Georgia that made it way to the Supreme Court.

Chief Justice Marshall again wrote to a well-considered decision ruling the Cherokee to be a nation with sovereign powers and that the laws of Georgia couldn't be enforced on Cherokee land.

A flaw in the system surfaced. President Jackson is said to have infamously responded by saying something like, "Justice Marshall has his ruling, now let him enforce it."

The Supreme Court had no power to enforce its ruling. So, the Indian removals continued as Jackson planned.

I'll bet Congress went right to work crafting an Amendment to plug that little oversight as soon as Jackson left office. But I'd be wrong. They didn't. The Supreme Court still does not have the direct power to enforce its rulings. "It relies upon deference for the Constitution and respect for the law for compliance to it judgments."

Had the Executive Branch not been willing to provide Federal Troops and law enforcement to implement the Courts rulings during the Civil Rights Movement what would have happened? Because we know the right thing does not insure, we will do the right thing? I'll be thinkin' on this conundrum for a bit.

Somehow it did work after the Bush v. Gore ruling.

But what if another "Andrew Jackson type" comes along? What happens when the Executive Branch doesn't respect the rule of law? Is there any way to force the Executive Branch to adhere to the Constitution? Let me check on those "checks and balances". I've got to think!

Without debate, without criticism, no Administration and no country can succeed – and no republic can survive. – John Fitzgerald Kennedy

ON THE RANDOMNESS OF THOUGHT
March 5, 2015

There was a time in my life when I assumed that by its very nature the process of thought was guided by some hierarchy of logic. I blindly believed we would spend more time considering the significant issues in life and our world than we would contemplating its trivia. Well, somewhere between my doctoral dissertation and my Social Security check, I discovered I was wrong. I'm certain I got the hint about the first time I let obsessing on silliness distract me from the serious and important.

Of course, those are just some random unorganized thoughts clattering around in my head, silly but fun.

For example, The Prime Minister of Israel, Benjamin Netanyahu, spoke to joint session of our Congress on the nuclear ambitions of Iran. Such a speech seems important enough to me to merit a comment or two especially when the Prime Minister openly compared Iran and its pursuit of nuclear weapons to Nazi Germany of the 1930s. He criticized the President of the United States for negotiating with Iran on the topic. But then the Congressional leadership invited him, not President Obama. But given the intertwined histories of our nations, I wouldn't have thought that mattered much who ask the man. It might be politically important to some, but it sure smells of political trivia to me.

Now this speech got ample coverage, ranging from Letterman to Jon Stewart to our somber and prized newscasters. Frankly, I found the comedians to be more expert in their insights than our esteemed anchor men (or women). At times we just struggle to ferret out the genuinely serious from the frivolous. I know I do.

There is one more thing I know. The whole Middle East thing disturbs me. To me its future looks remarkably like its past.

A son's remark has made me think back a notch in life. When I was just trying to get by, to keep the roof in tact and my family fed, well, keeping up with the woes of the federal government was secondary to the woes of my personal budget.

At these times it was the silliness in which I found meaning, a television program that gave my wife and me a laugh on the couch, or makes my children giggle. Books for us to read and read to our children could be found. Thank God for the funding of Public

Libraries. Could it be that silliness enriches us all? Maybe answers are not always found in the scowl of somber thought.

Have you ever considered that silliness might be as valuable as seriousness? Or maybe they are the same, just different. I'm going to have a coke and few peanuts; I'm going to have to think back, consider the really important and try to look forward from my back porch. I'm glad it is warmer and the snow has melted. I believe it is easier to think in the fresh air.

The wit makes fun of other persons; the satirist makes fun of the world; the humorist makes fun of himself.
— James Thurber

ART IS ART, IF IT'S ART?

Feb. 2014 redone for use on July 6, 2015

For as long as I can remember I have been told art is subjective. I tended to agree because it let me contend that "I like it" was adequate justification for a enjoying a painting or a watercolor. I could look at a Jackson Pollack and say, "I don't get it." I could look at Andy Warhol's can of Campbell's soup and say, "Huh!" I can look at a Norma Howard or a Jerome Tiger and say, "That is just wonderful." I can look at a Frederick Remington or a Charles Russell and declare, "That is just magnificent."

Art is designed for public consumption. Andrew Wyeth's hid his Helga paintings for sometime, but that is understandable. And he knew they would ultimately be publicly viewed. Did J.D. Salinger write more stories after <u>Catcher in the Rye</u> and just discard them? Did Harper Lee write after <u>To Kill a Mockingbird?</u> "Yes" and we get to read it this month. There will always be rumors about her role in Truman Capote's works, but "No". Authors want their works to be read, painters their works to be seen.

Art. There are books and poetry and sculptures, marble to wood craving. There is music and motion pictures. A book might be repeatedly read, a song that touches a personal emotion for no apparent reason, will be played over and over. How many times can you see a production of the same play?

I suspect along about now you are likely thinkin' how on earth did he get off on this tangent?

Well, the topic of tattoos arose in my family. I was told that it was now properly referred to as "Body Art". How about that?

See, times they have changed! Not sure where we started but we have arrived at body art as a social statement – or something like that. It's a generation thing and I'm thinkin' about it.

I don't like the spray paint on the sides of buildings but I get it. It is creative and meant to be viewed. I have on occasion taken a photo of such "Wall Art" to examine more closely at a later time. I also understand that the owner of the property might rightly consider it vandalism.

Being something of traditionalist I expect visual art to come from a studio, an environment that stimulates and enhances the creative recesses of the artist mind. Maybe creativity can be nurtured in a storefront behind a neon sign flashing "Tattoo".

The "Body Art" is often applied in locations even the owner can not see. Has the owner's property been vandalized? Huh, now that's an odd thought.

Anyway, it might make for one heck of "a show and tell" at the senior's center in about 50 years! "Body Art" sure is popular so there should be a lot to see.

Beauty truly is in the eye of the beholder. After all I find beauty in viewing my backyard through the mist of a Coca-Cola just pour over ice.

Show me a man with a tattoo and I'll show you a man with an interesting past. – Jack London.

THINGS OF UNNATURAL BEAUTY

Our back porch is small enough that there is a full view of the southern sky. It has been a comfortable afternoon warming up nicely after a rather chilly start to the day. About mid-afternoon I stepped outside, sat down and looked south. The sky was a bright high blue with only an occasional cloud drifting past. The conditions made seeing a jet drawing a straight white line into the sky easy to see and follow. As the plane moved closer to overhead the line and then the airplane became more distinct. The line I had first observed was beginning to disperse, taking on a fluffy appearance.

The plane moved closer to overhead, leaving an even more distinct trail as the movement of the aircraft became more discernable. I unquestionably over the years have seen this display many times and thought little of it. I don't remember it being as mesmerizing as it was today. Perhaps it was just that I took the time to really look at it. Anyway the whole display from creation to dispersion was quite beautiful.

Upon mentioning it, I was told to consider the amount of environmental contaminates that the jet engines where spewing into the atmosphere. Huh.

I never wondered about the quantity of contaminates the creation of this display might be emitting. I just didn't think about it. Perhaps I should have but I didn't. I did recall the attractiveness of an oil pump at sunset on the prairie. Then I got closer on that summer day and viewed it as an oozing wound cut into the ground.

Remember how much fun it was to swim and fish in the strip pits that seem to be all over the county? As a boy, diving off the banks into the cool water on a summer afternoon, how could I consider it to be anything but perfect? I now know others considered them to yet another scar cut into the natural prairie. I saw them as clear water.

I saw little difference between the early strip pits and Kerr Lake covering all that fertile bottom land around Tamaha. Both were created because people found a commercial benefit from creating each. Someone profited.

Once upon a time I could fish and swim in both of them. Now, I can sit on the bank and enjoy the sights and sounds of them. Wait a minute! What happened to the strip pits of my youth? What do you mean this is where they used to be? Yes, I know that is the Club Lake over there. Well, dang.

Thinking about it, water is a lot like snow. It can mask what lies beneath it. The more I think the more I'm convinced something doesn't have to be perfect or permanent to be pleasing. I have to take the time to be pleased.

I can't just glance at a Norma Howard watercolor and grasp the pleasure it brings. I have to really look. I stop and get out of my car on the hill to the north of the Lake John Wells. I gaze between the trees down onto the lake and toward the oak forest on the southern shore. It is beautiful. Beauty in our world is just not all that hard to find if we just look.

Take a minute. Look up. A commercial jet might be overhead. Enjoy.

Look deep into nature and then you will understand everything better.
– Albert Einstein

BUT IT IS MY MESS

Well, 20 degree early mornings seemed to have just suddenly arrived with little warning. Well, little warning except it is the middle of December. I sat down at my computer and looked around. A mess to my right, a mess to my left but I had an unobstructed view of my computer screen. I already knew it was cluttered because I cluttered it.

Maybe it is the weather. It just seems that when the cold holds me in the house I believe I should do something to – Well, you know – clean it up and throw it out.

Straightening up my mess, I can do that. It is just the rearrangement of clutter. It is that "throwing out business" that gives me trouble. Going through drawers because like a voyage of discovery. An envelope with 1999 ticket stubs in it. Now there are some good memories. I better keep those. Let me find a place to put them.

Please excuse the mess but I write and I read in this room. I sure there is logic in the previous statement but I can't find it now. I am convinced other folks have a similar room, used for similar purposes and yet their room is tidy. Can I rationalize that tidiness is a distraction to productivity or creativity? I'll bet their tidiness distracts them, using time in which they could be writing or some such task to straighten it up.

That is it – chaos liberates creativity. Ah, an illogical concept that I can make sound logical. With this level of excuse-making should I consider politics?

Okay, back to straightening up my mess. Look, three packets of 75 photos stacked here and there are yet another distraction. I find I am obligated to pause and take a peek. Oh, look at these photos of grandchildren and great-grandchildren. Then I place them back in the container and tell myself I'll get them in a photograph book soon. Maybe I'll do it during the next cold snap, maybe not.

I glance straight ahead at the large superbly framed photograph of a favored golf hole at Sedona Golf Resort. Family photos have been wedged into the crack between glass and frame, so many they now almost surround the original picture. I might still have a place for another photo or child's art work. The view from 12 Tee really is gorgeous.

Okay, my place is messy because I work in it. Really? – Well, that is my rationalization and I'm stickin' with it. I had this book out for something I was writing – what was it? Surely it wasn't that long ago. Okay I guess it was.

I hope it warms up soon. I don't do this very well. Can you imagine what would happen if I spilled my Coke? Well, I have and let me tell you it was ugly. I guess what is really dumb is that I have another Coke in here. I think Einstein had some neat quote about people who repeat the same mistake over and over again while expecting a different result.

I don't think he was talking about people like me.

If stupidity got us in this mess then why can't it get us out? – Will Rogers

Education

THE CREATION OF DISPOSITION
April 17, 2015

This week my wife let me know there was an interview on television that she thought I would find interesting. I did. I think Charlie Rose, whether on CBS or PBS, is one of the most prepared, insightful and objective interviewers on television or radio today. He was interviewing New York Times columnist David Brooks, a political writer and cultural commentator with a notable conservative bent, about his new book titled The Road to Character. A quote from this interview got me to thinking. Actual thinkin' can be perilous.

In response to a question, Brooks spoke of the difference between "resume virtue and eulogy virtue". Do I want a friend at my funeral just reading from my professional résumé? To what extent does a person's educational, professional or financial achievement reflect their actual character?

The more I thought a most intriguing question emerged. How do we actually acquire our character, our moral fiber? I don't believe we can learn it only from our successes. Personally, I believe I have acquired as much knowledge from my failures than from my successes, I know I have had an ample supply of each.

During the interview, Brooks noted that in 1950 the Gallup Organization asked high school seniors if they considered themselves to be "a very important person". 12% indicated that they did. The same inquiry was made of 2005 high school seniors and 80% indicated that they did. Well now, I don't know what but something has generationally changed.

The more I thought about it, I remember honesty in education as be integral. I am a fan of teacher's establishing the standards of measure for their classroom. I know in the 1950's a Stigler High School student received a report card for each subject that contained the number of students in the class who had attained a certain grade. Your grade was circled. B or C were the most common grades depending on the instructor, A's were generally few. I came to know my grades were directly related to my efforts. Had I questioned it, my grand-father would have promptly corrected me! I have no idea how much this might have changed but I am instinctually positive about the Stigler Public Schools.

I also believe none of us became who we are by formal education alone. I consider more important to be our family, our Church and the community; it was the adults I admired and attempted to emulate. Yet we turn out a little alike and a lot different. That makes knowing each other fun.

It strikes me that we can not all acquire the exact same thing in exactly the same way. We just aren't that much alike just read a newspaper. They are filled with stories that leave us shaking our heads and murmuring, "I just don't understand how anyone could do that".

Gosh, what a great question "Who am I?" is. Are we our "resume selves"? Are we our "eulogy selves"? And how in the heck do we get did we get that way? I said thinkin' was perilous. It is. But it is never a waste even if you don't get a conclusion. Think I'll open a Coca-Cola, sit out back and consider this whole idea some more.

A Bible and a newspaper in every house, a good school in every district — all studied and appreciated as they merit — are the principle support of virtue, morality and civil liberty. — Benjamin Franklin

AN ODE TO BEAN CHOWDER

SNS – May 14, 2015

Have you taken the grand venture the school of your grandchild or great-grand child makes available? This event will include lunch with your student followed by shopping at the school Book Fair. While it was titled Grandparents Day, we chose to believe that this must include great-grandparents. Bud's grandma joined us giving the group legitimate status.

So, for the preceding week I just knew that superb "old school classic bean chowder" was in my future. Being buzzed through the entry doors, checking in and placing a "sticky" on my shirt, we took a seat and waited. Then, Bud appeared and guided us to the cafeteria. A fun fact: 6 year old boys are fascinated with wooden canes. They are certain such a big stick must be a recreational device. This curiosity provided both fun and peril to the owner.

Alas, entry into the cafeteria did not bring the heady scent of school bean chowder. It didn't smell of anything. Trays were now Styrofoam, utensils are plastic. All appeared disposable to me.

The food choices reminded me of any fast food outlet. There was the choice of cheeseburgers or chicken nuggets, perfectly round and the size of a stack of 4 half dollars. The choice of beverage was a small carton of milk, chocolate or regular. We chose cheeseburgers, Bud took the nuggets. Fries, pickles and chunk pineapple completed either meal. I checked again and still found no bean chowder.

We found an empty table. I noticed Bud was reading the room as we sat. He later said, "This is the "time out table" but I think its okay". I know the purpose of a time out table. I was sitting where I belonged, Bud, his grandmother and his great-grandmother, maybe not so much. The food was tasty. The company was fun. Bud seemed proud to have us there.

The change of dining environment was immense. Coming in all shapes and sizes, speedy 6 year olds eat rapidly and noisily. They laugh, they talk loud and they have such huge smiles. All seemed anxious to reach the playground. Somewhere in the deep recesses of my mind, I remember that feeling. Huh, deep recesses – recess – maybe play should be important in our lives again. Monkey bars still look like fun. I can't jump out of a swing any more. But kids aren't allowed to do that anymore either.

The teachers well let me say it was nice to see adults who were not threatened by noise and loud play. They were comfortable with the fact that little boys and little girls play in a quite different fashion.

The stop at the book fair was educational. I didn't know there were so many books on sharks and river monsters.

By mid-afternoon I was on my small back porch popping open a Coca Cola. I still love the way it fizzes when I pour it over ice. Take a sip and the spray covers my upper lip. It must touch the little boy in me hidden not far below the surface.

I enjoyed Grandparents Day. But I did want school house bean chowder.

Everything I need to know I learned in Kindergarten. -- *Robert Fulghum*
(Share everything, play fair, Don't hit people, Clean up your own mess, Don't take things that aren't yours, Wash your hands before you eat, flush, etc.)

GET BACK UNDER YOUR DESK!

Publish 12-23-2015

It just hasn't been that many years ago that a teacher was barking instructions like a drill sergeant to me. In 1948, we were conducting school wide drills so that we could protect ourselves from a pending nuclear attack upon the United States by the Soviet Union.

"Hal get completely under your desk." "Fallout can be very dangerous." "Do not look toward the flash, it will blind you." "Hands over your head." Window coverings were drawn. Today such instructions may sound foolish and naïve.

I believed as did my classmates that such simple actions would protect us from a weapon we barely understood. An Atomic bomb sounded really big. The news trailers I had seen of Hiroshima and Nagasaki at the Time Theatre convinced me of their destructive power. I judged Oklahoma City or Tulsa was the closest cities at risk of an attack. Those were far enough away that hiding under your desk and looking away should provide adequate protection.

There was Bert the Turtle who would espouse "Duck and Cover" in a variety of Civil Defense bulletins. He carried his shelter on his back, we did not. So, you should learn to make like a turtle and "Duck and Cover".

I wasn't being uncooperative when I was told to get completely under my desk. I was just too long legged. In my struggles to discover a manner in which I could fit under a desk, I did become grateful that boys wore jeans and didn't have to wrestle dresses and skirts under the desks as the young ladies did.

Would I have ever thought of those times again? Maybe not, but a week ago I picked my great-grandson at school. He crawled up into his booster seat and snapped it shut. The click of the seatbelt is my indicator that it is time to precede. Bud settled into his seat and asked, "Can I get ice cream at QT?" I said, "Yes". I knew Billie would veto me if I didn't. Pleased with the prospect of Vanilla Ice Cream, he casually said, "We had an "active shooter" drill today."

The drill was exactly what sounds like. It was seven-year olds preparing for the circumstances that an active shooter invades their campus. Where do you hide, what doors will be locked? What on earth are teachers to do? Where Administrators walking the hallways carrying Glocks? Oh, I don't think that was included really in the drill. Huh – should it be? Nah. I was just thinking.

Oh well, I don't recall having sleepless nights from the "desk drills". I must have found some sense of sanctuary under that seat. I hope that the "active shooter" drills provide Bud with the same subtle assurance I must have found. But I didn't have the television news programming, so many stations covering the same event. You can only tell a little boy to go play in the yard so many times. We do what we can do.

I think I'll take advantage of this unseasonably warm afternoon to have a Coke on the back porch. Do you think an active shooter today is a more realistic possibility than a nuclear attack in '48? Still just thinkin'.

I'm not afraid of storms, for I'm learning how to sail my ship. – Louisa May Alcott

THE FUNNING AND FUNDING OF SCHOOL DAYS

In a recent "Throwback Thursday", the Thursday feature of the Stigler News Sentinel's Facebook page, there was a photograph of the 1961 Tamaha girls basketball team and their coach, Louis Frazier. It is my personal opinion that Coach Frazier was the finest basketball mind to coach in the small rural schools that dotted all of Haskell County in the 1940's and 1950's.

For me, the photograph revived a variety of childhood memories. I first was drawn to basketball in very early elementary school. During a week each spring, I spent hours in Stigler's WPA Gym watching the Haskell County Grade School Tournament. I believed it to be quite the event. My father was gone to World War II and my mother allowed me go to the gym alone. The independence was free. The Cokes were a nickel.

Each of the 4 county high schools had a gym. Interesting to me, just across the Canadian River there was Briartown, a dependent school with a gym. It wasn't a palace but it wasn't bad. It certainly had a lot of character. I wondered how such a tiny school could build a gym. It looked a little WPA, so maybe it was. Many of us played our first grade school tournament in that tiny gym.

Back to Louis Frazier, he was a man who took great pride in his family, his profession and his farm. I first knew him when he taught and coached basketball at Martin Box. Do you remember 100# boys and Anyweight boys and girls? 85# brackets? I forget. The Martin Box basketball facility was an open air, dirt floor field house. Coach Frazier made do. Then, Louis and Merle Frazier moved to the Tamaha schools. Louis got to build a gym. Ever wonder where the funds came from? I did. A lot of the labor was volunteer I believe. I still don't know.

With limited state aid, the small one, two or four room schools seemed to have what the patrons were willing and able to fund.

In a weekend article on the Tulsa Mayoral race, I discovered a most interesting fact about one candidate, a young man I had known a considerable length of time. I knew his grandfather and an uncle had been Mayor. Well, this I didn't know. It seems G. T's direct ancestor was an early Mayor of Tulsa (1899-1900) and he had provided the funds to begin the Tulsa Public Schools. I guess in the beginning all schools were local.

I hadn't thought about it but it seems private money was the initial foundation of almost every community school. Seems our ancestors dug into their pockets and tried to pay for the education they wanted their children to have. I'm not sure just when we became dependent upon funds from the state but we did. In the 1950's, the feds stepped in to public education, offering financial assistance and promised not to ask for anything in return. Huh – the feds educated us on "unfunded mandates". We already knew the concept "if you don't do it my way I'll take my ball and go home". We learned that in "playground".

Now, about 70 years later, repeated references on the news and in the newspapers to a lack of funding available for modern public education, I have found it difficult not to draw some type of comparison between today and yesteryear. I do feel that somewhere along the line we lost control. Of course, I always liked "playground" and Haskell County Grade School basketball tournaments better --- And the Kinta Tournament.

I just read an editorial titled <u>Save Our Schools.</u> Guess we got used to the State of Oklahoma doing it for us.

Do you think Coach Frazier could have built his gym today? Perhaps I'm foolish but I believe the volunteers are still there. Oh, well.

I went out to the back porch, really humid today. My smart phone says the dew point is 73. My cold coke still fizzes when I pour it into a cup of ice. You know, I'm just glad Coach Frazier got to build his gym. I'm glad he was able to open it up to independent teams from the whole county for nights of "match play". Gosh, it was fun. Truth be told, a lot of people had a lot of fun there. Don't forget the educational value of our games and our playgrounds.

My education began in my sand pile under a huge ash tree and progressed to the hardwood others had put in place for many of us.

An investment in knowledge pays the best interest. – Benjamin Franklin
The battle of Waterloo was won on the playing fields of Eaton. – Arthur Wellesley

EDUCATION WAS WHERE YOU FOUND IT
(So Help Me Find It)

I'm not sure at what point thinkin' about a topic becomes an active curiosity but I know it does. In this column over the years I have made efforts to tie our past to our present. Because of my personal interest and their place in our lore I find I have often have included the "one room schoolhouse".

I have no personal experience with these small schools. However I do understand these schools represented a clear commitment on the part of the parents in these tiny communities to provide a quality education for their children. Such schools thrived long before politicians used the words "consolidation" or "bus routes" to question their viability. Have you ever wondered how educationally or socially productive the hours spent on a school bus where? Again, I just don't know. But I do know I think about it along, wishing I knew more of the experiences of many of my friends and classmates.

Much of my knowledge of such schools is limited to the tales my uncle, Howett McBride, shared. He graduated from the University of Oklahoma just as the Great Depression was taking its full bite out of our economy. He returned to live with his parents at 605 N.W. "A" Street in Stigler. His first job was teaching at Perry School. He enjoyed telling us of saddling his horse which was pastured north of my grandparents' home on then vacant land. Of course, it was cold and frosty every morning with a north wind blowing.

A favorite story involved his arrival at the school one morning and going inside to build a fire in the heater. He saw a steady flow of liquid dripping through the ceiling. Upon investigation he discovered a still in the attic of the school. Now I have no idea as to the degree of truth the story held but what a great tale it was when he told it, filling out the saga in grand detail.

343

My uncle had fine and funny stories from his days in Kinta High School. He bought basketball uniforms from feeding out a pig on school scraps. There was a tale of a boy who had the misfortune of being overheard calling him "Booger Red", a backdoor acknowledgement of my uncle's full head of sandy red hair. It was a true debacle for a high school boy full of himself. It became a lingering story for his nieces and nephews. Well into adulthood we enjoyed the "Booger Red" tales.

After finding and marrying a sweet Kinta girl, Ada Barnett, my uncle moved to Bartlesville. He soon became an elementary school principal and then Coordinator of Elementary Schools. He hired a number of teachers with Haskell County roots and took great pride in them. However, I'll tell you he took the performance of anyone from Haskell County personally. If he hired you, you had better succeed. He remained in Bartlesville until his retirement but he never lost his educational roots in the countryside of Haskell County.

I have a favor to ask. If you attended one of those small rural schools in Haskell County would you write some of your recollections? What made your school distinctive? What about teachers, fellow students, the physical structure, just any memory associated with the school. Everything counts.

Email me at halmcbride@cox.net. Call me. Ms. Anita will give you the number. Write me at the Stigler News Sentinel.

I know request like this most often go unanswered. However you know how important I believe preserving personal histories to be. So I'm optimistic.

It would be nice to get enough stories to plagiarize. No. Wait. Let's not do that. Those political folks have given plagiarism a bad name. Also, I have a feeling Miss Lillian Riley would not approve. If you had her class, smile.

Education is not the filling of a pail but lighting of a fire. – William Butler Yeats

To educate a man in mind and not in morals is to educate a menace to society. – Theodore Roosevelt

GOING BACK TO SCHOOL

Do you recall red Big Chief tablets, laddie pencils and penmanship books? Penmanship, I recall making the repetitive vertical lines and ovals? I hear they don't do that any more. Writing in cursive is out. With "spell-check" on every device, is spelling and the Friday spelling test also near becoming extinct? Calculators have changed arithmetic.

Do you remember books filled with age appropriate stories called readers?

There were those fixed rows of school desk at Boone School. Let me think, do you believe education could have taken place if our rears were not in direct and constant contact with the desk seat? Did girls really have an easier time sitting still than boys did?

Nevertheless most students anticipated a return to school as fall approached. As a boy, I had a clear reliable indicator school was not far away. Fisher Truck Line and Prentice Truck Line would begin to arrive behind the Stigler 5 & Up bringing boxes filled with school books. The boxes were opened ensure the contents was correct.

At the time Haskell County was covered with small rural schools that provided an education through the 8th grade and the Stigler 5 & Up supplied their books. The 5 & Up was owned by my uncle and aunt, Vivian and Hubert Claunts.

I felt obligated to check out all the readers. Boxes full of books became a seat. Climate control consisted of a black General Electric oscillating fan, the blades covered by a cage of black curved strands of metal. The protective guard looked to be made of heavy wire but it wasn't. There were 4 settings on a bar that slid across the base of the fan. There was a clasp and a rod that adjusted the height of fan. The wear and tear of the years had collected its toll. The fan was old and the set screw on the height adjustment no longer held the fan in place. It gradually worked its way down until readjustment was needed. But I was grateful for that old fan.

After all this was duel between the heat of the store room and the intensity of my curiosity. I enjoyed the touch, the feel and the smell of a new textbook. I still do. This stalemate was broken when my uncle would bring me cold coke, tell me to make quick pass through the candy case and go home for lunch. My uncle was a good fellow.

My grandson, a post-graduate student, recently mentioned how many textbooks he had to buy. Out of habit, I felt like my eyes spun in my head until landing in a position and my mind went "cha-ching". Then I ask and found they were all on loaded into his iPad. Does that seem right to you?

I have the illusion that I might have some future use for what I read, even the words from a novel. So I have marked up every book I own. The margins are cluttered with my notes. It is satisfying.

The books on my Nook are highlighted but that just isn't the same. The Nook does allow me to enlarge the print to a comfortable reading size. I have reached a compromise with technology. My Nook neither feels nor smells like a book.

I love what I find written on the pages of books.

I like a teacher who sends you home with something to think about besides homework. – Lilly Tomlin as "Edith Ann".

I am always ready to learn although I do not always like being taught. – Winston Churchill

EDUCATION WAS WHERE YOU FOUND IT
(So Help Me Find It)

I'm not sure at what point thinkin' about a topic becomes an active curiosity but I know it does. In this column over the years I have made efforts to tie our past to our present. Because of my personal interest and their place in our lore I find I have often have included the "one room schoolhouse".

I have no personal experience with these small schools. However I do understand these schools represented a clear commitment on the part of the parents in these tiny communities to provide a quality education for their children. Such schools thrived long before politicians used the words "consolidation" or "bus routes" to question their viability. Have you ever wondered how educationally or socially productive the hours spent on a school bus where? Again, I just don't know. But I do know I think about it along, wishing I knew more of the experiences of many of my friends and classmates.

Much of my knowledge of such schools is limited to the tales my uncle, Howett McBride, shared. He graduated from the University of Oklahoma just as the Great Depression was taking its full bite out of our economy. He returned to live with his parents at 605 N.W. "A" Street in Stigler. His first job was teaching at Perry School. He enjoyed telling us of saddling his horse which was pastured north of my grandparents' home on then vacant land. Of course, it was cold and frosty every morning with a north wind blowing.

A favorite story involved his arrival at the school one morning and going inside to build a fire in the heater. He saw a steady flow of liquid dripping through the ceiling. Upon investigation he discovered a still in the attic of the school. Now I have no idea as to the degree of truth the story held but what a great tale it was when he told it, filling out the saga in grand detail.

My uncle had fine and funny stories from his days in Kinta High School. He bought basketball uniforms from feeding out a pig on school scraps. There was a tale of a boy who had the misfortune of being overheard calling him "Booger Red", a backdoor acknowledgement of my uncle's full head of sandy red hair. It was a true debacle for a high school boy full of himself. It became a lingering story for his nieces and nephews. Well into adulthood we enjoyed the "Booger Red" tales.

After finding and marrying a sweet Kinta girl, Ada Barnett, my uncle moved to Bartlesville. He soon became an elementary school principal and then Coordinator of Elementary Schools. He hired a number of teachers with Haskell County roots and took great pride in them. However, I'll tell you he took the performance of anyone from Haskell County personally. If he hired you, you had better succeed. He remained in Bartlesville until his retirement but he never lost his educational roots in the countryside of Haskell County.

I have a favor to ask. If you attended one of those small rural schools in Haskell County would you write some of your recollections? What made your school distinctive? What about teachers, fellow students, the physical structure, just any memory associated with the school. Everything counts.

Email me at halmcbride@cox.net. Call me. Ms. Anita will give you the number. Write me at the Stigler News Sentinel.

I know request like this most often go unanswered. However you know how important I believe preserving personal histories to be. So I'm optimistic.

It would be nice to get enough stories to plagiarize. No. Wait. Let's not do that. Those political folks have given plagiarism a bad name. Also, I have a feeling Miss Lillian Riley would not approve. If you had her class, smile.

Education is not the filling of a pail but lighting of a fire. – William Butler Yeats

To educate a man in mind and not in morals is to educate a menace to society. – Theodore Roosevelt

HOW MUCH AVAILABLE MEMORY

Have you noticed we no longer are required to recall what was once essential elements of day to day life? Like telephone numbers. I once remembered large groups of telephone numbers. Now I can barely recall my own. I just find the name in favorites and press. Or find the desired number in my contacts and press.

I was thinking, I wonder if memory is a fixed volume like say in a smart phone or an IPad. If so, I should have freed up some space by not having to recall so many telephone numbers. How many Gigabytes does my mind possess? What do you mean it can't be measured?

Okay, so memory is odd. I can't remember telephone numbers I call regularly. But I don't really dial a number. Wait, nobody dials anymore. Anyway, I just press a name.

Still, I can recall telephone numbers from 60 years ago. I could call Hays and Buchanan now. You just pick up the telephone and ask the operator for number 66. Oh, it doesn't work that way anymore. Well, perhaps it should. We might get to know each other better.

Thinking about it, tax time is upon us. Now there are some numbers that have changed. Remember when all you needed were the tax forms, a #2 pencil and a pad of paper. While there were more deductions, all the math you needed you learned in elementary school. But do you remember your first Texas Instruments Scientific Calculator? Mine was 1971. It took me through 16 hours of Graduate Statistics and some complicated tax compilations. The only computer I had access to took up half the basement in the Nursing School building at The University of Tulsa, required boxes of punch cards and fluency in Fortran. It didn't do personal income tax forms. I wonder how much memory that monster had.

Now that I am accustomed to Turbo Tax, sitting down at a table and staring at that pad of paper and a #2 pencil might be intimidating. Perhaps paralyzing. Like trying to remember the grandson's phone number to press into a land line.

I know this about taxes. They are conducive to a short memory.

The first weekend of March Madness is about over. It is neat having a part of it downtown this year. It brought men we knew as boys into town and into our living room for a visit. Memory blossoms.

What a schizophrenic season spring can be. Today is lavish. I'd likely go sit on the porch if the television wasn't filled with basketball and if I wasn't going to a first-grade baseball practice. I'm slowly warming up to this "machine pitch" stuff.

I can still remember the pitch count. How many gigabytes do you think that takes?

No man has a good enough memory to be a successful liar.
– Abraham Lincoln

MAKING THE REALLY IMPORTANT STUFF WORK

There was a time I believed that once we had educated our children my interest in education would wane. I was wrong. As your children have children your awareness of the significance of education will be revived. This sequence as it moves up and down is suggestive of a pattern of vacillating self-interest.

It is okay when a good healthy dose of selfishness fuels us into activity, revitalizing our interest schools and our community. I hate to mention it at this time but a few years back a politician's wife said about the rearing of children, "It takes a village". I think it does but she wasn't clear that the "village" recycles and renews itself. I have come to believe this cycling pattern is healthy for us as parents, grandparents, and so on. We get a breather in between and then are granted the privilege of doing a lot of it all over again. Well kinda. It depends.

Don't underestimate people who are making their second or third rotation through the activity, religious and educational systems. Have they changed over a few years? Yes. Are these vital community systems more the same than they are different? Absolutely. I recently heard an analysis that contended because the style and speed of communication has changed maybe we are not technology smart enough. A lady contended that knowledge is base knowledge even if it is transmitted in pencil through the US Postal Service. She asked, "How good are you guys at writing in long hand script?"

Have you noticed some news sources have recently suggested that Oklahoma is going to be last in the nation in spending on education? It does make for a stirring headline but what does it really mean. Well, if you're expecting an intelligent, insightful response in this piece I think you'll be disappointed.

Can education be measured by dollars spent? Will all children ever gain the same quantity of knowledge in a school? Not as long as a child's personal interest comes into play. We just acquire different skills as we make our way through our educational life.

In the News Sentinel over recent years, I have noticed far too many students receiving regional and national honors for it to be accidental. Some one has done something correctly. I also noticed the honor rolls are bulging. May I suggest that there is a village that values education?

When it comes time to "cut dollars" how do you really decide what should go? Those of you who have read some of my earlier columns know I'm not going to throw activities under the bus. A bus cost too much to risk damaging one. Have you heard those discussions about the relative merits of physical activities and intellectual activities? Are football and basketball of greater educational value than music and the performing arts? As much as I love competitive athletics I'd engage a discussion as to how many we might need. I sure my father and brother would have disagreed but I don't think fishing should become a school sponsored sport. On that I have to stop and think.

I'm going to have to retreat to my porch and give some really hard thought to this. The number of bubbles in the fizz of my coke suggests there has to be a lot of good ideas, new ideas and old ideas. Fizz is good.

I think I'll speak for those of us who can't carry a tune in a bushel basket, I wish I had learned more music appreciation. I still enjoy what I did learn. My parents paid Mrs. Rainey to teach me piano. I was an okay piano student and I am grateful for what Mrs. Rainey taught me. Oh, wait – Mrs. Rainey taught in her living room, not a classroom.

Maybe taxes don't always pay for the education we want our children to have. Maybe that is why it takes a village. Education can be like a blackberry bush if we allow it – full of thorns and chiggers but in the end everybody likes blackberry cobbler.

A man who has never gone to school may steal from a freight car, but if he has a university education he may steal the whole railroad. --- Theodore Roosevelt.
I never let my schooling interfere with my education. --- Mark Twain.

Family

LIVIN' IN MR. CODY'S HOUSE

July 18, 2015

The details of what's happening in Haskell County I now get from the Stigler News Sentinel. The days when all the news and the "dirt" just flowed into my home are gone. Between my parents days in the television shop, the tag office and the County Court House there were few happenings that I didn't here about. The News Sentinel does a fine job but somehow the juicy stuff gets left out. Newspapers are peculiar about publishing rumors. Well, maybe not all of them. Is the National Enquirer still in business?

Anyway I read that the original nursing home in Stigler was going to be torn down. Given its slab foundation and block construction, I suspect it past its expiration date some time ago.

Anything that building might have lacked in high quality brick and mortar, its administrator, Gib Cody, made up for with his personal care and concern. Gib had a unique sensitivity for his patrons. I'm suspect he learned much of it from his father who was a Methodist Minister and his mother, a minister's wife. Both are unique and demanding callings.

As she entered her 80's my Grandmother (Marvella) Lane twice fell and broke a hip. Each time she was told she'd never walk again. Each time she did. She was a 5 foot, 90 pound ball of grit and incredible determination. After her final fall she went to live in the Stigler Nursing Home.

She lived the latter years of her life there. However, she called it "Mr. Cody's House". She felt she was a guest there, a special guest. Seldom did a weekday pass that Gib didn't come in to visit her. Her mind never failed her until the final days of her life so these visits were important to her. Using her magnifying glass, she read her Bible, her newspapers and her True Detective magazines. Gib would knowledgably discuss these things with her, well, except for the True Detective.

Gib would tap on the door so that she could quickly discard her snuff. Its use was a closely guarded secret. She only allowed my father to purchase it for her. She kept her use discreet. Oh, we all knew but never saw the need to utter a word about it to her.

He was frequently quoted in her conversations. She adored him and felt everyone in the nursing home should feel the same way. Logic dictates that given the delicate nature of caring for others parents and the diverse nature of their individual health, some children would inevitably be dissatisfied. But Gib did his best and that was very good.

Gib Cody knew to his patients. My Grandmother Lane had a small glass of Mogen David Wine each evening before bed, about the size of a chipped beef glass. One night a well-intention nurse felt it was improper to serve alcohol in the nursing home and refused her the glass of wine. Morning came, Gib called my dad with a suggestion. By evening, "Doctor Tom" had written an order for the glass of wine. She could have a second glass upon request. As I said, Gib knew his patients.

The treasure here was not "brick and mortar". It was the devotion of one man. Summer is here. I'll toast Mr. Cody with a glass of ice cold sweet tea and thank him.

If you're too busy to come see me, you're too darn busy! --- Marvella Lane

FLY AWAY HOME

August 8, 2017

I have always heard the adage that one of the best parts of taking a vacation is coming home. It does seem that old sayings get to be old sayings because they contain a considerable truth. There is no bed like your bed, all the lumps are in just the right places.

This year I could not have ask any more of a vacation. The sound of the waves was relaxing. The sea breeze held the temperature in the high eighties. Clouds obstructed only one sunset. I depended upon my daughter-in-law to keep me appraised as to the overall quality of the sunrises.

The beach was totally free of seaweed and jelly fish. The surf was warm and soft. A visitor to the beach could sit his chair at the edge of the surf and plop down in it. The salt water just rolls over you. The resulting soak heals the soul and the bones – which ever happens to be ailing you at the moment.

Ideal for children, the summer beach gently slopes into the water and the surf breaks with no more than 3-foot waves.

This year I found that traveling with young children modifies my television viewing habits. It was "Shark Week" on the Discovery Channel. We did watch the local news but that was mostly coverage of what the hombres did on the boarder. The local weather was more of what happened today and less about forecasting tomorrow. Without the pending weather and Washington unrest to worry about, life just seemed calmer.

Vacations are supposed to be restful. This year was restful until we embarked upon our convoluted route home. For years our itinerary had been an easy Southwest Airlines (SWA) to Houston Hobby, then home to Tulsa. Nothing stays the same. This year SWA offered only 2 return flights, departing at 7 AM or 7 PM. I judged those to present a classic conundrum, one too early and one too late.

357

Flights from South Texas are limited. After considerable effort, followed by resignation, a mid-day return on United Express was booked. So, on our return venture, we were provided the full diversity of travel by regional airlines. Did you know different companies comprise "United Express"? I didn't but I do now.

Harlingen to Houston, aboard a Republic owned a new Embraer E170, the experience was beyond our most optimistic expectations. We "deplaned" at Terminal A.

It was downhill from here, both figuratively and literally. Our connecting flight left from Terminal B, a walk, an elevator, a train ride and a hike away. Once in B, we found a common waiting area for under a sign for about 8 gates. Come boarding time we were guided down into the bowels of Bush International Airport. Here were the gates, off a long seat-less hall way.

A traveling companion became convinced we had located the site to which the staff from United's recent incident involving the removal of a passenger from an aircraft had been reassigned. Their behavior supported this hypothesis.

No longer customers of Republic, it was out the doors and on to the tarmac we went. We boarded a vintage 44 passenger Embraer as if it were 1956. And yes, in the day, I traveled by DC-3 without complaint – but this isn't any longer the day.

I concede this classic aircraft performed like a jewel into Tulsa. The solidary flight attendant did serve me a coke.

Only the traveling is good which reveals to me the value of home and enables me to enjoy it better. – Henry David Thoreau

WORKING WITH RELATIVE NUMBERS
February 2, 2018

I recently received a couple of pieces of mail that were strong reminders of how relative numbers can be. Especially if those numbers are being used to calculate an individual's age. I think the truth is I simply try to ignore this entire concept of aging. Oh, recent realities have suggested that such an approach might be somewhat foolhardy.

First, I received an absolutely lovely invitation to a good friend's 80th birthday party. Now Jimmy Thomas and I were born one day apart. Noretta was born on Jimmy's birthdate a year later. For one day each February, Noretta and I are the same age, relatively speaking.

There is nothing like receiving an elegant invitation by U.S. Mail to make me think that age might just be both relative and concrete. Good Lord has that February really been so long ago.

I admire the contribution Noretta has made to Haskell County through the Historical Society Museum. Along with Beverly and Alice and Patti.

How many of you recall Hubert and Vivian Claunts, the Stigler 5 & Up and that marvelous candy case? They had two sons, my cousins, Boots and Tag. They have real names but few know them. Tag passed a number of years ago. Boots is still with us and will turn 99 in March.

Recently, I received an envelope by U.S. Mail with a clipping from the Red Rock News enclosed. The headline on the clipping read "Nearly 99 years, another hole-in-one". On January 3, 2018 at Canyon Mesa Country Club in Sedona, Arizona, Boots recorded his 14th hole-in-one.

Hole-in-Ones are a passion with Boots. He hunts aces like my brother use to hunt ducks. On the whole now Boots has his own tees, except for two holes where he can play from the red tees. Only on those two holes can he record an official ace. On the 3rd, he hit his ball long into slope and it trickled back toward the pin – then it fell in. It didn't matter that he couldn't see the ball rolling on the green, his companions did commentary. It doesn't matter that his friends now have to tee his ball up for him or that he can't retrieve the ball from the hole, it matters that he still swings the club.

Daniel Hargis of the Red Rocks News quoted Boots' mantra that allowed him to continuing golfing at his age. "Don't give up. Just keep trying. If you give up, you've had it." I'd add you have to golf with good friends. Friends who know all the exotic places you have driven your golf cart and play with you anyway.

Imagine, at 99 years of age, swinging at a golf ball almost every day. Just thinkin', wondering what the fizz of my Coke would say. It is all relative.

Old minds are like old horses; you must exercise them if you wish to keep them in working order. – John Adams

www.ingramcontent.com/pod-product-compliance
Lightning Source LLC
Chambersburg PA
CBHW071313090426
42738CB00012B/2693